HARDY THE CREATOR

HARDY THE CREATOR

A Textual Biography

SIMON GATRELL

CLARENDON PRESS · OXFORD

1988

Oxford University Press, Walton Street, Oxford OX2 6DP

Oxford New York Toronto
Delhi Bombay Calcutta Madras Karachi
Petaling Jaya Singapore Hong Kong Tokyo
Nairobi Dar es Salaam Cape Town
Melbourne Auckland

and associated companies in
Berlin Ibadan

Oxford is a trade mark of Oxford University Press

Published in the United States
by Oxford University Press, New York

British Library Cataloguing in Publication Data
Gatrell, Simon
Hardy the creator: a textual biography.
1. Fiction in English. Hardy, Thomas,
1840–1928—Critical studies
I. Title
823'.8
ISBN 0–19–812810–X

Library of Congress Cataloging in Publication Data
Gatrell, Simon.
Hardy, the creator: a textual biography/Simon Gatrell.
p. cm. Bibliography: p. Includes index.
1. Hardy, Thomas, 1840–1928—Criticism, Textual. 2. Hardy,
Thomas, 1840–1928—Publishers. 3. Authors and publishers—Great
Britain. I. Title.
823'.8—dc19 PR4755.G38 1988 88–737
ISBN 0–19–812810–X

Typeset by Colset Private Ltd.

Printed in Great Britain
at the University Printing House, Oxford
by David Stanford
Printer to the University

FOR PEGGY GATRELL

Preface

First of all there are many people who I want to thank for their help and advice. Michael Millgate and Dale Kramer have both twice read drafts of the book, and without their deep knowledge of the material, their generosity, and their encouragement, it would by no means have been completed in as short a time as ten years, and it would have been but a wan shadow of what it has now become.

Jon Evans also read the manuscript in its final form, and his enthusiasm was most infectious. Chapters have been read at different times by a series of colleagues as I have migrated around the northern hemisphere: Michael Cotsell, John MacVeigh, and Tony Bareham in Coleraine; Patricia Ingham in Oxford; and Jack Sweeney and Coburn Freer in Athens. Several of them had to disguise at best a mild enthusiasm for Hardy under the cloak of scholarship, and, all through, their commentary vindicated scholarship's power to transcend small personal preferences!

Conversation and correspondence with others has helped me formulate and reformulate ideas which have found their way into the book, and I want to thank them too: Bill and Vera Jesty, Pamela Dalziel, David Fleeman, Jim Gibson, Samuel Hynes, Suleiman Ahmad, Alan Manford, and Tom Hetherington.

To the acuteness and sensitivity of these people is owing much of what is good in these pages, and to their friendship much of my pleasure in writing them. I hope that when they glance through the book, they will not want to disown their foster-child.

Without the active co-operation of librarians and curators this kind of book would be almost impossible to write. Foremost amongst these, whenever the study of Hardy's texts is concerned, must always be Roger Peers, the curator, amongst other things, of the Hardy Memorial Collection in the Dorset County Museum. Without his responsive care all Hardy scholars would be the poorer, as I have cause to know after nearly twenty years of trying his patience and his good humour, and I must join with his name that of his assistant Paul Ensom. To the librarians of the Houghton Library at Harvard, of the Huntington Museum in San Marino, of the Humanities Research Center at the

University of Texas in Austin, of the Pierpont Morgan Library, of the British Library, of the Fitzwilliam Library at Cambridge, of the Library of University College, Dublin, of the Library of Congress, of the Signet Library, Edinburgh, of the Berg Collection at the New York Public Library, and of the National Library of Scotland—to all these go also my thanks for courteous and helpful service.

I am particularly grateful to those private individuals who have allowed me to look at essential material in their possession, to R.L. Purdy, Edwin Thorne, and Frederick B. Adams.

I must also belatedly acknowledge the assistance early on in the development of this book of the British Academy and the Leverhulme Foundation, whose financial generosity in 1977 allowed me to examine many of the manuscripts whose study forms the nucleus of this work. I hope they will feel that their patience has been rewarded. I am also grateful to Wolfson College, Oxford, for awarding me a Charter Fellowship in 1985, which provided me with the time and the place to put all my miscellaneous information into a shape that at least approximated to a book.

Eppie Azzarretto typed a good portion of the book and made sense of a ragged original, and to her my thanks go heartfelt.

Without the love and forbearance of Tita and Clym nothing could have been done.

About this Book

The conviction that underlies this book is that it is impossible fully to understand the works of a writer unless you first understand how those works came to be what they are. No criticism is in the end satisfying unless it takes at least implicit account of the creative history of the work or works in question, as far as it can be known. No reading is so rich as that which proceeds from a full awareness of the work's development.

This is not an original thought, and it is unsurprising that there has in recent years been a growth of interest in the way in which Hardy continuously reshaped his fiction. So far full scholarly editions of two of his novels have been published, and a number of writers have been concerned to examine the meticulous care with which he wrote and revised others.[1] These editions and critical studies have explored in more or less

---

[1] The editions are of *Tess of the d'Urbervilles* by Juliet Grindle and Simon Gatrell (Oxford: Clarendon Press, 1983) and *The Woodlanders* by Dale Kramer (Oxford: Clarendon Press, 1981).

substantial detail the development of the single work, but on the whole each novel has been seen in isolation, and there has been no real sense of a context into which to fit them. It now seems the right time to offer a rather broader overview; to suggest how insights into the development of separate texts might be seen in relationship to the growth of Hardy's career as a novelist, and to make generalizations about his approach to the creation and revision of his fiction as a whole. Hence the idea of a textual biography.

This book thus attempts to combine an outline of Hardy's career as a writer of fiction—his dealings with editors, publishers, and printers in England and America—with further investigations into his creative activity at the successive stages of the development of his fiction, through a detailed study of individual novels and stories, examples chosen to cover as much as possible of the corpus. This combination, it is hoped, should make possible some valid generalizations about the way that Hardy created his texts.

Of necessity the structure which has been evolved to accommodate these aims is a loose one. The primary commitment has been to the chronological sequence from 1868, when Hardy sent the manuscript of his first novel to Macmillan, to his death in 1928. Within this chronological sequence a developmental sequence is maintained, which introduces the study of manuscript before serial, of first edition before

---

There have been studies of the development of several of Hardy's novels. *Under the Greenwood Tree*: Simon Gatrell, 'Hardy's Changing View of *Under the Greenwood Tree*', *Notes and Queries for Somerset and Dorset*, 30 (1978), 315–24. *Far from the Madding Crowd*: Simon Gatrell, 'Hardy the Creator: *Far from the Madding Crowd*', in Dale Kramer (ed.), *Critical Approaches to the Fiction of Thomas Hardy*, (London: Macmillan, 1979), 74–99; Lawrence Jones, 'A Good Hand at a Serial', *Studies of the Novel*, 10 (1978), 320–34; Robert C. Schweik, 'The Early Development of Hardy's *Far from the Madding Crowd*', *Texas Studies in Literature and Language*, 9 (1967), 415–28. *The Return of the Native*: John Paterson, *The Making of* The Return of the Native (Berkeley: University of California Press, 1960). *The Mayor of Casterbridge*: Christine Winfield, 'The Manuscript of Hardy's *The Mayor of Casterbridge*', *PBSA*, 67 (1973), 33–58; Dieter Riesner, 'Kunstprosa in der Werkstatt: Hardy's *The Mayor of Casterbridge* 1884–1912', in Dieter Riesner and Helmut Gneuss (edd.), *Festschrift für Walter Hubner* (Berlin: Erich Schmidt, 1964), 267–326. *The Woodlanders*: Dale Kramer, 'Revisions and Vision: Thomas Hardy's *The Woodlanders*', *Bulletin of the New York Public Library*, 75 (1971), 195–230, 248–82; Philip Gaskell, 'Hardy, *The Woodlanders*, 1887', example 10 in *From Writer to Reader* (Oxford: Clarendon Press, 1978). *Tess of the d'Urbervilles*: J.T. Laird, *The Shaping of Tess of the d'Urbervilles* (Oxford: Oxford University Press, 1975); J.T. Laird, 'New Light on the Evolution of *Tess of the d'Urbervilles*', *Review of English Studies*, NS 31 (1980), 414–35. *Jude the Obscure*: Patricia Ingham, 'The Evolution of *Jude the Obscure*', *Review of English Studies*, NS 27 (1976), 27–37, 159–69; John Paterson, 'The Genesis of *Jude the Obscure*', *Studies in Philology*, 57 (1960), 87–98; Robert Slack, 'The Text of Hardy's *Jude the Obscure*', *Nineteenth-Century Fiction* 2 (1957), 261–75. Mary Ellen Chase's *Thomas Hardy from Serial to Novel* (Minneapolis: University of Minnesota Press, 1927) was an early pioneer in the field, and despite its many deficiencies, sometimes still offers a useful starting point for enquiry.

first one-volume edition, and so on; but at times the two are incompatible. Thus, although the book begins with a discussion of issues raised by the earliest surviving of Hardy's manuscripts, *Under the Greenwood Tree* (1872), this first stage in the growth of a novel or a story is so interesting that one example is not sufficient to illuminate each of its facets, and so the manuscripts of *The Return of the Native* (1878), *Two on a Tower* (1882), and *Wessex Folk* (1892) are also the subjects of detailed discussion. They have been considered separately within the chronological sequence rather than grouped together at the beginning of what might be called the creative sequence. The same kind of thing happens with Hardy's approach to serialization: though the first discussion comes in relation to *Far from the Madding Crowd* (1874) and *The Hand of Ethelberta* (1876), directly after the analysis of the manuscript of *Under the Greenwood Tree*, the nature of Hardy's attitude to magazine issue changed as he matured as a writer, and thus I have paused at the appropriate chronological moments to consider how Hardy handled the serializations of *The Trumpet-Major* (1880) and *A Group of Noble Dames* (1891).

Concluding chapters offer three kinds of reflection upon the preceding textual biography. The first shows, through a discussion of one novel, *Two on a Tower*, how it is possible and profitable to synthesize material from the study of each successive stage of Hardy's revision into a critical analysis of developments in the novel as a whole. The choice of a novel outside the familiar 'Novels of Character and Environment' grouping was quite deliberately designed to show that Hardy was critically and creatively active throughout his work. The second recognizes the fact that though this book is not designed as a handbook for editors of Hardy, much of the discussion is indirectly, and some of it directly, relevant to the problems faced by editors. It seemed worth while to gather the scattered material together and, approaching it through a brief study of the punctuation of the manuscript of *Far from the Madding Crowd*, to draw some more generalized conclusions about editorial choices and decisions. The third is a speculative finale.

These structural decisions have been made with an eye to logic and the comfort of the reader, and though they make for apparent complication when set out thus, the complications disappear as the narrative sequence is pursued.

S.G.

Athens, Georgia
May 1987

Contents

Illustrations

Grateful acknowledgement is made to the trustees of the estate of Miss E.A. Dugdale for permission to reproduce these manuscript leaves.

A Note on References

References to Hardy's Fictional Writings

Whenever manuscript material has been quoted, the folio number has been attached. When printed sources are quoted, then I have indicated the source of the quotation. I have chosen to use reliable critically edited texts wherever they are available. Where they are not, then I have fallen back upon the Wessex edition (Macmillan, 1912–13). This decision perhaps makes for some inconvenience, but any inconvenience is more than offset by the quality of the texts to which I refer.

References to Other Sources

There are three works to which I refer frequently and which I abbreviate in the text:

R.L. Purdy, *Thomas Hardy: A Bibliographical Study* (Oxford: Clarendon Press revised edition, 1968) is identified as Purdy.

R.L. Purdy and Michael Millgate (edd.), *The Collected Letters of Thomas Hardy* (Oxford: Clarendon Press, 1978–) is identified as *Letters*, followed by the volume number.

Florence Hardy, *The Early Life of Thomas Hardy* and *The Later Years of Thomas Hardy* (London: Macmillan, 1928 and 1930) are identified as *Early Life* and *Later Years*.

All other references are identified in the text or in footnotes.

Introduction

The Author and Publishing in late Victorian England[1]

In 1871, when Hardy published his first novel, Blackwood was about to begin the part-issue of George Eliot's *Middlemarch*, which was to bring the novelist more than £4,000; and Anthony Trollope's *Ralph the Heir*, which he later called 'one of the worst novels I have written',[2] was also appearing in parts, as well as running through *St. Paul's Magazine*. He had sold the rights for £2,500. Though Hardy certainly did not know these financial details, with the examples of Dickens, Thackeray, and Trollope before him he can have been in no doubt that it was possible both to write well and to make a living as a novelist.

He would have realized too that it was not simply a matter of being published in book-form. Serialization was essential. The part-issue of the George Eliot and the Trollope novels was the exception rather than the rule by 1871, for in the 1860s issue in parts prior to a book-edition was superseded, as a way of ensuring that the writer gained an income from two markets for the same piece of work, by publication in one of the rapidly growing number of periodicals that catered for the reader of fiction. Serial-issue was often more profitable than the first book-issue, since the conventionally established form for first-edition publication, in two or most often three volumes (the two- or three-decker as it is usually known), had normally a quite small print-run of five hundred to a thousand copies, and brought in only moderate financial reward for the author.

The price of these two- and three-deckers was established, well before the time that Hardy began writing, at 10s. 6d. a volume, excessively expensive even for the still predominately middle-class reading public. It was not unusual for well over half the edition to be sold at a discount of 50 per cent or more to circulating libraries, and in particular to Mudie's

---

[1] For an interesting discussion in amplification of some of the issues raised in this section, see J. A. Sutherland, *Victorian Novelists and Publishers* (London: Athlone Press, 1976). Sutherland confines his study to the period 1830–70, but almost all of what he says about the 1860s remained relevant during Hardy's career as a novelist.

[2] *An Autobiography* (1883), ch. XIX World's Classics edition (Oxford: Oxford University Press, 1980), 313.

Select Library in New Oxford Street. Guinevere Griest's book *Mudie's Circulating Library*[3] shows vividly the overwhelming power which this institution, along with that of W.H. Smith, possessed in maintaining the form and the cost, and to a certain degree influencing the content, of the first editions of novels in the mid- and late Victorian periods.

The basic subscription to Mudie's was one guinea a year for one volume, exchangeable at will; hence the three-decker allowed Mudie to lend one copy of a three-decker novel to three separate subscribers at the guinea rate. The high price, which Mudie himself very rarely paid, made it hard for publishers to sell copies to members of the reading public, especially when they could read all they wanted for a guinea a year; but publishers were content, since a more or less guaranteed sale to Mudie meant that a loss on even the unsuccessful first novel by an unknown author would be minimal. Thus, for a while the British public became book-borrowers rather than book-buyers. Hardy himself referred in letters to the first editions of his novels as 'library editions' (*Letters*, i. 60, 161–2).

The triangular correspondence between John Blackwood, J. M. Langford, and George Lewes (George Eliot's husband) over the success of *Middlemarch* is full of surprised comments about the large number of copies of the parts of the novel that were actually being bought by the general public. Lewes commented, 'The fact is the public has got out of the *habit* of buying books owing to its reliance on libraries', and continued with an anecdote about a lady who reported disgustedly that all thirty copies of *Romola* had been taken out of the library to which she subscribed, not even considering that she could buy it for 2*s*. 6*d*. at a nearby bookseller.[4]

Though Hardy profited financially from his association with periodicals and from the sale of three-decker novels to the circulating libraries, he also recognized that the conditions under which an author had to publish if he was to make a satisfactory living from his fiction imposed certain constraints on his writing, especially with regard to subject and treatment. To a considerable degree these most profitable avenues of publication and distribution required that the work they handled should conform to what the average middle-class Victorian father believed was suitable for his teenage daughters to read or to listen to. Mudie, emphasizing the 'Select' in the title of his library, and the editors of the fiction-carrying magazines, operated a virtual financial censorship, a

---

[3] Griest, *Mudie's Circulating Library* (Bloomington: Indiana University Press, 1970).
[4] *The George Eliot Letters*, ed. Gordon Haight (Oxford and Yale: 1955), 264–5.

restriction undoubtedly damaging to the development of fiction towards intellectual and moral honesty (though it is an open question whether these few individuals exerted their influence out of their own convictions, or in deference to the responses of the novel-reading public at large).[5] Hardy pointed out the effect of this censorship in his 1891 essay 'Candour in English Fiction':

The popular vehicles for the introduction of a novel to the public have grown to be, from one cause and another, the magazine and the circulating library; and the object of the magazine and the circulating library is not upward advance but lateral advance . . . the magazine in particular and the circulating library in general do not foster the growth of the novel which reflects and reveals life. They directly tend to exterminate it by monopolising all literary space.

By 1891 Hardy had sufficient experience of the tendency towards 'extermination' and was writing in this essay with hardly controlled bitterness.[6]

Often, if the first edition had not sold out within a few months of its first publication, the remaining copies were sold at a low price—remaindered—to a bookseller or to another publisher, who often bound the two or three volumes as one before putting them on the market. The rapidity of this process was again in part due to the power of the circulating libraries: if they would not take a sufficient proportion of the copies when the book was first published, or if Mudie refused to take it at all, then there was little hope for the expensive edition. Several of Hardy's novels were remaindered, including *Desperate Remedies*, *Under the Greenwood Tree*, *The Mayor of Casterbridge*, and *The Woodlanders*. On the other hand, three were successful enough to be reprinted in three volumes—*Far from the Madding Crowd*, *Two on a Tower*, and *Tess of the d'Urbervilles*. In each of these reimpressions Hardy made revisions—most often in direct response to the reviews of the first edition.

If the novelist were well known or the first edition successful, then

---

[5] The discussion in Griest, *Mudie's Circulating Library*, pp. 32–3, 82–4, and 140–55, bears on this question.

[6] 'Candour in English Fiction', in *Thomas Hardy's Personal Writings*, ed. Harold Orel (London: Macmillan, 1966), 125–33. The crushing of *A Group of Noble Dames* is examined in Chapter 5; the response to *Tess of the d'Urbervilles* is well known and may be found recorded in *Early Life*, pp. 290–1 and in the introduction of the Clarendon edition of the novel. It is worth noting in passing that Hardy's was only one of a sequence of attacks on the circulating libraries (Mudie's in particular). A contemporary of Hardy's, the novelist George Moore, had written in 1885 a pamphlet entitled *Literature at Nurse, or Circulating Morals*, in which he attacked the *de facto* censorship imposed by Mudie. The pamphlet was well received in the press and might be seen as causing the first genuine crack in the wall Mudie had built to enshrine the morality of fiction.

there would soon be an edition in one volume, often in the same or the following year. Mudie too had an influence upon this stage in a novel's production. Naturally enough, he was anxious to persuade publishers by all the means at his command to delay the issue of a more easily purchasable edition as long as possible, but his operation had another effect as well. It was his policy to sell off second-hand copies of novels that had ceased or considerably diminished their circulation, and publishers would attend to the price that Mudie could obtain for his used copies of their novels. If it was reasonably high, then clearly a one-volume edition would stand a good chance of success.

This edition would be much cheaper than the first edition, of course, usually around 6s., but it normally had a larger print-run, so it was not necessarily less profitable for the author.[7] These one-volume editions often appeared in a number of guises: in different qualities of cloth binding, and in illustrated boards, the 'yellow-back' issues mostly sold on W.H. Smith's railway bookstalls for a shilling or so. Most of Hardy's novels were issued in this variety of formats, especially those that were published by Sampson, Low in the 1880s and early 1890s.[8] Hardy almost always took the opportunity to revise that these cheap editions offered.

Hardy's last two novels, *Jude the Obscure* (1895) and *The Well-Beloved* (1897), had their first editions published in one volume, as part of the first collected edition of his work. They thus reflected the rapid extinction of the three-decker novel in the wake of the ultimatum issued by Mudie and Smith to publishers in 1894, in which they refused to pay more than 4s. a volume for novels, and demanded a twelve-month delay before cheaper editions were published. Griest (pp. 156–212) discusses in detail the reasons for the ultimatum—essentially that too many expensive novels were now being produced to allow for the profitability of circulating libraries run on the basis of the guinea subscription and

[7] Figures relating to the first one-volume issues of *A Pair of Blue Eyes* and *The Return of the Native* cannot have been particularly exciting for Hardy, however. The records of the King and Kegan Paul publishing house that issued these two novels in one volume in 1877 and 1879 respectively show that when they sold remaining stock to Sampson, Low at the end of 1883 the sum due to Hardy as two-thirds of the profits from the whole enterprise was £42. 17s. 9d.—£16. 13s. 6d. from *A Pair of Blue Eyes*, of which 1,500 had been printed, and £26. 4s. 3d. on *The Return of the Native*, of which 1,000 had been printed. (The records have been published by Chadwyck-Healey on microfilm as part of their series of archives of British publishers.) These figures, at least, suggest that Hardy had failed to capitalize upon the success with the reading public of *Far from the Madding Crowd*. This is borne out by the fact that he obtained well over £1,000 for the serial and first-edition rights of *The Hand of Ethelberta*, but decidedly failed to make four figures for the following novel, *The Return of the Native*.

[8] *A Pair of Blue Eyes, Far from the Madding Crowd, The Hand of Ethelberta, The Return of the Native, The Trumpet-Major, A Laodicean, Two on a Tower*, and *The Mayor of Casterbridge*.

carrying virtually all the new works published. Storage had also become a problem.

Other factors combined to make the end of the three-decker certain. Publishers began to accept that they could make as much profit from single-volume editions alone, and many novelists were anxious to write shorter fiction: Gissing, for instance, was glad to remove what he regarded as multiple-volume padding from the first-edition texts of some of his novels when they were reprinted in one volume. The most potent force for change, however, was pressure from the growing demand for new fiction in a cheap format from a rapidly increasing body of new readers, a development charted by R.D. Altick's seminal study *The English Common Reader*.[9] The last novel in three-volume form was probably published in 1897, only three years after Smith and Mudie's announcement, and with it came the end of the domination of the circulating library.[10]

By the time that Hardy began revising for his first collected edition in 1895, he had already had as many as five opportunities to change the English text of some of his novels. But the chances for alteration did not end there. Though none of Hardy's novels until *Tess of the d'Urbervilles* was protected in the United States by international copyright, American magazines and newspapers were prepared to pay at least as well as their British counterparts for serials and stories, and Hardy was soon sending duplicate proofs of his serials across the Atlantic. He also received small amounts for publication in book-form from his recognized publishers in America, despite the appearance of many unauthorized (pirated) editions of his work. These American issues meant that Hardy could, if he chose, revise his work yet again. And the same was true of the continental editions published by Baron Tauchnitz.

The first collected edition of Hardy's work, published by Osgood, McIlvaine in 1895–7, marks effectively the end of his career as a novelist, but it by no means marks the end of his interest either in the texts of his novels or in finding opportunities to maximize his revenue from them. In 1900–1, for instance, paper-bound editions of two of his novels were published, printed in very small type in double columns on poor paper;

---

[9] Michael Collie has a fascinating discussion of the revisions that Gissing made for the French translation of *New Grub Street* in 'Gissing's Revision of *New Grub Street*', *The Year-Book of English Studies*, 4 (1974), 212–24. Altick's book has most recently been reprinted by the University of Chicago Press in 1983.

[10] See e.g. Robert Lee Woolf, *Strange Stories and Other Explorations in Victorian Fiction* (Boston: Gambit, 1971), p. 61 n. 1: 'The latest three-decker in my collection (or known to me) is Algernon Gissing *The Scholar of Bygate* (3 vols.; London: Hutchinson, 1897).'

they cost 6*d*. a copy, and a hundred thousand of *Tess of the d'Urbervilles* were sold in a very few months. Hardy revised the texts. He started to publish with Macmillan in 1902, and the collected edition was brought out in a new format, including some slightly revised texts. In 1907 there was a pocket-issue (in which, for once, Hardy made no changes),[11] and then in 1912 the second fully revised edition appeared, Macmillan's Wessex edition. After this there was a de luxe limited edition in England, the Mellstock edition, and another, the Autograph edition, in America: in both of these Hardy made slight alterations. The last new venture in the history of the publication of Hardy's prose was the issue of a collected edition of his stories in 1927.

It will be seen, then, that the whole question of the development of the text of any of Hardy's novels or stories is closely bound up with, and to a degree directly affected by, the history of the book-trade in Britain and America; it raises issues connected with printing and illustrations, with critics and magazine editors, with binders and publishers. In fact, it involves a wide range of enquiry which it would properly take several separate books to satisfy; if this study cannot fully deal with all the issues it raises, then at least it will suggest the different directions that further investigation might take.

---

[11] Or at least none to the texts; he did revise two of the title-pages: *Under the Greenwood Tree* became *Under the Greenwood Tree or The Mellstock Quire*, and *The Mayor of Casterbridge: A Story of a Man of Character* has *The Life and Death of* prefixed to it.

1

Beginnings

1868–1875

Under the Greenwood Tree: The Manuscript

A textual biography should begin with a consideration of the manuscript of the author's first work; but textual studies of any sort are limited to what time, chance, and the author's whim have allowed to survive. There is nothing left of Hardy's first unpublished novel *The Poor Man and the Lady*, save certain fragments that found their way in a changed form into the three or four subsequent books, and the long story 'An Indiscretion in the Life of an Heiress' (1878) that Hardy cobbled together out of the coherent part of what remained. There will be something to say of these borrowings later, in connection with the manuscript of *Under the Greenwood Tree*.

The manuscript of his second novel, *Desperate Remedies*, has similarly disappeared. The first book-edition, published in three volumes by William Tinsley in 1871, is hard to find, since only 500 copies were printed, many of which were sold to the circulating libraries, while others were remaindered (sold to booksellers)—both transactions conducted at prices that did not cover the cost of production. It is unsurprising, given this kind of sales policy (in part forced on the publisher by Mudie and Smith), that Hardy lost £15 of the £75 that he had advanced towards the cost of producing and marketing the book.[1]

It was in the spring of 1872 that Tinsley paid Hardy £30 for the copyright of his third novel, *Under the Greenwood Tree*; it was the only time in his life that he sold a copyright and thus lost control of the novel and its profits, and it was not until seven years after his death that the rights finally reverted to his widow. However, the manuscript does survive, and offers the earliest possible view of Hardy at work.[2] In many respects the text that Tinsley purchased was close to the versions of the

---

[1] *Early Life*, pp. 109–12 and Purdy, pp. 4–5, where Tinsley's account for *Desperate Remedies* is reproduced. See also Sutherland, *Victorian Novelists and Publishers* (London: Athlone Press, 1976), ch. 10 for an account of Hardy's dealings with publishers over his first three novels. Sutherland points out the extremely low price (6s. instead of 31s. 6d.) that Mudie and Smith were charged for their copies.

[2] The manuscript of *Under the Greenwood Tree* is in the Dorset County Museum.

novel that we read today; but a study of some of the details of the manuscript shows in a remarkably clear way that Hardy had once a quite different conception of the novel.

The identification of different stages of development in any of Hardy's manuscripts can depend upon a variety of factors, and during the course of this book examples will be offered of them all. In the manuscript of *Under the Greenwood Tree* the most potent factor by far is Hardy's habit of giving his pages first a working number (most often at the top left-hand corner) and then, just before submitting them to the publisher, a final number (invariably at the top right-hand corner). Some manuscripts have two, and on occasions three, different systems of working numeration and their interpretation can become very complicated: *Far from the Madding Crowd* is a good example.[3] *Under the Greenwood Tree* has only one, but that one is very revealing.

What the working numeration shows is that throughout Hardy's early writing of the novel, and even during his fair-copying of it, *Under the Greenwood Tree* was a narrative which focused almost entirely on the characters making up the Mellstock choir, and on the loss of their church music-making. The story had a rather perfunctory love-plot attached to it, in which there was some uncertainty as to whether Dick Dewy the tranter's son or the innkeeper Fred Shiner would marry Fancy Day the schoolteacher. In the end we discover that Dick was successful, thanks to Fancy's stratagem of nearly starving herself to death for love.

It is impossible to know whether Hardy, reviewing what he had written some time in the summer of 1871, realized himself that as it stood his story would have scant interest for the middle-class female readership who stimulated the circulating libraries into buying multiple copies of novels, or whether he showed the newly copied manuscript to someone else, who suggested to him that if he really wanted to sell the story he would have to bring the romance to the foreground. Horace Moule, a close friend and literary man who had provided Hardy with his first introduction to the publishers Macmillan, seems a possible candidate for the role of friendly critic.

Whatever the stimulus, Hardy decided to raise the young vicar Mr Maybold from his simple role as the agent of change in church-music to become a suitor for Fancy Day, and considerably to increase the emotional complexity of the relation between Dick and Fancy.

[3] See Gatrell, 'Hardy the Creator: *Far from the Madding Crowd*', in Dale Kramer (ed.), *Critical Approaches to the Fiction of Thomas Hardy* (London: Macmillan, 1979), 94–6, for an example of this complication.

The late addition of three chapters, in which Maybold proposes to Fancy, is accepted by her, and then has to face the withdrawal of her acceptance (Autumn chapters V–VII), is not at first apparent from the manuscript, since the working numeration appears to run consecutively from the end of chapter IV of Autumn, from 154 through to 170. It is not until 170 is followed by 155 that it becomes clear that the chapters in question were added after Hardy had completed his working numeration.

This considerable development in the plot had complicating effects throughout the novel, and Hardy had to go back over earlier pages to add short passages, often on the verso of the preceding leaf, to prepare for Maybold's proposal. One of these is on the verso of fo. 42 (in Hardy's final numeration), and shows how in church on Christmas Day the vicar is as much attracted to Fancy as Dick is; another addition is on the verso of the leaf compositely numbered 71–72 and has Mrs Penny saying of Maybold, 'I fancy I've seen him look across at Miss Day in a warmer way than Christianity asked for.'[4]

Maybold's new feeling for Fancy had other effects. It gave his dismissal of the choir a more intimately personal motivation, and there is another insertion, this time on the verso of fo. 86, which makes the point. In the added chapters in Autumn there was also a conversation between Maybold and Dick Dewy which established an easy relationship between the two, and this allowed Hardy to add towards the end of the novel a sentence or two expressing Dick's puzzlement as to why the vicar, 'a man I like so much', wouldn't officiate at his wedding after all.

Another consequence of Maybold's interest in Fancy was that Hardy had to make her more interesting. On a single leaf at the end of Autumn chapter II, with a working number (145a) which shows that it was a later addition, there is Keeper Day's long explanation of why Fancy is too good for Dick, beginning 'Then I'll just tell 'ee you've come on a very foolish errand.' Originally Day had lived rather more exactly up to his reputation for 'halting well' in his talk, for the chapter had ended with his curt 'Then good night t'ye, Master Dewy.' An addition made to the same end was the detailed description of Fancy as 'our heroine' during the dance at the tranter's house; it would have been reasonable to say of the novel as it originally stood that it had no heroine.

Irregularities in the working numeration also make it possible to see that as far as the relationship between Dick and Fancy was concerned

---

[4] Such additions on the verso of the previous or occasionally the same page of material too extensive to be incorporated in the page are a feature found in most of Hardy's novel manuscripts.

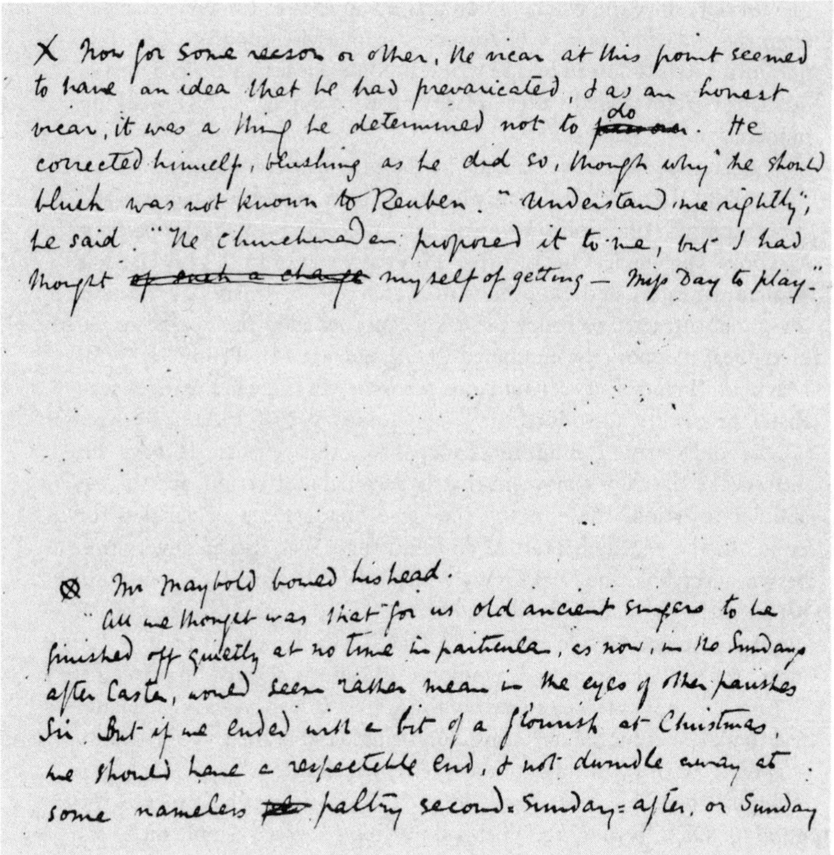
X Now for some reason or other, the vicar at this point seemed to have an idea that he had prevaricated, & as an honest vicar, it was a thing he determined not to ~~[illegible]~~ do. He corrected himself, blushing as he did so, though why he should blush was not known to Reuben. "Understand me rightly," he said. "The churchwarden proposed it to me, but I had thought ~~of such a change~~ myself of getting — Miss Day to play."

⊗ Mr Maybold bowed his head.

"All we thought was that for us old ancient singers to be finished off quietly at no time in particular, as now, in the Sundays after Easter, would seem rather mean in the eyes of other parishes Sir. But if we ended with a bit of a flourish at Christmas, we should have a respectable end, & not dwindle away at some nameless ~~pla~~ paltry second=Sunday=after, or Sunday

Figure 1: fo. 86 verso of the manuscript of *Under the Greenwood Tree* (see p. 9)

Hardy was chiefly interested in adding to it some moments of tension. The whole of chapter I of Autumn was added (as the left-hand numeration 136a–136g suggests), so that originally there was no dress-making to make Dick feel slighted, and no nutting to provoke a reconciliation. Hardy also added the gipsy-party at which Dick danced with a rich farmer's daughter; this stimulates a jealousy in Fancy that motivates her subsequent tale of flirtation with Shiner.

One last example symbolizes neatly the effect of this pattern of development in altering the balance of the novel. The close of chapter V of Winter, a chapter devoted to the choir's carol-singing, was rewritten specifically to link the vicar and Fancy together in the imagination of the tranter:

"Now putting two and two together," the tranter continued . . . "that is, in the form of that young vision we zeed just now, and this tenor-voiced parson, my belief is she'll wind en round her finger, and twist the pore young feller about like the figure of 8—that she will, my sonnies." (fo. 36)

The love-elements get everywhere, and it almost appears now as if the carol-singing had been designed solely to bring Dick, Fancy, and Maybold into conjunction.

The working numeration reveals that, in pursuit of balance between the choir and the lovers, Hardy also at this time deleted from the middle of Winter chapter II five pages of dialogue between the members of the choir. It was precisely this area of the novel that drew criticism from the first professionals who saw the manuscript, Alexander Macmillan and his reader John Morley. Macmillan wrote that 'the first 50 or 60 pages are really rather tedious & should at least be shortened by about one half', while Morley said: 'The opening scenes at the cottage on Xmas Eve are quite twice as long as they ought to be, because the writer has not enough sparkle and humour to pass off such minute and prolonged description of a trifle—*This part should decidedly be shortened.*' Macmillan, however, liked the novel well enough not to refuse it outright. He wrote in October 1871 that he could not accept it at once, since his hands were full of Christmas books, and sent back the manuscript. He asked at the same time if he might consider in the new year whether it would do as a spring or summer book, but this proposal was apparently never taken up.[5]

Some time between the receipt of his manuscript from Macmillan and its sale to Tinsley, Hardy acted on these criticisms and took out some

[5] Charles Morgan, *The House of Macmillan 1843–1943* (London: Macmillan, 1943), 96–9.

more of the choir's desultory conversation. This time it is disturbance to the final rather than the working numeration that indicates where the deletions occurred.

Chapter III of *Winter* was originally five manuscript pages longer than it is now; the leaf on which it ends has the composite final number 19–24, and presumably we have lost more conversation about local topics at the tranter's house. The numeration at the opening of *Spring* chapter II is very confused, but what is clear is that approximately three pages of dialogue amongst the members of the choir have been excised, probably on the subject of Mr Maybold.

Thus, the manuscript that Tinsley saw and liked enough to risk his £30 on had been transformed from a novel about the Mellstock choir and other local personalities to one in which the choir provided a picturesque background for the love-story. Indeed, this description echoes something that Hardy wrote in the letter to Macmillan that accompanied the manuscript: 'The accessories of one scene in it may possibly be recognised by you as appearing originally in a tale submitted a long time ago (which never saw the light). They were introduced advisedly, as giving a good background to the love portion' (*Letters*, i. 12). As we have seen, this was not Hardy's earliest sense of what he was writing in *Under the Greenwood Tree*.

Under the Greenwood Tree and *The Poor Man and the Lady*

Hardy's letter to Macmillan also raises questions about exactly what he took from *The Poor Man and the Lady*. There are two sorts of evidence available, and it is perhaps coincidental that they relate to the two narrative threads in *Under the Greenwood Tree*. Hardy's reference in the letter quoted above to the borrowing of 'the accessories of one scene' from the unpublished novel is supported by a note in *The Early Life*, where Hardy wrote of the execution of *Under the Greenwood Tree* that it 'had arisen from a remark of Mr. John Morley's on *The Poor Man and the Lady*, that the country scenes in the latter were the best in the book, the "tranter" of *The Poor Man and the Lady* being reintroduced' (p. 113). In fact Morley had written in his reader's report: 'the opening pictures of the Christmas eve in the tranter's house are really of good quality; much of the writing is strong and fresh' (Morgan, *House of Macmillan*, pp. 87–8).

When these witnesses are considered together they could be held to support one of three possibilities. It is most improbable that any of the business associated with the dismissal of the choir from the church-music formed part of the earlier novel. So it is most likely that either the first five chapters of the book (the carol-singing and its preparations), or chapters VII and VIII (the dance at the tranter's house on Christmas *evening*), or both of these episodes, in substantially the same form, were once in the manuscript of *The Poor Man and the Lady*.

What we know of the detail of the abandoned novel comes from the rest of Morley's reader's report, from a long letter of criticism sent by Alexander Macmillan (in the Dorset County Museum), and from an account of the plot by Sir Edmund Gosse derived from recollections of a conversation with Hardy on the subject, and published in the *Sunday Times* of 22 January 1928, just after Hardy's death. Though they mention nothing relevant to *Under the Greenwood Tree*, there is sufficient material in these documents to allow us to be sure that the story 'An Indiscretion in the Life of an Heiress' was cobbled together from portions of the unpublished novel. This intimate connection between the story and *The Poor Man and the Lady* means that similarities between the story and *Under the Greenwood Tree* may indicate material that was once in the discarded novel.

There are in fact a number of verbal parallels between *Under the Greenwood Tree* and 'An Indiscretion in the Life of an Heiress'. The most striking of these occurs in the chapter that follows directly upon the tranter's Christmas party:

He disguised his feelings from some suspicious-looking cottage-windows opposite by endeavouring to appear like a man in a great hurry of business, who wished to leave the handkerchief and have done with such trifling errands. (*Under the Greenwood Tree*, p. 63)[6]

This sentence can be compared with a fragment from the story:

On a certain day he rang the bell with a mild air, and disguised his feelings by looking as if he wished to speak to her merely on copy-books, slates, and other school matters ('An Indiscretion', p. 52)[7]

Although in the story the man is the schoolteacher, the similarity in the approach to the girl is, when taken in conjunction with the following pair of examples, too marked to be accidental:

---

[6] Page-references to the novel are from the World's Classics edition of *Under the Greenwood Tree*, ed. Simon Gatrell (Oxford: Oxford University Press, 1985).

[7] Page-references are to the sometimes inaccurate but generally available *An Indiscretion in the Life of an Heiress*, ed. Terry Coleman (London: Hutchinson, 1976).

Dick could have wished her manner had not been so entirely free from all apparent consciousness of those accidental meetings of theirs. (*Under the Greenwood Tree*, p. 96)

Mayne could have wished that she had not been so thoroughly free from all apparent consciousness of the event of the previous week. ('An Indiscretion', p. 35)

There is also some resemblance of rhythm and diction in the descriptions of the two heroines, and in the response the two men make to the sight of the girls:

An easy bend of neck, and graceful set of head: full and wavy bundles of dark-brown hair: light fall of little feet: pretty devices on the skirt of the dress: clear deep eyes: in short, a bundle of sweets; it was Fancy! Dick's heart went round to her with a rush. (*Under the Greenwood Tree*, p. 117)

The clear, deep eyes, full of all tender expressions; the fresh subtly-curved cheek, changing to tones of red with the fluctuation of each thought; the ripe tint of her delicate mouth, and the indefinable line where lip met lip; the noble bend of neck, the wavy lengths of dark brown hair, the soft motions of her bosom when she breathed, the light fall of her little feet, the elegant contrivances of her attire, all struck him as something he had dreamed of and was not actually seeing. . . . Mayne's heart, which had felt the rebuff, came round to her with a rush . . . ('An Indiscretion', pp. 35–6, 38)

If these and other similarities represent something more significant than unconscious self-echoing on Hardy's part, then it is reasonable to conclude that a number of situations in *Under the Greenwood Tree*, particularly those of which class-difference is a distinct element, do derive more or less directly from *The Poor Man and the Lady*. Many of the passages that parallel those in 'An Indiscretion' were late additions to the manuscript of the novel at the time when Hardy was complicating the love-strand, and perhaps he turned to *The Poor Man and the Lady* when confronted with this necessity. It has not often been remarked that *Under the Greenwood Tree* in its published form offers a somewhat watered-down version of the 'poor man and the lady' theme. Dick and his family are in economic terms not good enough to aspire to join with the Days, and, as I have argued elsewhere, Hardy's aim is, in the relationship of Dick and Fancy, to contrast the financial implications of 'not good enough' with the moral ones.[8] Hardy has scaled down the social contrast but retained the essence of the central situation of his first novel in this one.

---

[8] In the introduction to the World's Classic's edition of the novel.

Far from the Madding Crowd: *Serialization and Leslie Stephen*

Tinsley liked *Under the Greenwood Tree* enough to offer Hardy in July 1872 the important financial step of publishing his next novel as a serial in *Tinsley's Magazine*. At the same time the pleasant reviews of *Under the Greenwood Tree* had given Hardy more confidence, and perhaps he sought advice elsewhere on terms of publication. Consequently, he was able to make a more advantageous arrangement with Tinsley, who was happy to agree to pay him £200 for rights to the serialization and first book-edition only—quite a substantial sum for a still unknown author.

Publishing his novels in serial form rapidly became a way of life for Hardy, but it is difficult to be certain about the effect that pressures of writing against a deadline had on the nature and shape of his work. For this first serialization he was only one step ahead of the printer for most of the time; *A Pair of Blue Eyes* was, it seems, at best in an embryonic state when he sent his acceptance of the terms to Tinsley at the end of July, and the first part was due in early August for the September issue of the magazine. He wrote on 7 September 1872 that he had sent copy for the October issue (which actually appeared in mid-September) to Robson, the printer of *Tinsley's Magazine*.[9] This must have put Robson's compositors under considerable pressure, and there can scarcely have been much time for Hardy to read proof. One effect of the haste with which these compositors were forced to set *A Pair of Blue Eyes* was that they retained a considerably higher percentage of Hardy's own punctuation than they did for the earlier novel, which they could set at their leisure. (There is further discussion of the attitude of compositors towards Hardy's punctuation in Chapter 11.)

Tinsley's Magazine was not one of the most prestigious monthly journals of the day, and when in November 1872 Leslie Stephen wrote to ask whether Hardy would write a serial story for *Cornhill*, he quite naturally abandoned Tinsley and eagerly accepted the chance of appearing in what was perhaps the foremost magazine; it must also have been an incentive that Stephen offered twice as much money. It was *Under the Greenwood Tree* that had appealed to Stephen, and Hardy began to produce another story from the same fertile field of his invention.

Tinsley had made one or two trifling comments on *A Pair of Blue Eyes* as it went through his hands,[10] but it was from Leslie Stephen that Hardy learnt his first lessons in what was to become a topic of urgent concern to

---

[9] *Letters*, i. 18.
[10] Ibid. 20.

him. From the beginning there were things in Hardy's novels that offended against the conventional taste of the period—details or incidents that appeared to stretch to the limit (and sometimes beyond it), what a respectable family magazine of the sort that published and paid for serial fiction felt it could accept on behalf of its readership. John Morley had even felt that there was too much 'realism' in *Under the Greenwood Tree*, and Hardy was soon to discover with *Far from the Madding Crowd* what a nervous and conservative editor might ask him to remove from the magazine versions of his novels and stories.

There has recently been some debate about the effect that Stephen's advice concerning details of the *Cornhill* appearances of *Far from the Madding Crowd* and *The Hand of Ethelberta* had in helping to form the emerging novelist. The received opinion has been that his influence was on the whole benign, that Hardy was lucky to have so sensitive and acute an editor so early in his career. It may well have been that the friendship that grew between the two men during their direct literary association was of the first importance to Hardy, and that Hardy learned from Stephen; but Stephen was neither a novelist nor a poet, and it is difficult to see how he could have helped Hardy directly, save by channelling his energies in more profitable directions. It is moreover the case that Stephen was anxious to remove from both novels details and extended passages that offended his taste and his perception of that of the *Cornhill*'s readership, but which all readers of Hardy would recognize as characteristic.

The most substantial change that Stephen initiated in *Far from the Madding Crowd* was the exclusion of seven pages of the manuscript during the description of the shearing-supper. Stephen had suggested that the whole chapter might be omitted, but gave Hardy freedom to consult his own instinct in the matter. Hardy immediately wrote to Smith, Elder the publishers and asked for the return of the relevant portion of the manuscript so that he could 'reconsider one of the chapters'.[11] The reconsideration led to the removal of dialogue between the villagers, and of Baily Pennyways's news that he had seen Fanny Robin in Melchester. The deleted manuscript leaves were preserved in Hardy's papers and are now in the Dorset County Museum, but they may more conveniently be consulted in the *Thomas Hardy Journal* for May 1985, where they appear on pp. 41–4 as an accompaniment to an essay by Tony Slade discussing their significance. Though Stephen was

----

[11] Purdy, pp. 337–8; *Letters*, i. 27.

undoubtedly right in selecting this chapter as the weakest of those that describe the sheep-shearing and its aftermath, and thus the most suitable for deletion or contraction so that the action might be speeded up, it is also the case that it contains several details to which the fastidious editor must have objected. There is Pennyways's description of Fanny as a ruined woman, there is Laban Tall's vulgar way of eating a lettuce, and above all there is the suggestion of imminent sexual intimacy that Jan Coggan sees in the twinkle in his wife's eye.

Michael Millgate suggests that sometimes Stephen may have invoked Grundian considerations to mask critical advice and, though this is probably true, I should want to argue that in this instance Stephen used the need for narrative pace as a convenient excuse for covert censorship.[12]

Another of Stephen's suggestions was that Hardy might remove altogether Fanny Robin's baby; in this instance he accepted that his motive was prudery, and that the omission would injure the story. He added that, like the deleted sheep-shearing supper passage, it could be restored when the story was republished in book form. On this occasion Stephen sent the manuscript to the printers and said that Hardy could make whatever changes he felt were appropriate on the proofs.[13] The extent to which Hardy was willing to be ruled by Stephen may be gauged by considering the revisions to chapter LXIII that he made on the *Cornhill* proofs. For example, where Liddy, describing the contents of Fanny's coffin, originally told Bathsheba 'there's *two of 'em* in there', in the serial 'Liddy came close to her mistress and whispered the remainder of the sentence slowly into her ear'.

The most substantial cut was of a page and a third of the manuscript which describes Fanny and her baby in the coffin. Stephen must have objected to the lyrical and uncensorious treatment of the bastard and the erring mother. It is possible that he had other stylistic objections, but the passage is characteristic of Hardy's lofty style as it crops up throughout the novel, including as it does a literary quotation, a fanciful natural image comparing the baby's cheeks and plump fists to 'the soft convexity of mushrooms on a dewy morning', and a painterly comparison between Fanny's hands and those in Bellini portraits. It is bad enough, but Stephen might as well have objected to the whole novel.

As a result of his advice we have also lost the extremely moving and delicately expressed picture of the two in the coffin as companions of one kind, caught in incipiency rather than decadence: 'they both had stood

12 Michael Millgate, *Thomas Hardy: A Biography* (Oxford: Oxford University Press, 1982), 160.
13 Purdy, p. 339.

on the threshold of a new stage of existence'. This paragraph as a whole represents a central strand in Hardy's conception of states of being and becoming. With this passage present we would also be able to enter much more readily into the impulse that later moved Troy to kiss Fanny, and we would sense more vividly that it was not purely one of remorse. As Hardy wrote, 'the youth and fairness of both the silent ones withdrew from the scene all associations of a repulsive kind'.[14]

Although Hardy never restored the sheepshearing supper pages, he was sufficiently concerned by the impact of censorship on this scene to take some steps to remedy the matter, not in the first impression of the first edition, which was published in 1874 before the serial had finished its run in *Cornhill*, but in the second impression issued a year later, and more extensively in the one-volume cheap edition of 1877. There were ten or so small reversions to the sense of the manuscript, but there was no attempt to restore either the text of Liddy's whisper to Bathsheba or the description of the couple in the coffin.

There is other evidence in the manuscript and correspondence of Stephen's censoring pencil, and some excisions from the proofs were made by him without consulting Hardy. These were mostly done because of the religious offensiveness or the coarseness of Hardy's manuscript expressions, and it is tempting to wonder whether the change from the 'buttocks' of a sheep to its 'back' was prompted by Stephen, or whether he was responsible for the new and rather unpleasant moral tone of Gabriel Oak's attitude towards the murderer Boldwood in chapter LV:

Gabriel's anxiety was so great that he paced up and down, pausing at every turn and straining his ear for a sound

became in the serial:

Gabriel's anxiety was great that Boldwood might be saved, even though in his conscience he felt that he ought to die; for there had been qualities in the farmer which Oak loved. (p. 296)[15]

The first shows real agitation, the second a kind of patronizing by Oak of Boldwood which seems out of character. Whether this was what Hardy

---

[14] The passage occurs on fos. 2-232 and 2-233 of the manuscript, which has recently been donated by Mr Edwin Thorne to the library of Yale University.

[15] Page-references are to *Far from the Madding Crowd*, ed. Robert C. Schweik (New York: Norton, 1986).

wanted we have at least license to doubt, in the light of Stephen's frequent interventions elsewhere.

This editorial activity sets a pattern which can be traced with variations through most of Hardy's novels. As has been seen, though Hardy restored some of his original readings at various times after the serialization, many remained as Stephen had suggested. It is impossible to say whether in preparing for the first edition Hardy considered each case and made a decision, but it seems quite unlikely, and that leaves the editor of the novel with an important decision of his own to make. So much, of course, depends on whether the individual editor feels that his sense of the author's final intentions for his work is the overruling consideration. If that is the case, then he is right to leave out the deleted sheepshearing passage, and to accept Hardy's later revisions to the toned-down version of Fanny Robin and her baby, as Robert Schweik does in his recent edition of the novel.

But another view is possible. If it is felt that the cancelled and unrestored passages were deleted not because the author thought or accepted that they were bad work, but because they did not suit some externally imposed canon of taste or publishing expedience, then there is a perfectly respectable case for restoring the excised readings to an edited text. This poses a different kind of burden of judgement on the editor, but then editing consists largely of making choices between alternatives of approximately equal validity.

The Hand of Ethelberta: *Serial Proof-Sheets*

Hardy's next novel, *The Hand of Ethelberta*, was also overseen by Leslie Stephen for *Cornhill*. The manuscript of the novel has been lost or destroyed, but by chance the proof-sheets for the serialization have survived, and they show further evidence of Stephen's influence as editor.[16] In Maitland's biography of Stephen there are extracts from letters to Hardy that refer to two passages in the novel:[17] 'I doubt . . . whether a lady ought to call herself or her writings "amorous." Would not some such word as "sentimental" be strong enough?' This was in May 1875, and in August he wrote: 'I may be over particular, but I don't

---

[16] In the collection of R.L. Purdy.
[17] F.W. Maitland, *The Life and Letters of Leslie Stephen* (London: Duckworth, 1906), 276.

quite like the suggestion of the very close embrace in the London churchyard.' By October he was able to say, referring to the embrace, 'I think you have much improved the rose-leaf incident.'

Hardy responded positively in both these instances. The first of them comes in chapter X, where originally Ethelberta said of her poems to Lady Petherwin, her mother-in-law: 'It would be difficult to show that because I have written so-called amorous and gay verse, I feel amorous and gay' (p. 84).[18] This speech embodies a central idea of the first part of the story, analysis of the relationship between what one creates and what one feels, but Hardy was quite prepared to alter 'amorous'—though he did not take Stephen's alternative, chosing 'tender' instead. If the change calmed Stephen's sensibilities, it did not ultimately satisfy Hardy, since he revised the passage again for the Wessex edition of 1912, in which 'tender and gay' becomes 'gay and amatory', returning to the sense, if not the wording, of the original.

Slightly later Lady Petherwin asks Ethelberta: 'And you think the verses may tend to misrepresent your character as a gay and amorous one, when it is not?' (p. 85). Again Hardy altered 'amorous' in proof, trying 'reckless' first, and settling finally for 'rapturous'. This version was retained in 1912.

The rewriting of the scene in the churchyard was more substantial, indeed the most substantial in the whole proof, requiring an extra piece of paper for Hardy to complete it. It occurs in what is now chapter XXVIII, and centres around a rose that Ethelberta was wearing 'on her bosom'. Originally one of her admirers, Neigh the son of a horse-knacker, snatched a swift embrace, and was discovered by Ladywell with rose-petals caught in the breast of his waistcoat. Ladywell made the correct inference that the petals had been shed by 'the pressure of heart to heart'; Neigh denies it, however. To remove the embrace required many sentences of alteration, and Hardy replaced it with a scene in which Ethelberta herself offers Neigh the petals from the rose while he, in taking them, 'pressed her fingers more warmly than she had given him warrant for'. He puts the petals in his pocket-book, whence they fall during his conversation with Ladywell. It is hard to agree with Stephen that the incident has been improved by the revision. In the earlier version Neigh is made to look rather ridiculous by his hasty and unwanted embrace in the churchyard, and Hardy was justified in aiming for such an effect. Neigh is pretentious, and in the new version he comes off with too much of his dignity intact.

[18] References to the text of *The Hand of Ethelberta* are to the Wessex edition of 1912.

There is one other small revision that may with a certain amount of confidence be ascribed to Stephen's influence. In chapter VIII Hardy wrote: 'Christopher, with lightened spirits, voice to correspond, and eyes *ensuite*', and in proof *'ensuite'* was altered to 'likewise'. Warrant for supposing that the editor was responsible for the change may be found in another extract from Maitland's biography: 'Such was his disgust for a French word in an English sentence, that I am proud of having caught him using *éloge* in his old age' (p. 265). It seems certain that there were other changes made at Stephen's suggestion, and it is a pleasant pastime, though ultimately unprofitable, to examine each of the proof-revisions to try to find evidence of his hand elsewhere.

The Hand of Ethelberta is like a number of Hardy's novels, in that the primary process of creation was continually interrupted by the need to revise proof for earlier episodes. In this instance Hardy had not even completed half of the novel when the first episode appeared in the *Cornhill*. Thus some of his words paradoxically had achieved the permanence of print, while the whole upon which they ultimately depended for their meaning was not yet in more than a primitive form. It is hardly surprising that Hardy should have come to regard serial publication as tentative, undertaken while a novel was still in flux.

It is the more or less invariable experience of novelists that as their writing progresses characters will develop in ways not foreseen at the outset, and themes will surface as of primary significance that had not been envisaged when work began. Different writers will have different methods for coping with this within the manuscript, but the writer of a serial under conditions of publication similar to those for *The Hand of Ethelberta* has few options. The appearance of an episode in print fixes it for the time being, so that revision in the light of subsequent developments in the novel has to be held over until the whole is re-examined in preparation for the book-edition. Hence it is also unsurprising to find that Hardy accepted whatever opportunities were offered by the proof for the successive serial episodes to take into account ideas that came to prominence in his evolving creation.

An example of this is the beginning of part four of the serial (chapter XIV). It opens with a discussion between Ethelberta's brothers Dan and Sol, and Christopher Julian, about the possibility of their going to practise their crafts in London. After the brothers have explained the range of their capacities, Christopher comments with irony (in what may be presumed to be the manuscript reading): 'You can both do too much to stand the least chance of being allowed to do anything. Sol, you must be a man who can look thoroughly at a door to see what ought to be done to it, but as to looking at a window, that's not your line.' When Hardy came to read the proofs of this passage he replaced the full stop after 'anything' with a comma, and added: 'in a city, where limitation is all the rule in labour. To have any success'. This generalization makes the point more explicit for the reader. As an isolated example this would have local interest, but in the same episode there is a further instance of the same kind of change. Sol and Dan do go to London, and work for a time in Ethelberta's house. On one occasion she says to Christopher of them: 'My brothers, you perceive . . . represent the respectable British workman in his entirety, and a touchy individual he is, I assure you, on points of dignity' (chapter XVII, pp. 129–30). In reading the proof Hardy saw another opportunity to introduce the town/country opposition, and added to the speech: 'dignity, after imbibing a few town ideas from his leaders.' It is a further small suggestive detail that both of these changes are second attempts, Hardy being dissatisfied with his first revised version—evidence that he thought particularly carefully about them.

The contrast between country and town life and values becomes a significant theme in the novel, and it may plausibly be suggested that these two revisions in proof of an early episode (made as he was writing into the second half of the novel) indicate that Hardy considered he had not given the theme the attention that he now felt it warranted.

There is another small group of instances of proof-revision suggesting Hardy's retrospective concern that a point that was becoming important as he neared the completion of the novel had not received sufficient emphasis in earlier episodes. In half a dozen places he underlined the painful effect on Ethelberta's relations with members of her family caused by her attempt to rise socially far above them.

A novelist not working under the constraints imposed by this pattern of simultaneous creation and publication has much more freedom to look back through his narrative once he has finished it and revise the opening in the light of the conclusion. Hardy in this novel and elsewhere did not have that freedom, and these small proof-revisions are all that he had time and license from the publisher to make.

In fact there are on average two or three revisions on every page of these proofs for *Cornhill*. For the most part they are details in phrasing or characterization of local interest, almost all of which immediately strike the reader as improvements, but which make their greatest impact cumulatively. Interspersed with these are larger, more significant changes, some of which I have already looked at; and another is on the leaf of proof reproduced in Purdy (p. 22), where a passage is added that gives us a further small insight into Christopher Julian's introspectiveness. There are also quite substantial alterations to the letter that Ethelberta receives from her father in chapter VII, but such large-scale changes are rare. As a brief example of the more normal scope of the revision, the following has several points of interest (it comes from chapter XXXI of the novel, and read thus in the proof that Hardy received from the printer): 'the outlook from the window, which presented an unusual combination of bucolic scenery with marine. Upon the irregular slope between the house and the quag was an orchard of aged trees' (p. 256). Hardy made three changes: the first replaced 'an unusual' with 'a happy', reflecting in the cliché more accurately the description that follows, in which there is more of the conventional than the unusual. Then he decided that 'bucolic' was quite the wrong word, too patronizing and not descriptive enough, and as if to compensate for his previous commonplace addition he chose 'grange' to replace it. The third change was a correction of the charming compositorial error that transformed 'the quay' to 'the quag'.

For a novel of this length Hardy found surprisingly few compositorial errors, and it seems clear that the printer's reader did an efficient job in eliminating the obvious blunders. On the other hand a few of those that remained for Hardy to deal with are suggestive for the student of the relationship between compositor, text, and author. In chapter XXIII, for instance, the compositor set 'a dear new angel met at last night's hall', which Hardy revised to 'a dear new angel met at last night's dance'. Hardy must have written 'last night's ball' in the manuscript, and thus a small question is thrown up: Would Hardy have revised 'ball' to 'dance' if the compositor had not made the error and so drawn his attention to the word? It can be suggested that 'dance' reflects more accurately the slightly informal and impromptu nature of the occasion, and there is no doubt that the word represents a conscious choice on Hardy's part at the moment of revision. What this example and a handful of others like it also show is that to a small degree at least the production of the substantives of the text, as well as of the punctuation, is a co-operative process between writer and printer.

Despite Hardy's extremely clear handwriting, there are combinations of letters that cause compositors problems. In chapter XV for example, the context of the passage suggests that 'shyly' was misread as 'slyly',

and similarly in chapter XXXIII 'slyly' was misread as 'shyly'. One of
the pairs of words that always causes problems in Hardy's hand is 'home'
and 'house'; in chapter XXI the proof read 'home', and Hardy changed it
to 'house' (which was presumably also the reading in the manuscript).
This example is a slender staff of support for editors of many of Hardy's
texts, who will be confronted with what appears to be 'house' in the
manuscript and 'home' in the printed texts, and who wish to return to
the manuscript reading. It is unlikely that Hardy would have noticed all
occurrences of this particular mistake in proof.

Another kind of mistake the compositors often make when setting
Hardy's prose is to confuse initial 'f' with initial 'g', and in this case the
most experienced reader of Hardy's hand is sometimes left uncertain.
There is an example of this on p. 17 of Dale Kramer's Clarendon Edition
of *The Woodlanders*. Marty South comes out of her firelit cottage into the
utter darkness of Little Hintock: 'her eyes were fresh from the blaze, and
here there was no street lamp or lantern to form a kindly transition
between the inner glare and the outer dark.' As Kramer's textual note on
the word 'glare' points out, it is very hard to tell whether Hardy wrote
'flare' or 'glare'. The editor is on safe ground in choosing to retain the
compositorial reading, since Hardy must have read it at least five times,
and probably more, during the novel's publication history, and he saw
no need to alter it. My interpretation of the manuscript evidence,
however, is that Hardy originally wrote 'flare', even though it is the
more unusual word in the context. Another pair of words that is easy to
confuse is 'flow' and 'glow' when used by Hardy to describe the action
of blood in a girl's cheeks during a blush.

Though it is true that the amount of revision revealed by these proof-
sheets is not particularly large, this is only to be expected, given both the
rapidity with which the printers would require the return of proof and
the fact (already alluded to) that, at least for early episodes, Hardy was
revising text whose ultimate conclusion he had not yet firmly
established.

But it is also the case with Hardy, as probably with most writers, that
once a piece was set in type it acquired a kind of permanence that would
need a more than average act of will to break into, except for the
correction of manifest errors. One of the questions that this book raises
concerns the stage at which Hardy's texts became, as it were, fixed for
him, so that revising them was no longer an act of creation but one of
refinement. As a first contribution to this enquiry, it is worth suggesting
that Hardy very soon, perhaps from the beginning with the frantic rush

over *A Pair of Blue Eyes*, began to see serialization as no more than a temporary measure, to be superseded by the relative permanence of book-publication. Thus, the serial versions of many of his novels still seemed to him to be in a state of becoming. Hardy's sense at any time of the completedness of his work is a vexed though important question, and one that will be discussed further at different points in the rest of the book.

The Hand of Ethelberta was a financial landmark for Hardy. From English and American sources he was paid around £1,500 for the serial and first-book rights of the novel—not because of any intrinsic merits of its own, but because of the great critical success enjoyed by *Far from the Madding Crowd*. An important effect of this considerable amount of money (as much, for instance, as George Gissing received for ten of his novels)[19] was that it gave Hardy the opportunity to pause for a while, and take a more deliberate look at the kind of writer he was, and the kind of writer he would like to become.

[19] See Michael Collie, *George Gissing: A Bibliography* (Toronto and Buffalo: Toronto University Press, 1975), *passim*.

2

Intermission

1876

Dealings with America

At this short pause in his career as a novelist Hardy began the series of commonplace books that have become known as his 'Literary Notebooks', which have been so brilliantly edited by Lennart Björk.[1] They are witness to a period of intense and omnivorous reading in Hardy's life, and they reflect his growing desire to develop more widely the cultural contexts of his fiction. Hardy must, I think, have been preparing himself for what he anticipated would be a different kind of novel; and though *The Return of the Native*, seen in the progression of his fourteen novels, does not seem radically different from *Far from the Madding Crowd*, still every reader will admit that there is a new flavour to the narratorial voice, and a fresh self-consciousness about the novel's design.

The financial independence that had allowed this 'sabbatical' (as Björk calls it) was provided just as much by revenue from the United States as from England. It had not taken Hardy long to learn that though the lack of international copyright legislation meant that he could expect relatively little profit from the sale of his books in America, editors were able to be generous in their payment for advance sheets of serials. Smith, Elder offered Hardy £700 for serial and first-edition rights for *The Hand of Ethelberta*; *The New York Times* paid him £550 for the serial rights alone.

Hardy's interests in America were first looked after by Henry Holt, who published all of Hardy's novels until 1886 and *The Mayor of Casterbridge*. Holt educated Hardy in the problems for foreign authors of publishing in the States, helped him to find an outlet for some of his serials and stories, and paid him as large a royalty on the book-editions as he claimed he could (10c. a copy, for the most part). Then from 1878—when they serialized *The Return of the Native* in their *New Monthly Magazine*—Harper and Brothers became more and more

---

[1] Lennart Björk (ed.), *The Literary Notebooks of Thomas Hardy*, 2 vols. (London and Basingstoke: Macmillan, 1985).

associated in America with Hardy's work. They also published in
Harper's Weekly all of Hardy's earliest stories, forming in this respect an
unspoken partnership with the English *New Quarterly Magazine* (edited
by Kegan Paul, who soon became Hardy's friend) which established
Hardy as a significant writer in this genre. In 1887 Harper and Brothers
eventually took over as Hardy's 'authorized' publishers in America.[2]

Separate publication in England and America offers potential for
textual confusion, but this does not seem to have occurred with any of
the earlier novels. Although Hardy sent to America advance sheets of
some of his early serial stories, it seems probable that these were clean
revises on which he made no further alterations, since sample collations
of *The Hand of Ethelberta* and *The Return of the Native* in their American
serialization show that they only differ from their English counterparts
in such matters as punctuation, spelling, and styling.

The publication of *The Trumpet-Major* in *Demorest's Monthly Magazine*
(1880) represents Hardy's first distinctively different American serial
version. From sample collations it appears that Hardy sent *Demorest's*
proofs of the English serialization in *Good Words*, and that he was
subsequently forced through editorial intervention to make bowdlerizations for *Good Words*. Thus, it was only in America (until the
publication of the first edition of the novel) that the text was available in
the form that Hardy intended (see also pp. 55–6 below).

A Laodicean and *Two on a Tower* each had only one setting in serial
form (the former was published by Harper's simultaneously in both
countries, the latter had no separate printing in England). It was not
until *The Mayor of Casterbridge* and the novels and stories that followed it
that distinctive British and American serial versions became the rule, and
to preserve the chronological sequence these texts will be discussed in
Chapter 5.

Hardy's correspondence during this year in which he wrote nothing
substantial shows that he was anxious to try to get as high a financial
return as possible on his earlier novels. In March 1876 he asked George
Smith of Smith, Elder whether they might not issue a cheap edition of
Far from the Madding Crowd or *A Pair of Blue Eyes*, adding:

My reason for suggesting a cheap edition of one or two of my previous stories
for the coming summer is that I do not wish to attempt any more original

---

[2] For more detailed information on Hardy's relationship with Henry Holt, see Carl Weber,
Hardy in America (Waterville: Colby College Press, 1946), and Seth Weiner, 'Thomas Hardy and
his First American Publisher', in *Princeton University Library Chronicle*, 39 (1978), 134–57. Weber
also outlines Hardy's dealings with Harper and Brothers.

writing for a few months, until I can learn the best line to take for the future; &
the interval would be a convenient one for reading over and amending any
previous book. (*Letters*, i. 43)

The publishers were apparently not ready for cheap editions; it was not
until the following year that they issued *Far from the Madding Crowd* in
one volume. In the same letter Hardy enquired about getting in touch
with Baron Tauchnitz, saying in this instance that he had the impression
'that to be in his list is a sort of advertisement for future works'.

It had taken five years and five novels for Hardy to explore all the
avenues open to the moderately successful author; his productivity had
been quite enormous, the result of his drive to write, his desire for
celebrity, and his need for money. It was not surprising that he needed a
rest.

3

The Manuscript of The Return of the Native

1877–1878

The novel that Hardy began to write at the end of this fallow period was
The Return of the Native, and there is substantial evidence to show that, as
with *Under the Greenwood Tree*, what the readers of the serialization of
the novel in *Belgravia* were confronted with was quite different in some
respects from the story that Hardy commenced.

In fact, despite its abundance of fair-copy leaves, *The Return of the
Native* is one of the more complex of Hardy's manuscripts, careful
examination revealing that there were sometimes two earlier versions of
pages that now have almost no alterations.[1] Though Hardy used two
kinds of paper in the manuscript of *Under the Greenwood Tree*, this variety
proves unhelpful in resolving questions about stages in the development
of the narrative. As far as *The Return of the Native* is concerned, however,
such evidence is invaluable. We have also to be grateful for Hardy's
economical habit of reusing for fresh text the verso of sheets he had
earlier discarded. These rejected false starts on what are now the backs of
existing leaves often provide the best evidence of the early direction of
the narrative, and are frequently referred to in what follows.

Another aspect of many of Hardy's manuscripts not significant in a
study of *Under the Greenwood Tree*, but important here, is Hardy's
uncertainty over the names of characters and places. Just as it is possible
to identify several layers of the manuscript of *Tess of the d'Urbervilles* by
the presence of the various first names Hardy gave his heroine—Love,
Cis, Sue, Rose-Mary, and Tess—so it is possible to say that leaves in the
manuscript of *The Return of the Native* bearing names like Avice,
Toogood, Candle, or Brittan (subsequently discarded by Hardy in
favour of Eustacia, Wildeve, Cantle, or Yeobright) are survivals from an
earlier version of the novel.

To begin with the question of the paper. There are two varieties of

---

[1] A photofacsimile of the manuscript of *The Return of the Native* has been published by Garland
(New York, 1986). The introduction by S. Gatrell discusses in more detail some of the points made
in the following pages.

paper that Hardy used when writing *The Return of the Native*, and these two varieties mark a division of the manuscript into two sections. Any of the leaves in the earlier part—up to fo. 220 in Hardy's numeration—may have belonged originally to a version of the narrative quite different from that which now survives. For although a considerable number of the leaves in this first section are fair copies of a very fresh kind, these fair copies are also written on the earlier stock of paper (with a few exceptions towards the end of the first section). Leaves after fo. 220 are on a different stock of paper, and while they may have adjustments in detail, rarely show evidence of substantial transformations in plot or character.

We know from surviving correspondence that Hardy sent a portion of the manuscript to several editors before it was finally accepted by *Belgravia*.[2] It seems reasonable to hypothesize that what John Blackwood of *Blackwood's Magazine*, Leslie Stephen of *Cornhill*, and George Bentley of *Temple Bar* saw was an early version of some or all of the pages up to fo. 220; it would then follow that many of the fair-copy leaves in the first half of the manuscript represent a rethinking and rewriting done either in response to their criticisms, or after the story was finally accepted by Chatto and Windus. There is, as far as the paper is concerned, what might be thought of as a transitional stage in the manuscript; it occurs between fo. 210 and fo. 220. What seems to have happened is that Hardy, when making the revision to the first part of the manuscript, first used up for new, fair-copy leaves all available sheets of the original stock of paper, including those which he had set aside because they contained false starts. He exhausted this paper before completing the revision and for the new versions that he made of fo. 211 and fos. 213-19 he had to open a new package of paper, paper that from fo. 221 of the manuscript onwards is used exclusively. It is of course the case that if the rewriting represented by the fair-copy leaves in the first part of the manuscript had been done *after* fo. 220 had been completed, then they would all have been written on the newer paper. A further piece of evidence to support the argument that Hardy revised up to fo. 220 before creating any more of the printer's manuscript is that the longest surviving name from the early versions of the texts, Avice Vye, occurs for the last time on fo. 206, the last appearance of the character before fo. 220.

Almost all of the discussion that follows will therefore be concerned with these first 220 pages.[3]

---

[2] *Letters*, i. 47, 49-50.

[3] In what follows I am indebted to the pioneering work of John Paterson, whose *The Making of The Return of the Native* (Berkeley: University of California Press, 1960) was the first substantial

It is impossible now to be certain how Hardy first envisaged the beginning of his novel (whether, that is, he always had in mind the description of the heath), for the first chapter is almost all fair copy, and only the second leaf seems to be a survival from an earlier stage in the history of the manuscript's development. While this leaf does suggest that the now famous opening was from early on a part of Hardy's scheme, the evidence is not conclusive. What does seem clear, though, is that the second chapter is now not at all the same as it once was, and the track through the manuscript that leads to this conclusion may be taken as typical of the complex paths which Hardy's textual critics have frequently to follow.

Chapter II ends with an extra-numbered leaf (fo. 12a), and it is tolerably clear from their state that both fos. 12 and 12a are replacements, and that fo. 11 probably is also. These pages contain the description of what the reddleman saw as he rested his horses on the Heath, looking up at Blackbarrow (as Rainbarrow was called before the first collected edition of 1895), and there is available a certain amount of evidence to suggest why the rewriting was made. On fo. 14 of the manuscript, in the midst of the description of the bonfires visible from the top of the tumulus, the following passage is cancelled: 'Amid these glares the little window [under] the hill, which the woman had watched, though still shining just the same as ever, was barely visible. In its tininess, its faintness, & its whiteness, it was to these as a glow-worm among lamps.' On fo. 17, Fairway, indicating the abode of the 'new-married folks', now points 'towards a dim light in the direction of the distant highway, but considerably to the west of where the reddle-man was resting.' In an earlier cancelled version he had pointed 'to the dim light in the valley which had been observed by the solitary woman.'

These revisions are the first part of the track; and it would be possible to guess that Eustacia—or Avice as she would have been called then—instead of standing motionless on the top of the barrow as she does now, observed from afar, was in an earlier version seen by the narrator rather than the reddleman, and described looking down at a light in the valley below her. But the trail goes further and has a more surprising twist: on the verso of fo. 18 there is a false start for an unnumbered leaf; this reads: 'of night, a sound which modulated so naturally into the rest that its beginning and ending were hardly to be

---

examination of the development of a Hardy text. I cover much of the same ground as Paterson, but my interpretations of the manuscript evidence are rather different.

distinguished. The bluffs had articulated, the bushes had articulated, the heather bells had articulated, at last articulated the woman.'

It is easy enough to discover the leaf on which Hardy began this passage again; fo. 60 starts: 'of night a sound which modulated so naturally into the rest that its beginning and ending were hardly to be distinguished. The bluffs had broken silence, the bushes had broken silence, the heather-bells had broken silence; at last so did the woman.' The immediate inference from this close identity would be that fo. 18 was a replacement leaf written some time after Hardy had reached fo. 60; but there are one or two other factors that suggest a different solution.

There are two cancelled passages on fo. 60 that have a bearing on the question. The second new paragraph on that leaf once began: 'Far away down the valley a faint shine had recently made its appearance: it came from a cottage window.' The same paragraph once ended: 'Her eyes were steadily fixed thereon as if the interior and its occupants could be seen.' It is possible in view of these suppressed descriptions to suggest with some confidence that this heavily revised leaf, stranded amidst a stretch of fair-copied leaves, once had a place much nearer the beginning of the manuscript; the numeral 60 at the top of the leaf replaces an earlier cancelled number that is not absolutely legible, but which might be either 15 or 75. There is no apparent reason why it should have been 75; on the other hand, when taken in conjunction with the fact that the current fos. 14-21 were at one time numbered 19-26, so that there would have been room for an earlier fo. 15, there does seem some warrant for believing that it was indeed 15. As a fragment of supporting evidence, it is worth noting that the current fo. 18 is the first of a sequence of three leaves that have false starts for other leaves on their versos—fos. 19 and 20 have material that now appears respectively on fo. 14 and fo. 16; this makes it more probable that the false start on the verso of fo. 18 should be for what was once fo. 15.

And there is further still to go: fo. 60 is the fourth leaf in chapter VI of the novel as it was finally arranged; the three preceding leaves describe how Eustacia Vye returns to Blackbarrow after the heathfolk have left their bonfire; they give a sense of her figure and bearing, and go on to the virtuoso evocation of the sounds of the heath at night in the wind. The first of these leaves (fo. 57) is almost unemended fair copy in Hardy's hand, while the next two are unrevised fair copy in the handwriting of his wife Emma. The earlier version of all this material may well originally have been intended for the opening movement of the novel—for Avice's first rather than her second appearance—and the leaves that these fair copies replaced may well once have been numbered 12–14. It is thus likely that instead of the remote view of her silhouette against the skyline that we have now, our first encounter with this central character was to have been much more intimate; though in both arrangements there is narrative emphasis upon her apparent harmony with the heath, one of the central paradoxes in a character who claims to despise it.

As to why Hardy made such a change, there are a couple of likely reasons, both connected with the letter of criticism that John Blackwood sent Hardy when saying that *Blackwood's* was booked up for the immediate future. The relevant passage is: 'The doubt that occurs to me is whether you are right to occupy so large a portion at the beginning of your story without a thread of light to throw an interest round the rugged characters you so vividly paint.

There is hardly anything like what is called Novel interest.'[4] It may have been that Hardy, responding to this commentary, decided to break the darkness of his opening chapters with the more commonplace humanity of Diggory Venn and old Vye in conversation; this also allowed him to indulge his penchant for distant and remote views of significant events, and it added a small touch of mystery in the unresolved identity of the occupant of Venn's caravan. It is also possible that Hardy thought of the advancement of the bonfires into a more prominent position as 'a thread of light'.

The manuscript unravelling that I have attempted here would be of relatively little textual interest, were it not the case that it is also involved in one of the two considerable changes in the structure of the novel that can still be identified. The two passages on fo. 60 which describe the light from the cottage window and the woman's observation of it were, as I have noted, both revised. The first became: 'Far away down the valley the faint shine from the window of the inn still lasted on', and the second: 'She lifted her left hand, and revealed that it held a closed telescope. This she rapidly extended, as if she were well-accustomed to the operation, and raising it to her eye directed it exactly towards the light beaming from the inn.' The two points of significance to be drawn from the revisions are the replacement of the cottage by the inn, and the suppression of the word 'occupants'. In the novel as it is now, Eustacia is looking down at the inn in an attempt to see whether Wildeve and Thomasin have returned together from Southerton where they were that day to be married; and to see whether Wildeve will respond to her bonfire-signal. The earlier versions suggest a different situation; originally Thomasin and her husband-to-be were intending to return to a cottage (and it is here relevant that Thomasin's husband was not originally to have been an innkeeper). It seems also that there was more than one person to be seen in the cottage, and thus that both had indeed arrived there before the woman began her observation. These conclusions are confirmed by an alteration on fo. 28 to a remark made by Fairway. Originally it went: 'we can drop down across to the Quiet Woman, and when we've had a wet there we'll draw up-along and strike up a ballet in front of the married folks' door.' For the revised version Hardy omitted 'and when we've had a wet there we'll draw up-along', so that the 'married folks' door' became that of the inn.

All this represents one manifestation of a radical rethinking of an important strand of the plot, a change that spreads filaments throughout the first half of the novel and may have affected the second half also; it is that rather than returning home on the evening of her abortive marriage-attempt, Thomasin originally spent a week in Southerton with her assumed husband, and was back in Egdon for a now unknowable period of time before discovering that she was not married to him.

There are only two surviving pieces of evidence that provide the basis for this conclusion: the first is on fo. 126 where Thomasin and Mrs Yeobright are talking about Thomasin's position after her return from Southerton unmarried. Thomasin says; 'Why don't people judge me by my acts? Now look at me as I kneel here, picking up these apples—do I look like a lost woman? . . . I wish all good women were as good as I!' As well as embodying one of Hardy's most deeply held convictions in the first sentence, this outburst provokes the following response from her aunt (as she is now, though in earlier drafts she was her mother):

Strangers don't see you as I do . . . They judge from false report. Well it is a silly job, and I am partly to blame.

So it appears in the final manuscript version, but earlier there was a slightly different speech:

Strangers don't see you as I do . . . They judge from report, and you were away a week with him. Well, it is a sad job, and I am partly to blame.

There is no ambiguity here. It also seems from this quotation that Thomasin must have learned that she was not married fairly soon after returning to Egdon, since Mrs Yeobright says nothing about her staying in the cottage on the heath; perhaps Toogood (as Wildeve was at first called) told her the truth in some brutal fashion after meeting with Avice by Mistover on the first night of their return.

The second central passage is on the verso of fo. 160, which contains a false start for material now on fo. 103; Diggory Venn is talking to Avice/Eustacia of Thomasin and Toogood/Wildeve, and in the version on fo. 103 he says: 'It is quite a secret. It is that he may refuse to marry Thomasin after all.' But earlier there was a different secret: 'His wife Thomasin has found that she is not lawfully married to him.' Since in the later conception the marriage-ceremony was not even attempted, this must relate to the time when the two lived for a week at Southerton, and for a few hours at least on Egdon. This latter is confirmed by a passage on fo. 18 in which Grandfer Cantle (or Candle as he was earlier) originally said:

Yes, they went away up the country to do the job, and neither vell nor mark was seen of 'em again till an hour or two ago when they came home man and woman—wife, that is.

After revision it became:

Yes, this morning at six o'clock they went away up the country to do the job, and neither vell nor mark have been seen of 'em since, though I reckon that this afternoon has brought 'em home again, man and woman—wife, that is.

One side-effect of this change is materially to reduce the unconscious irony that lies behind the Grandfer's slip of the tongue at the end of his speech.

None of the other twenty or so revisions that are made to accommodate Hardy's altered plot-line is quite so explicit, and their significance has to be illuminated by the changes already discussed. Characteristic is that on fo. 27, a fair-copy leaf, in which Fairway originally said: 'What do ye say to giving the new man and wife a bit of a song to-night afore we go to bed? When folks be married 'tis as well to look glad o't, since looking away won't unjoin 'em.' There is nothing here to suggest that Thomasin and Wildeve had been away a week, but because Hardy decided to make the plot-change, he also felt constrained to add '—being their wedding-day' after 'bed', and 'just' before 'married'.

This example occurs before it is generally known that Thomasin is in fact unmarried still; later in the novel there is a group of changes that alter the perception that others have of her position, once it has been established. Some of them are one-word alterations, others are slightly more complicated, but all have a similar effect in reducing the intensity of the response to her adventure in Southerton.

There is one further development in this area of the plot; at some intermediate stage in the evolution of Hardy's thinking he considered making Thomasin refuse to marry Toogood/Wildeve. On fo. 196 a sentence began: 'On the Sunday morning following the week of Thomasin's marriage'; at some later revision-period 'marriage' was changed to 'refusal to marry'; later still it was altered back to 'marriage'. The leaf is relatively early, as the numeral has been altered from something now unrecoverable, and it is only as an addition to the text that it names London and Paris as the locations of Clym's employment.

There is what may most satisfactorily be interpreted as a further occurrence of this fleetingly established development, on a false start of a leaf numbered 96, which Hardy reversed and used to write fo. 186. It reads:

he tells me nothing—least of all about you.
    He is no friend of mine. However perhaps you could hardly have heard yet in the circumstances, so few people know. This is the matter: my marriage with Tamsin will not take place.
    No immediate word came from Avice.

It seems most likely that it is Toogood/Wildeve who speaks here of his marriage, and that he is referring to Thomasin's decision to refuse it, rather than to any determination of his own.

There is insufficient evidence to decide whether Hardy made this short-lived change to his plot before or after removing Thomasin's cohabitation with her assumed husband. If, however, it can be imagined that Hardy once thought of Thomasin living for a week with Toogood under the impression that she is married to him, and then through the strength of her personality, her truth to herself, refusing to marry a man whom she no longer loves when he is driven to make amends, it would reinforce the still perceptible relationship between Thomasin and Tess Durbeyfield. It would then be possible to consider this version of Thomasin in some ways a precursor of Tess. It might also indicate that one strand of *Tess of the d'Urbervilles* is a working out of an idea that he felt unable to pursue in *The Return of the Native*. Proceeding further into the realms of speculation, the comparison gives rise to the likelihood that Thomasin's child would, had her refusal to marry survived, have been illegitimate and thus akin to Tess's baby Sorrow. The relative insignificance of Thomasin in the surviving version—once she is safely married—may have been the direct result of Hardy recognizing that he could not examine her in the role that he had originally conceived for her, and thus losing interest in what had become a more commonplace personality.

It seems almost certain that Hardy changed his fundamental conception of the novel in response to the comments of one or other of the magazine editors to whom he showed the first part of the serial; he would almost certainly have been told that his story was unpublishable unless he bowdlerized this element of the plot. It is possible that he might have come to such a conclusion without external prompting, but in view of his record with later novels, especially *Tess* itself, this seems less likely. It is probable that the eclipse of Thomasin was one of many involuntary changes of direction imposed on Hardy by the contemporary taboos governing the publication of serial fiction.

The second structural revision is less easily defined, based as it is upon evidence of Hardy's changing sense of the natures of his characters and the roles he marked out for them. Diggory Venn, Eustacia Vye, and Damon Wildeve are all rather different people in the novel we read from those Hardy first imagined and began to write about. Take Diggory Venn: in Hardy's earliest conception he did not carry Thomasin home in his van from Southerton, because he had no van, and because Thomasin would have come home with Toogood; he did not appear like a red ghost to the bonfire-makers on Blackbarrow; he did not meet Mrs Yeobright; in fact he first appeared in the novel as the occupant of a tent discovered by the little boy Johnny (Christian Candle's nephew in an early reading) as he goes home from Avice Vye's bonfire. He expressed no emphatic interest on hearing that Toogood was, on the day of his return, meeting with Avice, even though supposedly married to Thomasin.

It is also possible that Venn originally had no romantic interest in Thomasin. As is so often the case, there is not enough evidence to be sure on this point; it is at least worth noting, however, that when Venn overhears the second meeting between Avice and Toogood, Hardy has to indicate in an addition to the text on fo. 94 that Venn was aroused to strategy because 'stung with suspicion of wrong to Thomasin'. What he overheard at that interview cannot now be known, since the dialogue has been completely rewritten; the only hint is on the verso of fo. 186, a leaf already referred to above. It is the false start of a leaf numbered 96, and begins with Avice speaking: 'he tells me nothing—least of all about you.' To this Toogood responded: 'He is no friend of mine'. The only candidates for the identity of 'he' are Avice's father (as Jonathan Vye once was) or else Venn himself—which would then imply some kind of relationship between him and Avice of a kind that no longer exists.

It is equally impossible to know what Avice and Diggory spoke about in the chapter now called 'A Desperate Attempt at Persuasion', since all but the first leaf of it too has been rewritten; but the cancelled title, in the form of a brief snatch of verse, might have introduced a different kind of dialogue, one based directly on Avice's personal animosity towards Thomasin:

> Woman oft has envy shown:
> Pleased to ruin others' wooing,
> Never happy in her own.

Whatever followed, it is certain that as a result of the conversation Venn did not propose himself as a suitor for Thomasin, nor did he arrive at Bloom's End just in time to hear Wildeve's triumph.

The next meeting between Venn and Eustacia, involving Eustacia's volte-face over Wildeve and Venn's agreement to act as her messenger, is all late fair copy, and so again anything might have been decided between Diggory and Avice; though to judge from a cancellation at the foot of fo. 189 it cannot have been what it is now. Reporting on the marriage of Thomasin and Wildeve, Venn originally kept quiet from the Yeobrights the fact 'that since his compact with Avice and the coercing measures they had employed, he had kept strict watch on Wildeve, and had reported upon his movements every day to that beauty ensconced among the hills.' This earlier version is clearly not appropriate as a summary of how Wildeve was persuaded in the later arrangement to marry Thomasin; again there is the tenuous suggestion of a closer relationship between Diggory and Avice than is ever seen between Venn and Eustacia.

It is also possible that Thomasin was in on the secret: a question concerning her niece put by Mrs Yeobright on fo. 191 prompts the thought; it was twice revised. At first it read: 'Did she seem to know that her [?] would be there?' in which the key word is quite illegible; then it became 'Did she seem to know that Miss Vye would be there?'; and finally it read 'Was there an arrangement that Miss Vye should be there?' Venn slides around the question, and his evasiveness clearly suggests that at one time it had some point.

No more can even be conjectured about the earlier Diggory Venn. Subsequently, however, when Venn had fully taken on his role as protector of what he sees as Thomasin's interests, Hardy still had to add, on the verso of fo. 245, a passage accounting for his appearance to gamble by the light of glow-worms with Wildeve. Also, the chapter in which he harasses Wildeve to the extent of using a gun to keep him away from Eustacia (with the characteristic effect of precipitating an open meeting between them), and in which he consults with Mrs Yeobright on the matter of Thomasin's comfort of mind, was a late addition to the novel, perhaps made in response to two needs—for more matter to fill a serial episode, and to provide a sufficient reason for Yeobright to go to the Nunsuch house to hear the worst.

There remains a final detail to be looked at in this context. During a conversation at Bloom's End after the mummers' performance, one speech on fo. 162 was originally attributed to Diggory, though there is no other evidence that he was ever at the party. There are two alternative explanations for the seeming misattribution. The more straightforward is to say that it was simply a slip of the pen, and was corrected as soon as Hardy realized what he had done (though there is some difficulty in imagining why Hardy should have made such a slip in the first place). The more complicated is to accept that Diggory was once at the Yeobright's party; this would mean that he was once a part of the Egdon community, a fellow of Fairway and the Candles, and not the isolated character that he seems to have been in both early and later versions. As usual there is no straightforward answer, but the possibility of social equality between Venn and the heath-dwellers introduces a factor which underlies the changes to all the characters in the novel, a factor which may be called 'gentrification'.

At one time every character in the novel was to have been more or less on a socially equal footing. The local aristocracy, as we perceive them now, the aloof Eustacia Vye and the utilitarian Mrs Yeobright, were originally distinguished from the other heath-folk by the force of their personalities, rather than by superior social standing, claimed by themselves or accepted by others. Eustacia's grandfather, Avice's father, was originally not a naval gentleman, but on fo. 6 wore an 'obsolete' coat and gaiters, and spoke to Diggory Venn as to an equal rather than as to an inferior (fos. 8–10); Avice's mother was thought to be a witch by one of the heath-folk (fo. 31), and thus was probably also a heath-dweller; Avice herself may have been born and passed her childhood on the heath—consider the implication of the difference between the cancelled version of a passage on fo. 75 and its replacement:

Egdon was her Hades, and she had imbibed all that was dark in its tone and

Egdon was her Hades, and since coming there she had imbibed much of what was dark in its tone.

Mrs Yeobright originally spoke to the bonfire-makers as to equals (fos. 34–8); her strength of personality rendered her superior (in force of character) to the others, but not her birth or pretensions. Clym, at his home-coming party, and Thomasin in her letter to Venn, use dialect to a degree that is rare with them elsewhere, and which is revised as soon as Hardy has them drift higher in the social scale. Clym originally was to go no further afield in his employment than Budmouth, and his status was to have been well below that of manager.

With Venn the process was slower of accomplishment, and perhaps achieved more reluctantly; it is not until the first collected edition of 1895 that his social credentials are fully established, and his considerable transformation from apparent vagabond to bourgeois respectability is complete.

The most radical change in this respect within the manuscript is that from Toogood to Wildeve. We know of the early identity of the character through a now-cancelled addition on the verso of fo. 21, that was intended for insertion into a superseded fo. 22: 'O no. They may call him Conjuror Toogood, and white witch, and what not, but you all know what the man really is is a herbalist, and to gie him his due he's very knowing in some most racking complaints.' This is evidently an intermediate version; on the original fo. 22 he must have been described in a sinister or superstitious way, and the verso addition would then have been made to add some realism or common sense to the description, with perhaps a deliberate echo of *Silas Marner*.

The name Toogood survives in cancellations as late as fo. 150, where Avice, in considering Clym, asks herself 'What was Toogood? Interesting but inadequate', and thereby suggests a more substantial figure than the 'quak' that he was called by Fairway on fo. 23; it may be that Hardy had in mind by this time someone who might be thought of as a prototype of Vilbert in *Jude the Obscure*. There is, though, very little of the medical Toogood left in the novel, since all his early appearances have been rewritten in the name and personality of Wildeve. Nevertheless, the survival of these few details is perhaps the strongest testimony to the quite different novel that had once existed in Hardy's imagination; there must have been immense differences in behaviour and character between the quack/conjuror Toogood and the elegant, idle, and sensitive innkeeper Wildeve.

It has been received opinion for many years now that the change Hardy made to the character of Avice Vye in developing Eustacia was the most fundamental upheaval in the novel. But on a close examination of the manuscript it appears that, while Hardy considerably altered his view of her character, he did nothing so profound to her as he did to Toogood, and the revisions he made are closely connected to the general wave of gentrification that struck the text.

John Paterson has attributed 'diabolism' and 'satanism' to the early Avice, but his argument is based on one manuscript reference only. Paterson says of Avice:

She was originally described, however—and this, significantly, represents the novel's first reference to her by name—in more pejorative terms: in the opinion of the peasant chorus, "Avice Vye [was] a *witch*" (fol. 31).[5]

It is worth quoting the whole of the cancelled passage from which Paterson's brief quotation comes:

What? inquired Timothy Fairway.
A witch, said the woman firmly. Young Avice Vye is a witch, as her mother was afore her.
"That's new to me I own

Because the leaf that precedes fo. 31 is fair copy, we cannot be certain of the relationship between the two, but if the speakers have not altered in the rewriting, then the 'woman' referred to is Susan Nunsuch. In context Paterson's quotation loses much of its power; it is far from being the generalized opinion of the heath-dwellers, since Fairway has never heard it said of her before. Furthermore, it is probably the opinion of the one character in the novel who believes in witchcraft, and who practises near the end the only, rudimentary, act in that field. In the novel as it stands Susan Nunsuch's attitude to Eustacia is continually being undercut by the narrative—the only support it gets is when Mrs Yeobright says that good girls do not get taken for witches even in Egdon. There is nothing in the manuscript as it survives to indicate that there was ever to have been a different attitude to the business of witchcraft.

In this context it is also worth noticing that the two episodes that involve Susan Nunsuch in her anti-witch activities against Eustacia were probably late additions to the novel; they give some colour to the need for such a plan of education as that which Clym proposes, but they also

---

[5] Paterson, p. 18. See n. 3 above.

illustrate a paradox in Hardy's nature and in his writing. We are expected to view witchcraft through the rational eyes of Clym; yet at the same time Eustacia dies within minutes of the melting of her wax form over Susan Nunsuch's fire, and though there are other sufficient causes of her death, we cannot forget the close coincidence of the two events. It is not exactly that Hardy wants to have it both ways, but rather that, as with Christianity, he is himself rationally sceptical but emotionally sympathetic, and that both qualities coexist within him.

Once the initial assertion that she is a witch is robbed of its authority, the quotations that can be found to support Avice's satanic origins are not convincing. As noted above, it is probable that the earliest presentation of Avice is on fo. 60, (fo. 15 in an earlier arrangement); this leaf had Avice looking down from Blackbarrow on the cottage that contained Toogood and Thomasin, home from their 'honeymoon' in Southerton. She makes a sound, and in the earliest version

what she uttered began as a sighing, & it finished as a [?] titter of derision. The mockery implied by this laugh might either have been [directed] at her own previous sigh, or at something in her mind.

Slightly later 'titter of derision' became 'satirical laugh', and later still 'gentle laugh', while 'mockery' became 'amusement' and '[directed] at' became 'derived from'. The final version is simply:

What she uttered was as lengthened sighing, apparently at something in her mind.

There is a similar transformation on fo. 62, where Avice's skirt gets caught by a bramble; in all there are four different versions of her response to this incident. The first runs:

it tore nothing & it injured nothing about her; yet the woman uttered hot words of passion as she loosened it & passed on. The immediate cause was quite insufficient for the mood, & it was plain that she had peviously been charged brim-full with anger, which here found a temporary leak.

The second increases the intensity by adding after 'passion' the phrase '& sounds worthy of Tisiphone' (also early evidence of Hardy's schematic attempt to relate his narrative to the classics). The third is the definitive change:

Instead of putting it off and hastening along she yielded herself up to the pull, & stood passively still. When she began to extricate herself it was by turning round and round on her axis, & so unwinding the prickly switch. It was plain that she was in an idle mood.

This is completely different from the first versions: passivity against activity, idleness against anger; but the final version takes the difference still further. The last sentence is altered to read: 'She was in a desponding reverie.' Thus in passages on two pages it is possible to trace the same transition from anger or passion to idleness and to melancholy. There are further relevant examples in the immediate vicinity, and instances could be multiplied from the 'Queen of Night' chapter, but the point has been sufficiently made: that the difference between the two conceptions is rather between an actively and a passively passionate character than between a witch and a romantic heroine.

It is interesting in this context to note that in the letter of criticism of the earliest version of the novel that John Blackwood wrote to Hardy there occurs the following paragraph:

Avice is a remarkable character and might have been educated in Paris.

This suggests that romantic adventure and unconventionality were already the keynotes of her character; witches are not generally educated on the Continent. It is also possible that this brief comment was the spark that sent Clym from Budmouth to Paris.

After the 'Queen of Night' chapter most of the changes Hardy makes which differentiate Avice from Eustacia are part of the general process of gentrification, stressing her social superiority to the heath-folk— superiority in her own eyes to all others in the novel. Thus, on fo. 116 she asked herself originally: 'What was a man worth whom another woman did not value', but later her self-questioning ran: 'What was a man worth whom a woman inferior to herself did not value'; and on fo. 166, when Avice is at the Yeobright's party, she complains to herself: 'Nobody here cares for me'; Eustacia, however, laments: 'Nobody here respects me'. Even Mrs Yeobright, herself raised considerably in social standing in revisions to the novel, grudgingly acknowledges Eustacia's position; when commenting on her appearing, to give away Thomasin, Mrs Yeobright said at first: 'How very remarkable. Avice Vye.' After revision this became: 'How very remarkable. Miss Vye. It is to be considered an honour, I suppose.'

There is no comparable transformation worked on the character of Clym Yeobright; the gentrification that moves his jewellery shop from Budmouth to Paris, and his occupation in it from assistant to manager, is all; and whilst this makes it easier for the reader to understand where he got his ideas on education and life in general, and provides the attraction for Eustacia that might not have been needed to catch Avice's imagination, it makes no fundamental difference to his nature.

The only substantial change to affect Clym is a plot-revision. Originally, when Mrs Yeobright knocked on the door of the cottage at Alderworth on the day of her death, she saw Eustacia's face at the window, and blamed her exclusively for the refusal to let her in. Some time later Hardy was pondering ways of getting Clym to discover the truth of what had happened at his door that afternoon, and realized that he would have to make some alterations to earlier passages in order to make the revelation convincing; at the same time he may have felt that he needed a stronger justification for Clym's uncontrolled violence towards Eustacia when he confronts her with the accusation. The backward trail began when he decided to use Johnny Nunsuch as the bearer of the truth. There had to be some convincing reason for Clym pursuing the matter further, and so he added the conversation between Diggory Venn and Mrs Yeobright in which she tells him that she was planning to visit Alderworth and that she had forgiven her son and his wife (fos. 300–1). Then he had to add Mrs Yeobright's 'woman cast off by her son' speech to Johnny Nunsuch, and his (still rather odd) appearance at her deathbed to repeat her words. Then he had to go further back and introduce the presence of Clym's furze-cutting equipment beside the closed door, thus implicating him in Mrs Yeobright's sense of rejection. It is also true that the leaf on which Johnny tells Clym of all he saw that day has an extraordinary number of lines on it (45 as opposed to the norm of 26 or 27), and is most probably a late addition. The effect of all these revisions is to enable Clym to feel more intense self-reproach before he learns the truth, and more comprehensible anger after learning it.

The only other alteration worth mentioning is the addition to the last page of the novel of some details of what Clym preached in his new sermons on the mount—that he left 'alone set creeds and systems of philosophy'. On the whole Hardy seems to have been secure within himself about Clym, though many critics have felt that his characterization is the failure that undermines the core of the novel.

So far I have examined some of the scattered and fragmentary manuscript evidence that allows the investigator to hypothesize concerning Hardy's early conception of his narrative. The irrecoverable truth would be considerably more complex than anything suggested here, for, as we saw at the beginning of the chapter, there are many different layers in the text, and often it is just not possible to suggest priority, or to follow a logical sequence of implications; we know that much is missing because of the large amount of fair copy. The interested reader will do well to compare what is said here with what Paterson wrote over twenty-five years ago, and then to go to the manuscript himself, where he will be able to exercise his own re-creative imagination.

As a conclusion to this study of *The Return of the Native*, it seems worth looking at a few important incidental details that illustrate Hardy's revising at its most characteristic; details that show why revisions reveal so much of the artist.

Hardy seems characteristically to have written fast at first (to get his original conception down on paper), providing a sometimes flat narrative which he then went over again more slowly, the number of reviews depending upon the pressure of serial deadlines.

An example of the subtlety with which Hardy approaches his creative rereading is on fos. 212–13 of the manuscript, during the episode in which Clym joins those who are trying to rescue the Vyes' bucket from the bottom of their well. Clym has met Eustacia only once, and that in mummer's costume, and without discovering her identity for certain; nevertheless, something about her has caught his imagination. For her part, Eustacia has been dreaming about him as a potential beloved and saviour from the darkness of the heath. Yeobright takes the place of Fairway as the man controlling the rope:

The grapnel was again lowered. When its smart impact upon the water was heard, Yeobright knelt down, & leaning over the well began dragging the grapnel round & round as Fairway had done.

"Tie a rope round him—it is dangerous," was said in a soft & anxious voice from behind.

This is how it was at first; when he came to consider it again, Hardy allowed his creative imagination to settle on the tiny incident, and altered it to read:

The grapnel was again lowered. Its smart impact upon the distant water reached their ears like a kiss, whereupon Yeobright knelt down, & leaning over the well began dragging the grapnel round & round as Fairway had done.

"Tie a rope round him—it is dangerous," cried a soft & anxious voice somewhere above them.

The effect of the kiss on the passage is almost magical: it anticipates Eustacia's deepest desire, and forces her to declare her presence (the reader knows it is her at once because the word has, without his realizing it, prepared him for her appearance); in bringing Clym and Eustacia together it activates the grapnel in the well as a symbol of their relationship—they meet across it here, and begin the fruitless excavations into their personalities that their marriage embodies.

And then there is the change to the location of Eustacia's voice. Earlier it was earth-bound, but now it is a disembodied, spiritlike voice that comes out of the air; for a moment it seems that the kiss has drawn forth a spirit of love, though the next paragraph destroys the illusion in placing her at a window of the house. Even this is appropriate, for the 'above' is turned thereby into a reinforcement of Eustacia's social superiority.

Another example that is characteristic in a different way can be found in Hardy's description of the furniture in the Quiet Woman. Originally it read:

Most of them were sitting round the room in seats divided by wooden elbows apportioning stalls, & these were carved with the initials of many an illustrious drunkard of former days, who had passed his days & his nights between them. (fo. 232)

The mild irony of 'illustrious drunkards' and the suggestion of the bestial in 'stalls' are the only details of interest here. When reading through what he had written Hardy may first have been arrested by the potential in 'stalls', and, while retaining the touch of the farmyard, he added an extra satirical dimension:

Most of them were sitting round the room in seats divided by wooden elbows like those of cathedral stalls, which were carved with the initials of many an illustrious drunkard of former times, who had passed his days & his nights between them, & now lay as an alcoholic cinder in the nearest churchyard.

Not only is there now the juxtaposition of cathedral and drunkard, but there is also one of Hardy's more delightful pieces of graveyard humour; especially pleasing is his use of 'the nearest' instead of some place-name, as if their cinders, like their living selves, could only stagger to whatever was handiest.

It is also possible to see Hardy working with an eye to the novel's overall conception; on fo. 316 Mrs Yeobright sits down in the spot where she falls asleep and is bitten by an adder: 'a little patch of heather intruded upon the path; & she sat down amid its feathery arms.' Comforting enough, but Hardy decided to alter it. The question raised is whether the change was inspired by something that he wrote in the final episode: 'It was very pleasant to Thomasin, when she had carried the child to some lonely place, to give her a little private practice on the green turf & shepherd's thyme, which formed a soft mat to fall headlong upon when equilibrium was lost' (fo. 412). It seems reasonable to suggest that Hardy deliberately underlined the final movement of the novel from death to life when he altered the first passage to read: 'a little patch of shepherd's thyme intruded upon the path; & she sat down upon the perfumed mat it formed there.'

The last example to be considered here seems crucial as we consider the central unanswerable question at the climax of the novel: did Eustacia deliberately throw herself into the stream? There is no definitive narratorial statement, but there are plenty of previous references to her desire for death; on the other hand, it is a rain-filled and stormy night, and Thomasin shows how easy it is to miss the path. The balance, though, seems to be weighted towards suicide, and it was partly to redress that imbalance that Hardy made a very simple but telling change. The narrator describes what Wildeve and Yeobright heard as they stood in the road: 'it was the plunge of a body into the stream adjoining'; this is the original reading and it implies the volition of a diver. The final version, 'it was the fall of a body into the stream adjoining', suggests only the passivity of an accident. Hardy is likewise deliberately non-committal about other crucial incidents in other novels; the violation in *Tess of the d'Urbervilles*, for instance, was revised several times, both in the manuscript and afterwards—and each time the revisions seem to be made in the interests of maintaining a balance of probability between the violence of rape and the acquiescence of seduction (though it remains a violation however you imagine the action, just as Eustacia's death seems necessary, whatever the role of her will in the matter). It is as if the narrator in either case is unwilling to commit himself at the critical moment, although it might equally be suggested that the situation has been deliberately left inconclusive in order to force the reader to reflect with greater attention upon the events that surround it.

There is another facet of the manuscript of *The Return of the Native* which was not a factor in *Under the Greenwood Tree*: the presence of some leaves written in the hand of Emma Hardy. As we saw earlier, Hardy got his future wife to make a fair copy of the manuscript of *Desperate Remedies*; and though she had nothing to do with *Under the Greenwood Tree* or *Far from the Madding Crowd*, after their marriage in 1874 her handwriting appears in almost all of the remainder of her husband's novel manuscripts, and in several of his stories. From the kind of mistakes that are made in the passages in her hand, it seems probable that she mostly wrote from Hardy's dictation, though occasionally the evidence points to her having copied an earlier draft. There are almost no examples of places where she has made any change to the text other than the correction of an obvious error in transcription; on leaves that she wrote out the revisions are nearly always in Hardy's hand.

It is not difficult to imagine that making fair copy of a number of leaves in considerable haste to meet a serial deadline was a tiring business, and that Hardy was glad of the help; it also seems likely that Emma was anxious to share as far as possible in the creative life of her husband. Her assistance was particularly useful when Hardy was preparing duplicate manuscripts for *Two on a Tower*, and essential when he was composing *A Laodicean* lying ill in bed. About the latter he wrote in *The Early Life*:

from November onwards he began dictating it to her from the awkward position he occupied; and continued to do so—with greater ease as the pain and haemorrhage went off. She worked bravely both at writing and nursing till at the beginning of the following May a rough draft was finished by one shift and another. (p. 188)

According to Purdy (p. 38), the manuscript of *A Laodicean* was burned by Hardy, and so cannot offer any evidence about Emma's role as amanuensis. In this context, it is interesting to note that of the five novel manuscripts that have substantial numbers of leaves missing, it is possible to hypothesize that in at least three of them there is some connection between the gaps and Emma Hardy's hand.

There is much circumstantial evidence to suggest that over a hundred leaves of the manuscript of *The Mayor of Casterbridge* were removed by Hardy, when he presented it to the Dorset Natural History and Archaeological Society in 1911, because they were all or part in Emma's hand. Five of the nine occurrences of her writing are false starts on the versos of current leaves, and, where it is possible to read the numeral of the false start, either that leaf in its later version, or the one before it, or both are missing (see Figure 2). The other four are all in the first line of their leaf, and in each case Hardy has attempted to disguise his wife's writing, and the previous leaf has been removed. Furthermore the four fragmentary leaves in the manuscript are all directly related to missing leaves, indicating that material has been cut from them because they too contained some of Emma's writing.

There is no evidence of this kind in any of the other defective manuscripts, but it may just have been that Hardy was more efficient in effacing the traces of his wife's writing. It seems likely that the combination of a sense that if his manuscripts were to be permanently preserved they should contain only his own script and a certain irritation that occasionally stories were aired about the role that Emma had played in the creation of the novels would be enough to cause him to destroy those pages that she had copied.

He may well have done this to *The Trumpet-Major*, from which fourteen leaves are missing. The manuscript was presented to King

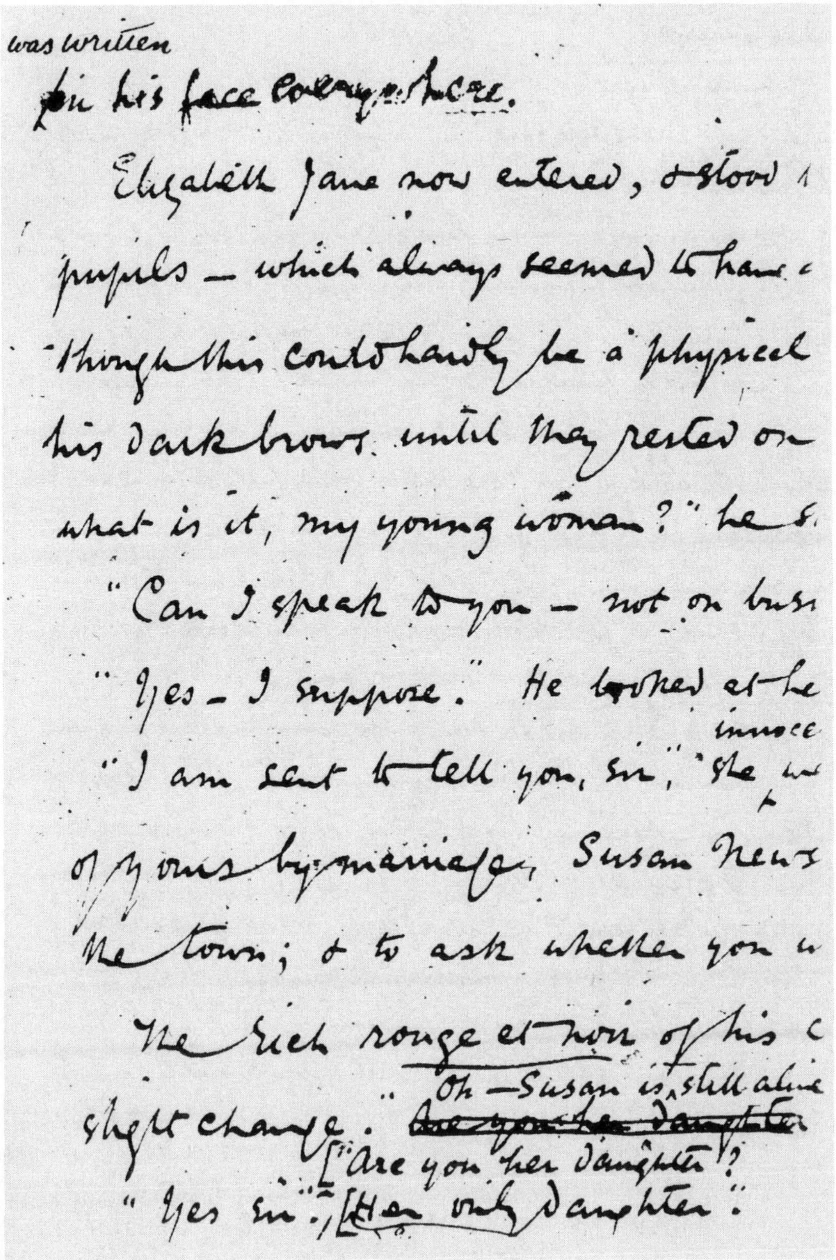

was written

in his face everywhere.

Elizabeth Jane now entered, & stood .

pupils — which always seemed to have .

though this could hardly be a physical

his dark brows. until they rested on

what is it, my young woman?" he s.

"Can I speak to you — not on busi

"Yes — I suppose." He looked at he

innoce

"I am sent to tell you, sir," the we

of yours by marriage, Susan New

the town; & to ask whether you w

the rich rouge et noir of his c

slight change. ~~Oh — Susan is still alive~~

~~Are you her daughter~~

["Are you her daughter"?

"Yes sir." ~~her~~ *only daughter."*

Figure 2: fo. 94 of the manuscript of *The Mayor of Casterbridge*

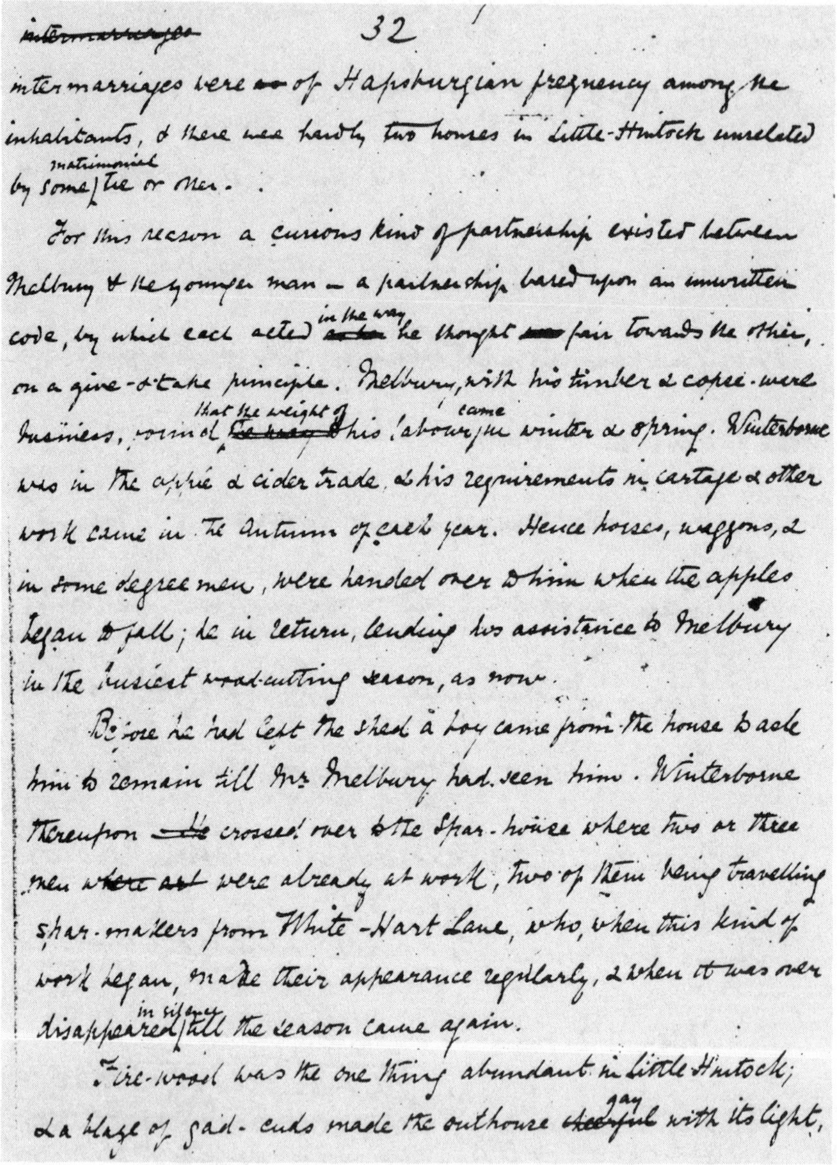

32

intermarriages were — of Hapsburgian frequency among the
inhabitants, & there was hardly two houses in Little-Hintock unrelated
by some/the or other.
matrimonial

For this reason a curious kind of partnership existed between
Melbury & the younger man — a partnership based upon an unwritten
code, by which each acted in the way he thought fair towards the other,
on a give-&-take principle. Melbury, with his timber & copse-wood
business, found that the weight of his labour came winter & spring. Winterborne
was in the apple & cider trade, & his requirements in cartage & other
work came in the autumn of each year. Hence horses, waggons, &
in some degree men, were handed over to him when the apples
began to fall; he in return, lending his assistance to Melbury
in the busiest wood-cutting season, as now.

Before he had left the shed a boy came from the house to ask
him to remain till Mrs Melbury had seen him. Winterborne
thereupon crossed over to the spar-house where two or three
men were already at work, two of them being travelling
spar-makers from White-Hart Lane, who, when this kind of
work began, made their appearance regularly, & when it was over
disappeared in silence till the season came again.

Fire-wood was the one thing abundant in Little-Hintock;
& a blaze of gad-ends made the outhouse gay with its light.

Figure 3: fo. 32 of the manuscript of *The Woodlanders*; the first five words,
and the remainder of the leaf from 'Melbury' in line 7, are in Emma Hardy's
hand.

George V, also in 1911, and though one page in Emma's hand still survives, Hardy may have overlooked it, since the missing fourteen occur in a single sequence. With *Tess of the d'Urbervilles*, which lacks thirty-nine pages, the case is more problematical, since not only is there no evidence of the kind that helped to make this inference virtually certain for *The Mayor of Casterbridge*, but it also seems on the surface unlikely that as Hardy and his wife grew further apart, and the subjects of his fiction became less and less to Emma's taste, he would have asked her to copy leaves for him. On the other hand, these thirty-nine do occur in the first third of the novel, where the manuscript is at its most worked over, and recopying might therefore have been thought most necessary. No other reason for the omissions has been forthcoming, and the fact that this manuscript too was presented to a public collection (this time the British Museum) adds a little weight to the possibility that she did after all copy some leaves of *Tess*, and that Hardy removed them.

When we come to the case of *Jude the Obscure*, from which there are fifty-nine pages missing, it seems even more unlikely that Emma would have had anything to do with the manuscript, though her handwriting does appear in a false start on the verso of one leaf. What she wrote there, however, bears no relation to the novel as it survives, and may never have been part of *Jude*. In this instance another explanation for the missing leaves has been advanced: that there is some coincidence between them and passages that required bowdlerization. This is, however, not true for every missing page; moreover, this manuscript was also given to a public collection, the Fitzwilliam Museum in Cambridge.[6]

A Pair of Blue Eyes offers a quite different case, for only three of the eleven serial episodes survive, and Hardy never had possession of the manuscript after it was sent to Tinsley for his magazine. The manuscript also contains three leaves with Emma's handwriting on them. Her hand survives too in other novels which were not presented to public collections; in *The Return of the Native*, which was Clement Shorter's reward for having the other novels bound in 1908,[7] in *Two on a Tower*, which was never returned from America, and in *The Woodlanders*, which he did not ask Shorter to have bound and which remained in his library until his death. See Figure 3 for a characteristic leaf written partly by Hardy and partly by his wife.

---

[6] Patricia Ingham, 'The Evolution of *Jude the Obscure*', *Review of English Studies* NS 27 (1976), 34.

[7] In *The Great Victorians* ed. H.J. and Hugh Massingham (London: Ivor Nicholson and Watson, 1932), Edmund Blunden records Hardy as saying that the novels bound on Shorter's instructions were so badly done that they had to be re-bound, probably for their presentation to various institutions in 1911. (I am grateful to Michael Millgate for pointing out this reference to me.)

4

Researching the Story
1878–1882

The Trumpet-Major: *Serialization and First Edition*

What Hardy did in 1875–6 might be thought of as research of a general sort, but the background fabric of the book that followed it, *The Return of the Native*, came fundamentally from his experience and imagination as much as *Under the Greenwood Tree* or *Far from the Madding Crowd*. For his next novel, however, he began to reach beyond his own knowledge, and he started working in the British Museum library on the history of the Napoleonic period. There is another notebook, the 'Trumpet Major Notebook', edited by Richard Taylor, which charts this more specific research.[1] This notebook contains not only transcriptions from newspapers and journals of the period, but also Hardy's drawings of details of dress and equipment. Some of his reading indeed, found its way directly into the novel: the episode in which the militia are drilled on a Sunday morning is a celebrated example.

It seems that Hardy had entered a different phase in his creative life (though one that was in the end to prove unprofitable), for this kind of research was also important in his preparations for *Two on a Tower* in 1881. Although Hardy knew the names of the stars and where to find them, he had no experience of astronomy as a serious pursuit, and he paid a visit to the Royal Observatory at Greenwich in order to test the feasibility of his plan that the novel should contain an observatory established at the top of a hollow memorial pillar. He also enquired about the processes involved in the grinding of a lens.[2]

The only hint we have that Hardy undertook this kind of specific preparatory work for earlier novels is in a fragment of manuscript that relates to *Far from the Madding Crowd*.[3] Hardy himself wrote on it in red

---

[1] *The Personal Notebooks of Thomas Hardy*, ed. Richard H. Taylor, (London and Basingstoke: Macmillan, 1978), 115–86.

[2] See *Letters*, i. 96–7 and *Early Life*, p. 195.

[3] Now in the Dorset County Museum. The fragment is discussed at greater length by Christine Winfield in 'The Manuscript of Hardy's *The Mayor of Casterbridge*' PBSA 67 (1973), 36–7 and in my 'The Early Stages of Hardy's Fiction', in *The Thomas Hardy Annual*, 2 (1984), 25–7.

ink: '*Far from the Madding Crowd* Some pages of 1st. draft. (Details of sheep-rot—omitted from MS. when revised)'; it seems unlikely that it ever formed part of the manuscript of the novel, but more relevantly, it also seems from the text of the fragment that he had to consult a shepherding manual or encyclopaedia about sheep-rot.

This detail comes as a timely reminder that though Hardy was brought up in a thoroughly rural environment, and was quite evidently familiar with different kinds of agricultural work and life, yet there would still be areas where his knowledge would have to be reinforced by reference to some authority.

In 1879, though, Hardy came up against a different kind of authority. With *The Trumpet-Major*, editorial censorship entered a new phase for Hardy. There is no concrete evidence to show how far *The Return of the Native* was affected by pressure from the editors of *Belgravia*, but there is ample to reveal the way in which the Revd Donald Macleod, the editor of *Good Words*, imposed himself upon the text of *The Trumpet-Major*.

On 20 June 1879 Macleod wrote to Hardy about the novel, and the letter needs to be quoted extensively, as it is an expression, more open than most, of what would best have satisfied almost all of the serial editors whom Hardy encountered during his career as a writer of fiction:

We are anxious that all our stories should be in harmony with the spirit of the Magazine—free at once from *Goody-goodyism*—and from anything—direct or indirect—which a healthy *Parson* like myself would not care to read to his bairns at the fireside. Let us have as much humour (oh that we had more!) and character—as much manly bracing fresh air—as much honest love-making and stirring incidents as you like—avoiding everything likely to offend the susceptibilities of honestly religious & domestic souls.

Do forgive this homily! But we have had such bothers in the past in consequence of a want of clear understanding beforehand on matters like this that I think it best to be frank.

You will not, I hope, for a moment imagine that the statement of such views implies any possible doubt as to your sympathies being in perfect harmony with the lines laid down—It is all the other way!

This last paragraph reads ironically in the light of Hardy's later experiences; but, as far as *The Trumpet-Major* was concerned, he can have had few qualms on receiving the letter.[4]

When it came to dealing with what Hardy had actually written, there were some differences of opinion. Purdy notes how Hardy recalled, some

---

[4] The letter is in the Dorset County Museum.

forty-five years after the event, the degree of editorial interference he suffered during the serialization of the novel:

I met Dr. Macleod whenever he came to London and discussed small literary points with him, all of which I have forgotten except two: that he asked me to make a lover's meeting, which I had fixed for a Sunday afternoon, take place on a Saturday, and that swear-words should be avoided—in both which requests I readily acquiesced, as I restored my own readings when the novel came out as a book. (pp. 32–3)

Hardy's memory was only slightly at fault; in fact he made the meeting take place on a Monday, but almost all the consequent changes were returned exactly to the manuscript reading when they appeared in the first edition. There were occasional small adjustments of the kind that Hardy was always making, but only two serial readings remained, one of which, ironically enough, was the addition of 'Monday', which was not removed until the Osgood collected edition in 1895. It must have seemed odd to readers of the first edition that Bob, at the end of one volume, says that Matilda is arriving on Monday, but at the beginning of the next goes to meet her on Sunday.

Although Hardy complied carefully with the letter of Macleod's request, he was allowed to retain the following passage:

The office was next door to All Saints' Church, and the afternoon sermons at this church being of a dry and metaphysical nature at that date, it was by a special providence that the waggon-office was placed close to the ancient fabric, so that whenever the Sunday waggon was late, which it always was in hot weather, in cold weather, in wet weather, and in weather of almost any other sort, the rattle, dismounting, and profane noises outside completely drowned the parson's voice within, and sustained the flagging interest of the congregation at precisely the right moment. No sooner did the charity children begin to writhe on their benches and adult snores grow audible than the waggon arrived (p. 140).[5]

The only bowdlerizing change here from the manuscript was the substitution of 'profane noises' for 'swearing'; otherwise this characteristically wry look at church practices passed the minister's editorial eye (it was not his church that was being ridiculed).

Well over half of the specific references to Sunday and its activities in this episode were interlinear additions to the manuscript, including the 'swearing' just alluded to, and this fact gives rise to the thought that

___

[5] Page numbers refer to the Wessex edition of 1912.

Hardy might deliberately have been testing Macleod. The details of John Loveday's suggestion in chapter 18 that Matilda Johnson had been intimately acquainted with members of the—th Dragoons, deleted for the serial in *Good Words*, had been similarly a late addition to the manuscript. As our knowledge of Hardy's attitude to serialization and serial editors grows, it becomes more and more probable that he consciously attempted to slide incidents and phrases past them that he was sure they would not take—though it is surprising to find that it is possible to say this of so early and relatively uncontentious a novel as *The Trumpet-Major*. It can more plausibly be posited of his last few novels and stories, of which it can be said either that Hardy deliberately provoked a Grundian response, or else that he was almost unbelievably sanguine, and repeatedly so, about what editors would stand.

As far as the swear-words mentioned in Hardy's note are concerned, almost all of them were either removed or toned down for the English serial, though neither they nor the references to Sunday travelling were changed for the novel's American serialization in *Demorest's Monthly Magazine*—either Hardy sent off proofs to New York before Macleod had a chance to interfere, or else he made a deliberate decision to allow his United States readership to read the uncensored version. Only a proportion of the bowdlerized versions were returned in the first edition to the form found in the manuscript and the American serial; some were caught later in the two collected editions, but a considerable number still remain in the weaker form enforced by the editor of *Good Words*.

It is hard to find complete runs of *Demorest's Monthly Magazine* (essentially a fashion magazine that included fiction), and the copy I consulted (University of Illinois Library) lacked half of the episodes. However, a comparison of this fragment with *Good Words* shows that the editor must have asked Hardy to delete other passages, including a sentence on the value of diluted spirits in restoring good-humour (tobacco was all right as far as Macleod was concerned), a passionate embrace in the rain, and a description of how Anne's waist was encircled by Bob's arm.

It seems likely too, that after a discussion with Macleod, a footnote 'Historically true' was added in *Good Words* to the drilling of volunteers before church on a Sunday; the episode of *Demorest's* was missing in the run I examined, but the note is not in manuscript or the first edition. There are other places in passages I was unable to examine where it is reasonable to suspect that Hardy was forced by Macleod to alter his manuscript reading, and failed to return to it in the first edition. A good candidate is the omission of 'and kissing your partner' from Festus Derriman's taunt: 'No dancing on the green, Lockham, this year, and kissing your partner in the moonlight' (ms fo. 197, p. 232). Others are the removal of coarse or irreverent words, as when 'like the ark when carted away' was changed to 'like the ark when sent away', or when 'dress with the waist under the armpits' was changed to 'dress with the waist under the arms'. However, only a full collation of the American serial will reveal the complete story.

It seems, from the continued appearance in the first edition of some of Macleod's bowdlerizations, that Hardy did not use early proofs as copy for the first edition, and the editor of the novel would have to decide whether he would be justified in returning to the American serial readings in places where editorial interference still remains in place. There is certainly a good prima facie case for doing so.

The Trumpet-Major is the first novel in which Hardy made a conscious effort to restore in the first book-edition the majority of the changes enforced on him by serial publication; a good point at which to pause for a moment and consider the relationship between serial and first edition of Hardy's novels in more general terms.

It was a matter of economic necessity for late Victorian publishers, and thus a matter of concern for authors, that the first edition of a serialized novel should be issued before the story completed its run in the magazine. Mudie, Smith, and the others would (if the novel were a success) be flooded with demands for the book from readers avid to know whether the heroine was indeed saved from her precarious position, in the last chapters, and they would be compelled to order the book in large numbers. In fact, Hardy's correspondence shows that he was soon alive to this aspect of the importance of getting the book out before the serial finished. He wrote on 21 September 1878 to Chatto and Windus, the proprietors of *Belgravia*, where *The Return of the Native* was soon to end: 'It would be convenient for me to publish the library edition of the *Return of the Native* as it is usually done, that is, somewhat before its conclusion in the magazine, & I have thought that it might appear a month before the last number without prejudice to *Belgravia*' (*Letters*, i. 60). It apparently took him a little longer to appreciate fully the other reason for early publication; that it diminished the scope the libraries had to circulate bound copies of the serialization rather than the three volumes of the book. In an unpublished letter of 30 October 1883 to Walter Besant (drawn to my attention by Michael Millgate), Hardy speculated that the poor sale of the first edition of *The Trumpet-Major* to

Mudie was the direct result of the library having circulated bound copies of the *Good Words* serial issue. Hardy added that the financial failure of Blackmore's *Christomel* was undoubtedly caused by the first edition having been delayed until after the serial had ended. He also noted that, as an out-of-town subscriber to Mudie's Library (and thus not able to inspect the books he was to be sent), he had received such bound serializations, even occasionally copies made up and circulated before the last serial episode had appeared!

The implication for the author of this rapid publication was often that he or she was forced to revise (if revision were contemplated at all) while the primary impulse of creation was still fresh and alive. An example of this in Hardy's work is offered by *The Woodlanders*. Hardy sent the ending of the novel in manuscript to the editor of *Macmillan's Magazine* on 8 February 1887. He must, at about the same time as he was completing the story, have been revising proof for the March episode of the serial. A week later he wrote to Macmillan about the first edition, saying that he would 'send a revised copy of the story for the printers [of the book edition] in the course of a few days', and asking for proofs of the April episode (the concluding one) for this purpose (*Letters*, i. 161–2). Thus, Hardy's work on all three stages—manuscript, serial, and book—overlapped in a continuous sequence of creation.

However, as far as Hardy was concerned there was a distinct difference between serial and book versions of his work, the difference between a transient and a permanent form. Though he would almost certainly derive less money from the first edition than from the serial, it was the form in which his novels would be read by the critics, it was the form of his novels upon which the growth of his reputation would depend. But most importantly, for most novels it was the first time that he had an opportunity to consider the work as a whole, quite free from editorial interference (though not perhaps from that of Mudie), and for most it was also the edition in which Hardy made the largest number of revisions.

Despite all these considerations, though, there are several notes to friends that express at this stage a certain weariness with the business of revising, a sense of having skimped the task of preparing the book for its critical ordeal. Hardy was emphatically not one of those writers who wants to forget a story as soon as it is published, yet it is possible to imagine that after the process of writing the manuscript, and reading proofs and revises for the serial, considering the novel again might have been a deadening job, whatever the imaginative vision that had inspired the work. To make revisions and read proof and revises for the book before the serial had even finished its run must severely have taxed the imaginative stamina and commitment even of Hardy, an author dedicated to the improvement of his work. Thus, while it is feasible, it may (for some novels at least) be too simple, to see the first edition as representing the first appearance of the work in a form embodying the whole initial creative experience.

The Trumpet-Major offers a good example of the kind of changes that Hardy felt able to make for his first editions, beyond the reinstatement of censored details. The single series of alterations with the greatest cumulative effect is the grotesque mock-heroic dimension added to Festus Derriman. The first encounter with him begins with a song; in *Good Words* 'a voice was heard', but in the first edition 'a deep stentorian voice was heard'; and, when the figure projecting the voice appears, instead of the entry of 'a young man', in came 'a young man, about the size and weight of the Farnese Hercules'. In the serial 'the man . . . went on' with his song, but now we read 'the colossal man . . . went on in tones that shook the window-panes'. This introduction to Festus is characteristic of revisions throughout the first half of the novel. Having once established the new conception he was anxious not to overdo it, and there is very little of this kind of change more than half-way through the text; still, where he was once 'half-fledged', he is 'ponderous', where formerly he spoke, now he 'thundered', and later he is described as being 'a match for one of Frederick William's Patagonians'.

It must be supposed that Hardy realized that in the serial he had left Derriman half-way between realism and artificiality, and decided now to push him into farce. In the process he becomes a less serious suitor for Anne, a more dramatic contrast with the ordinary people at the centre of the novel, and a more suitably theatrical accompaniment to Matilda Johnson. The episode of this (now) huge man chasing Anne across a meadow becomes analagous to the story in *Tess* about William Dewy and the bull.

There are some other important revisions to the narratorial commentary. Two of these are connected with what was the greatest difficulty Hardy faced throughout the novel; making the interrelationships between Anne and the two brothers convincing, especially towards the end, where the alternation of Bob and John in Anne's heart is rather rapid. At the end of chapter XXXVII Hardy wrote:

He had resolved for his only brother's sake to reverse his procedure before it was too late, and guide Anne's mind in the direction required.

He realized that this offered inadequate motivation for John's self-denial at a time when he finally seemed to be turning Anne's love towards himself; and the passage became:

He had resolved for the sake of that only brother whom he had nursed as a baby, instructed as a child, and protected and loved always, to pause in his procedure for the present, and at least do nothing to hinder Bob's restoration to favour, if a genuine, even though temporarily smothered, love for Anne should still hold possession of him. (p. 338)

By stressing the depth of the emotional tie John feels to Bob and by reducing his contemplation of active promotion of Bob's cause to a passive withdrawal, Hardy has given a more plausibly motivated piece of analysis. A little later, in chapter XL, as a result of John's selflessness, Anne is about to forgive Bob yet again. In the serial she says:

A too easy pardon is apt to make folk repeat the fault. Do you repent?

The tone of this was wrong, and Hardy realized that a narratorial intervention here would help to disarm some of those readers who might feel that it was too obvious that Anne was choosing the wrong man. Therefore, the speech is replaced by:

Youth is foolish; and does a woman often let her reasoning in favour of the worthier stand in the way of her perverse desire for the less worthy at such times as these? She murmured some soft words, ending with 'Do you repent?' (p. 366)

A third, and perhaps more important, change is that to the last sentence of the novel; originally John Loveday left the mill, 'to blow his trumpet over the bloody battle-fields of Spain.' It may be that the addition to the sentence was Hardy's first ending to the story, and that he was talked out of it by Macleod (though there is no manuscript evidence to suggest it). In the first edition the passage reads: 'to blow his trumpet till silenced for ever upon one of the bloody battle-fields of Spain.' John's death seems required; how intolerable it would have been to return to Bob and Anne! The logic of the story leads the reader to be grateful for his death, to feel that it comes as the only fitting end; and, though it adds a sombre tone to an otherwise romantically coloured tale, it shows more clearly the kinship that *The Trumpet-Major* bears to most of Hardy's novels. An underlying conviction that many of them share is the sense that we had better not have been born, a belief that grew stronger as Hardy grew older. Both Tess and Jude desire death, and we are glad to acquiesce at least in Jude's; Pierston in *The Well-Beloved* also wants to die, and it is Hardy's grim joke that he does not. But earlier, too, Boldwood's imprisonment (in *Far from the Madding Crowd*) and Ethelberta's marriage are death-in-life situations from which death will come as a kind release; Eustacia Vye says she wants to die, and her wish is fulfilled; Viviette Constantine's death in ecstasy is felt to be the happiest end possible for her; and Henchard's death above all is an embodiment of the doctrine that we had better not have been born. It is another of the paradoxes experienced by readers of Hardy that, while sensing the power of this extreme position, it is more than balanced for them (until Jude at least) by the strength of the life-force that Hardy infuses into these characters.

Finally, it seems reasonable to conclude from the changes noted and the many others not mentioned that, once the serialization was finished, Hardy had a clearer idea of what his novel had turned out to be. He could judge what limited but important revisions needed to be made before the text became fixed in book form and the critics were able to have their say about his achievement.

Two on a Tower: *Manuscript, Serial, and First Edition*

Complications for Hardy in the process of preparing copy for the first editions were sometimes caused by his not having the revised material for the last two or three serial episodes; for *The Hand of Ethelberta* for instance, he had to ask Smith, Elder to set from the serial sheets and let him make revisions on the proofs for the book.[6] When he came to the first edition of *Two on a Tower* Hardy faced even greater difficulties, since the novel was being serialized in America only, and serial sheets for the last two episodes were not available either to him or to the publisher. Indeed, the textual complexities caused by Hardy's decision to accept the offer of serialization in the *Atlantic Monthly* are intricate, but their unravelling is fascinating.

Carl Weber first outlined the problems in his essay, 'The Manuscript of Hardy's *Two on a Tower*';[7] what I hope to do here is to explore further the evidence he presented, and to consider at the same time what the implications of the study are for the present state of the text of the novel.

The surviving correspondence between Hardy and T.B. Aldrich, the editor of the *Atlantic Monthly*, contains information about a couple of

---

[6] *Letters*, i. 43.
[7] *PBSA* 40 (1946), 1–21.

important details that attempt to resolve the logistic problems confronting an English author writing a serial story for an American magazine. We learn that Hardy sent a duplicate copy of the manuscript of each episode 'to guard against accidental loss', and we discover that, since there would be insufficient time for proofs to be sent to England, corrected by Hardy, and then returned to Boston, Hardy agreed—for the only time in his career—to the publication of a novel without his proof-revisions. In this connection he wrote to Aldrich: 'If you notice an obvious error please correct it on your side.' The editor replied that his proofs would 'be read with sympathetic care'.[8]

Only one of the two manuscripts of *Two on a Tower* has survived; it was kept by Aldrich and is now in the Houghton Library of Harvard University. It is to a degree misleading, though, to think of the Harvard manuscript as one of two separable and distinct copies. The most obvious indication of its composite nature is that, of the eight episodes, only the first four and the last bear the names of the compositors who set the serial; and collation confirms that the surviving manuscript of the fifth, sixth, and seventh episodes was not used as copy for the *Atlantic Monthly*. Weber plausibly suggests that when Aldrich was on holiday in Europe the printer's copy manuscript was not preserved, and to make up his copy he had to use the duplicate for those episodes. It is impossible to know whether what survives for any episode is the first or second copy sent by Hardy.

As I have already mentioned, a further complication surrounds Hardy's preparation for the English first book edition. In order to be sure of securing British copyright, the novel had to be published in volumes at about the beginning of November 1882, thus anticipating the publication of the last serial number in America. Collation shows that Hardy used the *Atlantic* serialization as the basis for his revision of the first three-quarters of the novel. The seventh episode would not have reached him till around the end of October, too late for his preparation of the first edition, and so he used a third manuscript as copy for the last quarter of the English book-text. It is impossible to know whether Hardy made and retained a third manuscript copy of the whole novel (there is no evidence that he did so), or whether he made specially for this purpose a third copy of the last two episodes.

There would be no particular problem for the textual critic if these various manuscripts were identical, but this was far from the case, and

[8] *Letters*, i. 103; Aldrich's letters to Hardy are in the Dorset County Museum.

my purpose here is briefly to indicate through examples some of the ways in which the text of the novel that we read today may have to be modified in the light of its early history.

The problems are at their simplest in the first half of the novel, where the manuscript that survives was used by the American compositors to set the serial, and where for the first edition Hardy made his revisions on a copy of the serial and sent that to the printers. Here the line of transmission of the text is clear, and there are only two kinds of change that need to be considered: compositorial errors and editorial alterations.

The first point to be made is that because Hardy saw no proofs of the serial he can have been responsible for none of the differences between the printer's-copy manuscript and the published serial. It then becomes a question of what attitude one should take to those differences.

Compositorial error must be eradicated from the text wherever it appears, however many times Hardy subsequently read copy and proof containing the error and did not himself catch it. Most compositorial mistakes that survive the scrutiny of the printer's reader and the serial editor do not disturb the general sense of the passage in question, and there is no reason to expect that Hardy, preparing copy or reading proof against time, should have noticed them. For the most part the errors have no interest for the critic, but occasionally the uncorrected compositorial misreading does alter in a small way the effect of a sentence.

An example of this occurs during the first visit of the young astronomer Swithin St Cleeve to Welland House, the home of his patroness Lady Constantine (chapter VII). In the course of his inspection of the contents of the library he was offered a meal, and (in the manuscript version) when it was served he 'was agreeably surprised to see a whole pheasant' (fo. 64). In the serial and all subsequent texts we read that St Cleeve 'was greatly surprised to see a whole pheasant', and a glance at the manuscript shows how easy it was for the compositor to confuse the words. When he first entered Welland House Swithin was mildly ill at ease in the unaccustomedly aristocratic surroundings, but it might be suggested that 'agreeably' hints, as 'greatly' does not, that he has begun to come to terms with the great house and its body of supercilious attendants. It is a small point, but the return of 'agreeably' to the text of the novel is necessary, as is the return of other words mis-set by the compositors. The manuscript leaf is reproduced opposite.

When we come to editorial interventions the matter is not so clear-cut. It would be possible to argue that since Hardy authorized Aldrich to make changes he thought essential, and since he did not repudiate the

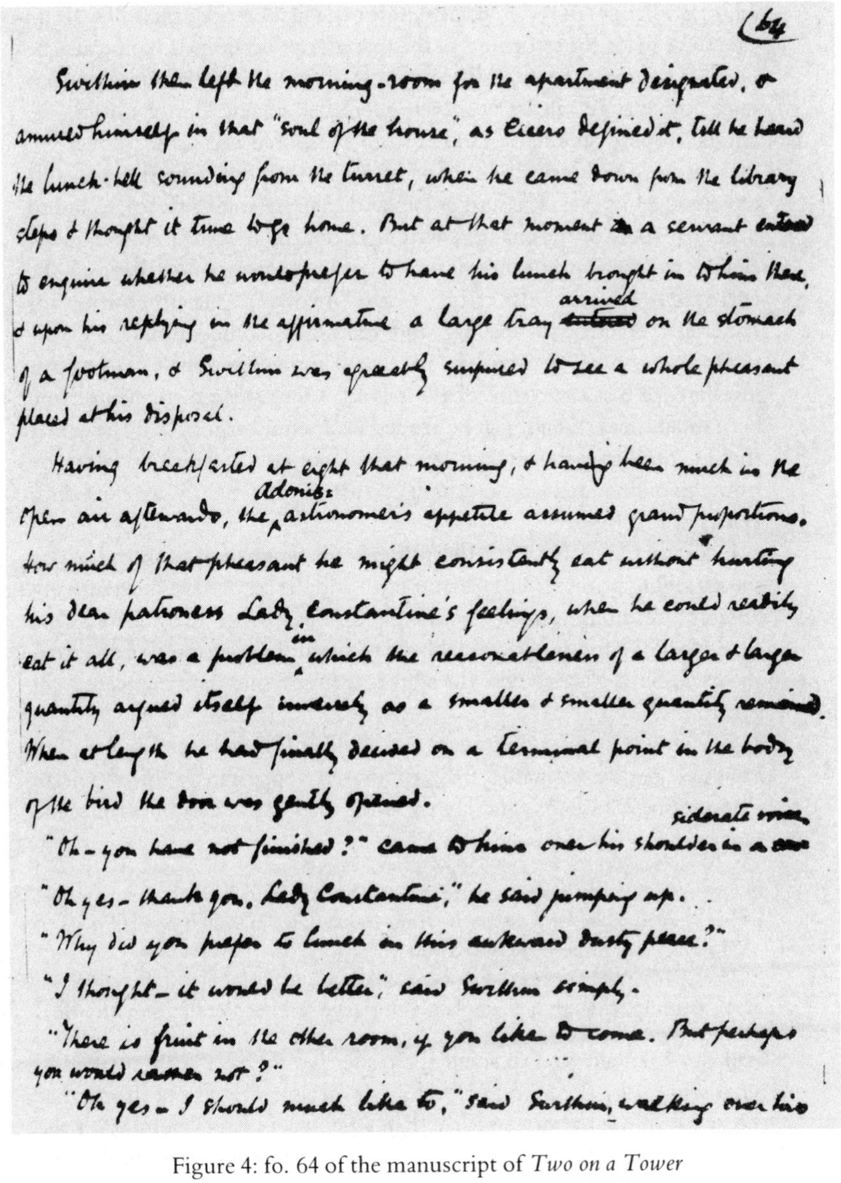

(64)

Swithin then left the morning-room for the apartment designated, & amused himself in that "soul of the house," as Cicero defined it, till he heard the lunch-bell sounding from the turret, when he came down from the library steps & thought it time to go home. But at that moment ~~a~~ a servant entered to enquire whether he would prefer to have his lunch brought in to him there, & upon his replying in the affirmative a large tray ~~entered~~ arrived on the stomach of a footman, & Swithin was greatly surprised to see a whole pheasant placed at his disposal.

Having breakfasted at eight that morning, & having been much in the open air afterwards, the Adonis-astronomer's appetite assumed grand proportions. How much of that pheasant he might consistently eat without hurting his dear patroness Lady Constantine's feelings, when he could readily eat it all, was a problem in which the reasonableness of a larger & larger quantity argued itself inversely as a smaller & smaller quantity remained. When at length he had finally decided on a terminal point in the body of the bird the door was gently opened.

"Oh — you have not finished?" came to him over his shoulder in a considerate voice.

"Oh yes — thank you, Lady Constantine," he said jumping up.

"Why did you prefer to lunch in this awkward dusty place?"

"I thought — it would be better," said Swithin simply.

"There is fruit in the other room, if you like to come. But perhaps you would rather not?"

"Oh yes — I should much like to," said Swithin, walking over his

Figure 4: fo. 64 of the manuscript of *Two on a Tower*

editorial changes in revising the text for the first edition, then there is no case to be made for returning to the manuscript version. It would also be possible to argue the opposite view that, despite Hardy's authorization, once any change can be positively identified as not Hardy's own, the altered reading should be excised from the edited text of the novel.

These are tenable positions of principle that require no further thought or action. However, it is also possible to examine each difference, and to note that some of the changes deriving from the *Atlantic*'s editorial staff clearly rectify Hardy's mistakes, whereas others go well beyond the correction of 'obvious error' (some involving the imposition of American practice in spelling and grammar, some displaying over-pedantic responses to Hardy's style, and some representing a positive interference in the texture of the novel). Once these distinctions have been established, then it can be argued (as I would argue) that the editor should consider each instance of editorial alteration, and should exclude from his edited text those changes that he can justify as exceeding Hardy's directive.

In all there are some sixty-five places in the first half of the novel where the surviving printer's-copy manuscript and the serial have substantively different readings, and it would be tedious to list them here. One example of what might reasonably be thought the correction of an error, and a couple of places where the editors went beyond their mandate, will suffice.

Swithin in chapter V returns to Welland House from his trip to London to investigate the rumoured appearance of Viviette Constantine's husband, and Hardy in the manuscript describes the scene thus:

In one hand he had a valise, a great coat on his arm, and under his arm a parcel which seemed to be very precious, from the manner in which he held it.

"Lady Constantine?" he asked softly.

"Yes," she said, in her excitement holding out both her hands, which he shook warmly, though he had plainly not expected her to offer one. (fo. 46)

Had this been allowed to stand the reader would have been justified in wondering why the parcel (containing a large lens) was not dropped at this point in the narrative rather than a few pages later, along with the greatcoat, and why the valise did not bang Viviette on the thigh as he took her hands; the removal of, 'which he shook warmly' by the editor was indeed a sympathetic action, and no one could doubt that the serial version should remain in the text.

On the other hand, a situation that recurs in the serial is the replacement of an unusual word in Hardy's manuscript with a more conventional one. When Swithin 'smacked his forehead with his hand' (fo. 48), the editor must have found the verb surprising and rather vulgar, for he changed it to the more expected and literary 'smote'. This goes beyond the correction of error and becomes a mild form of literary censorship. It is an admirable characteristic of Hardy as a writer both in prose and verse to surprise us by the felicitous use of an ungainly word, and to attempt to smooth out Hardy's calculated roughnesses is to do him a disservice. Hence I would argue that 'smacked' and several other similar words or phrases should be restored to any edited text.

Another recurrent stylistic situation is the removal by the *Atlantic* staff of apparently redundant words. For example, in response to Swithin St Cleeve's description of the sky as 'a horror', Lady Constantine comments in the manuscript: 'A new view of our old familiar friends the stars' (fo. 37). The serial omits from this the word 'familiar', presumably on the grounds that old friends are bound necessarily to be familiar—pedantic reasoning that pays no attention to the fact that in speech one is not necessarily logical, and which does not take into account the rhythmical and rhetorical effect of the word. Again there is no question but that 'familiar' should be reintroduced into the text.

This example-by-example approach places a burden on the editor to make a large number of decisions, and to justify each decision; but, in the case of this novel, I do not see how anyone wishing to offer the reader a text in a form which contains as much as possible of what one can be sure Hardy actually wrote or consciously authorized can do otherwise than take on this burden.

Where the fifth and sixth episodes are concerned, although there is the added complication of a manuscript that was not printer's copy, the ground rules remain essentially the same. For instance, in the bishop's letter of proposal of marriage to Lady Constantine (chapter XXXI) there occurs the passage: 'a mind comprehensive as yours will perceive the immense power for good that you might exercise in the position in which a union with me would place you' (fo. 259). This is how the *Atlantic* and all subsequent texts read. The most ready inference that the reader will draw from this passage is that the bishop refers to Viviette's prospective social position; but a revision to the Harvard manuscript has 'spiritual' inserted before 'position', and the addition of the adjective substantially alters the tenor of the bishop's suggestion.

Now, at this point in the novel there are two possible explanations for the difference between the manuscript and the serial: one that the American editor objected from some unfathomable religious scruple to the idea of a woman being in any sort of spiritual position, the other that the printer's copy manuscript did not have the interlined word.

It is worth considering for a moment how the latter situation might come about. It is to be supposed first of all from the physical state of some of the leaves that Hardy was using paper and ink that were specially manufactured for a copying process. This is suggested by the excessive blurring of the writing, the dramatic show-through of the writing on to the verso of the leaf, the mirror-image impressions on the verso of a number of leaves, and the unusual care that Hardy took to pack each page with as much material as possible—echoed only in the manuscript of 'The Romantic Adventures of a Milkmaid', written the same year. I do not know what that process was, but, taking the Harvard manuscript as evidence, either it produced two copies identical in appearance as well as content, or else Aldrich preserved the top copy (implying that, for whatever reason, the lower was used to set episodes five, six, and seven).

After the dual copies were made, mostly by Hardy, but sometimes by his wife Emma (and presumably the text of each episode must have reached some kind of final state for him to start making the copies in the first place), the two identical texts must have been subjected to Hardy's usual further revising. From the evidence that we have, most of these revisions were entered accurately in both versions, but a number of changes were entered in only one. Some of these discrepancies can best be explained by imagining that Hardy continued revising the second copy while the first was already in the post to America; but since it appears that *both* copies within one episode had independent revisions, this explanation cannot cover every case. The independent revisions in the copy first sent (whichever it was) must have occurred through negligence in transferring Hardy's revisions from one copy to the other.

In terms of the example under consideration, the point that arises from this process of copying and revision is that, whether Hardy neglected to ensure that his addition of 'spiritual' was made on both copies of the manuscript sent to Boston, or whether the *Atlantic* editors rejected Hardy's addition, for the editor the decision remains the same—the word must be reinstated in the edited text.

The editor's task becomes more difficult in a situation like the following: the Harvard manuscript (*not* printer's copy at this stage, it must be remembered) had originally this version of an exchange

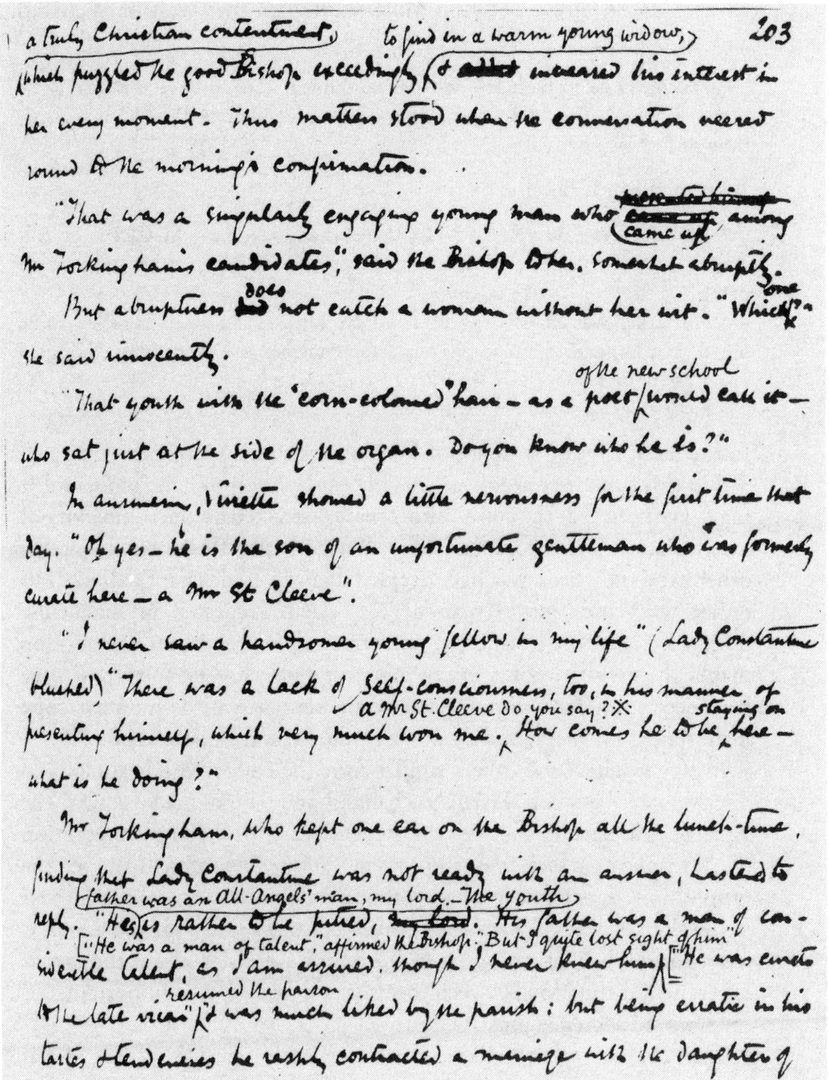

a truly Christian contentment, to find in a warm young widow, 203
which puzzled the good Bishop exceedingly, & increased his interest in
her every moment. Thus matters stood when the conversation veered
round to the morning's confirmation.

"That was a singularly engaging young man who came up among
Mr Torkingham's candidates," said the Bishop Other, somewhat abruptly.

But abruptness does not catch a woman without her wit. "Which?"
she said innocently.

"That youth with the 'corn-coloured' hair — as a poet/woman call it of the new school —
who sat just at the side of the organ. Do you know who he is?"

In answering, Viviette showed a little nervousness for the first time that
day. "Oh yes — he is the son of an unfortunate gentleman who was formerly
curate here — a Mr St Cleeve".

"I never saw a handsomer young fellow in my life" (Lady Constantine
blushed) "There was a lack of self-consciousness, too, in his manner of
a Mr St Cleeve do you say?
presenting himself, which very much won me. How comes he to be here staying on —
what is he doing?"

Mr Torkingham, who kept one ear on the Bishop all the lunch-time,
finding that Lady Constantine was not ready with an answer, hastened to
Father was an All-Angels' man, my lord. The youth —
reply. "He is rather to be pitied, my lord. His father was a man of con-
["He was a man of talent," affirmed the Bishop. "But I quite lost sight of him"
siderable talent, as I am assured, though I never knew him [. "He was curate
resumed the parson
to the late vicar" it was much liked by the parish: but being erratic in his
tastes & tendencies he rashly contracted a marriage with the daughter of

Figure 5: fo. 203 of the manuscript of *Two on a Tower* (see p. 68)

concerning St Cleeve between Mr Torkingham (the vicar of Welland) and his bishop:

"How comes he to be here—what is he doing?" . . . "He is rather to be pitied, my lord. His father was a man of considerable talent, as I am assured, though I never knew him."

After revision it became:

"A Mr St Cleeve do you say? His father must have been St Cleeve of All-Angels', whom I knew. How comes he to be staying on here—what is he doing?" . . .
    "His father was an All-Angels' man, my lord.—The youth is rather to be pitied. His father was a man of considerable talent, as I am assured, though I never knew him."
    "He was a man of talent," affirmed the Bishop. (fo. 203; see p. 67)

In the serial the last sentence of Mr Torkingham's speech was omitted, and in this case there are three possible explanations for the omission. It may have been that the compositors were distracted by the complexity of interlineation at this point and accidentally omitted the sentence. On the other hand the editor may have decided that it was inelegant to have 'His father was' and 'was a man of . . . talent' repeated in such close proximity, and felt justified in removing the sentence since the bishop makes the essential point in the following speech. Or, thirdly, it may have been that Hardy himself deleted the sentence in the printer's-copy manuscript, but neglected to do so in the Harvard manuscript.

In this instance and others similar to it the editor who is anxious to discriminate between Hardy's changes and those made across the Atlantic will have to consider the evidence carefully. Here the retention of 'affirmed', which demands some antecedent statement of the proposition, does point to a hand other than Hardy's at work, and either of the alternative explanations is plausible. Once Hardy's involvement is judged improbable then, as far as the editor's decision about the text is concerned, distinction between the other two causes is unimportant, for the omitted sentence must be restored.

The chapters that make up the seventh episode of the serial (XXXIII–XXXVII, fos. 269–312) are those which present the greatest textual complexity since, in addition to the surviving manuscript and the inferred duplicate manuscript used as printer's copy, there is an inferred third manuscript used as copy for the corresponding chapters in the first edition. Such an inference is demanded, since it is only in the portion of the text of the first edition corresponding to this and the final serial episodes that the *Atlantic*'s editorial changes are not accepted. It is not possible here to go into all the combinations of readings that are found in this section; one or two examples will have to suffice.

As Swithin prepares, at Viviette's behest, to leave Welland, he thinks over her motivation: 'it crossed his mind that Viviette might have reasons for this separation which he knew not of. There might be family reasons—mysterious blood necessities which are said to rule members of old musty-mansioned families' (chapter XXXVII, fo. 306). This is how all the printed versions read, and how the passage appeared at first in the surviving manuscript. But there were two late changes to the manuscript that did not get transferred to print. In order to underline further Swithin's new sense that Viviette might not be acting completely voluntarily, that she might be under pressures he knows nothing of, Hardy added 'had cruelly thrust upon her' between 'have' and 'reasons'. While considering this change he must have noticed the repetition 'family . . . families', and as a result he altered 'families' to 'lineages'.

At first sight this example seems like those examined earlier, but the third manuscript makes a decisive difference. It is difficult to conceive of a reason for the *Atlantic* editor to have left out the added words, or for him to have rejected Hardy's elimination of the repetition; and there is no particular confusion in the manuscript that might offer a reason why the American compositor should have overlooked the changes. In addition, however, for either of these individuals to be held responsible for the omission of the alterations from the serial, some similar reason would have to be found for their omission from the first edition. It is marginally possible that Hardy decided himself to omit these identical late revisions in proof for the first edition, but, taking into account the nature of the changes, it is more plausible to argue that Hardy neglected to transfer the revision to two out of the three manuscripts than to rely upon such an improbable coincidence of opinion between author and American editor. The fact that there are more than twenty similar examples that would also have to depend upon such a coincidence confirms this view. Hence, I would argue here, as before, for the inclusion of the latest manuscript readings in the edited text, though they appear in no printed version hitherto published.

One other example: Hardy began by writing the first sentence of chapter XXXIV as follows: 'Sunday morning came, and brought with it a new and unexpected shock' (fo. 276). Then he altered it at once to: 'Sunday morning came and complicated her previous emotions by bringing a new and unexpected shock.' The first edition, and thus presumably the manuscript that was copy for the first edition, follows this reading, but in the *Atlantic* the phrase 'with it', left out of the revised manuscript version, appears after 'bringing'. In this case it is possible to suggest either that Hardy revised the manuscript used as printer's copy for the serial differently from the other two, or that the *Atlantic* editor thought it more correct to retain 'with it'. A third possibility is that the American compositor misunderstood Hardy's manuscript intentions. For the editor, the authority of the existing manuscript and the first edition must in this case outweigh the possibility that the *Atlantic* reading represented Hardy's final thought on how the revised passage should read.

Although there were also three manuscripts of the last chapters of the novel, for the final episode the Harvard manuscript is once again printer's copy, and it is impossible to know what variations the now lost second serial manuscript might have contained. This situation presents its own alternatives to be resolved.

For instance, the phrase 'only the skeleton of a telescope' appears thus in the first edition and as a first version in the manuscript (fo. 317), but it reads 'only the rames of a telescope' in a revised version in the manuscript and in the serial. It seems most probable that Hardy accidentally failed to transcribe this change (which is one of a series of alterations that increase the dialect content of Mrs Martin's speech hereabouts) into the copy of the manuscript he used for the first edition, and thus that 'rames' should be incorporated into an edited text.

Another way in which these last two episodes are of interest is in confirming that Hardy felt no need to make for the first edition the kinds of changes that the *Atlantic* editor made for the serial. As one generic example, split infinitives in the magazine's copy are corrected, but those in the first edition's manuscript go unaltered into the published text. This is further substantial support for an editorial policy of excluding many or all of the earlier *Atlantic* changes from a critical text.

It is the combination of the necessity for duplicate and triplicate manuscripts, with the exuberance of Hardy's continual need to revise, that gives rise to these textual ambiguities in *Two on a Tower*. When a well-established novelist feels that a fair copy of a work, involving what must have been a relatively expensive form of duplication, needs revision to the extent that he cannot ensure that the same changes are made on each copy of the manuscript, then we have a vivid measure of the power of the unresting search for an ideal form that motivated him as a creative artist.

5

Hardy and the Graphic

1883–1891

During the winter of 1882–3 Hardy was writing what he called a 'short novel', but what, since its inclusion in the volume *A Changed Man* in 1913, has usually been described as a long story. 'The Romantic Adventures of a Milkmaid' was planned to appear in one of the special issues that the weekly journal the *Graphic* published twice a year, once in the summer to catch the holiday trade, and once at Christmas. These extra numbers of the magazine were more substantial than the normal weekly copies, and Hardy showed his professional versatility in meeting happily the demand for a tale of a length somewhere between the usual short story and the novel. The appearance of 'The Romantic Adventures' in the summer issue of 1883 marks the beginning of Hardy's nine-year connection with the *Graphic*. During that period only one of his important works, *The Woodlanders*, was not first published there.

Very little is known about the composition of 'The Romantic Adventures of a Milkmaid'; *The Early Life* includes the single entry, for 25 February 1883: 'Sent a short hastily written novel to the *Graphic* for Summer Number'. The only relevant letter that survives is addressed to the editor of the magazine, Arthur Locker, and simply announces that the story is nearly ready.[1] We thus have no idea what Hardy's dealings with the editor were; but a note that he appended in 1927 to the story in his study-copy of *A Changed Man* (in the Wessex edition) gives a hint that Locker may have had some influence on its final shape: 'Note: The foregoing finish of the Milkmaid's adventures by a re-union with her husband was adopted to suit the requirements of the summer number of a periodical in which the story was first printed.' It is always possible that Hardy's professionalism extended by now to an awareness of what would be most acceptable in terms of narrative line to the average

---

[1] *Early Life*, p. 205; *Letters*, i. 115.

magazine editor (there was, the reader will recall, a similar note appended in 1912 to the ending of *The Return of the Native*, and another at the same time to the 1879 story 'The Distracted Preacher'), but it is equally possible that he had continually to be reminded that serial readers liked a happy-ever-after ending.[2]

With 'The Romantic Adventures of a Milkmaid', the only independent evidence of Hardy's attitude towards the ending, and indeed towards the fabric of the tale as a whole, is to be found in the history of the development of the text.

Hardy's sense of the 'Romantic Adventures' as 'hastily written' is borne out to a degree by the changes of mind that the manuscript reveals; it is as if he had not allowed himself enough time for reflection before making the fair copy of the story. At the beginning, for instance, when Margery (the milkmaid in question) first encounters Baron von Xanten (the cause of her romantic adventures), in a deleted passage in the manuscript she witnesses his preparations for suicide, taking a revolver with its 'dull blue gleam' into his hand, and placing 'his finger on the trigger' (fo. 6). In the later version there is no more than a hint to the reader that he was thinking of killing himself; Margery herself only realizes that he is very unhappy: 'He started up with an air of bewilderment, and slipped something into the pocket of his dressing-gown' (fo. 7). It may be a further measure of Hardy's haste that there remained uncancelled on fo. 27 of the manuscript a reference to the occasion when Margery 'begged him to spare his own life', a remnant of the old plot that Hardy deleted in proof for the *Graphic*. Hardy half changed his mind again when he revised the text for the story's first English book edition, adding after 'dressing-gown' to the quotation from fo. 7 above: 'She was almost certain that it was a pistol.' Later, he also added that 'Margery had sufficient tact to say nothing about the pistol', thus avoiding the melodrama, but reintroducing the certainty.

Following this change of direction in the manuscript there are several cancelled details that show that Margery was originally to be less self-confident in her relations with the Baron—she did not imagine, for

---

[2] Hardy's study-copy is in the Dorset County Museum. A few years later William Blackwood wrote to Hardy, concerning the story 'The Withered Arm' which Hardy was to publish in *Blackwood's Magazine*: 'On the margin of proof I have made a few suggestions for your consideration' (9 December 1887). Hardy's response is lost, but three weeks later Blackwood wrote: 'The little change you made of making the farmer die a natural death & as a chastened man was a decided improvement' (30 December 1887; letters in the Dorset County Museum). Perhaps this was one of Blackwood's hints to Hardy. But it is at least clear that the editor was involved to a degree in the creative process in this case, as has already been seen elsewhere.

instance, that, in order to fulfil her wish to go to a Yeomanry Ball, the Baron might take her himself (fo. 15). There are hints, too, that the Baron was to be less scrupulous than he eventually is; a deleted passage of narratorial comment runs: 'It was noticeable that, either from reckless-ness or want of thought, he had said nothing to remind the unthinking Margery of any possible harm which might accrue to her fair fame by these proceedings' (fo. 16).

As far as the conclusion to the novel is concerned, the manuscript appears to refute almost as far as possible the claim in Hardy's 1927 note quoted above (that the changes were made to comply with the *Graphic*'s scrupulous morality), for the Baron is thoroughly virtuous in the earliest version of the plot that survives. The end of the story involves a series of carriage- and horse-rides: Margery thinks that Jim, her secretly married husband, has run off to London with a handsome widow, and the Baron insists on her getting into his carriage and pursuing him. Meanwhile, Jim (who has only been simulating love for the widow in order to make Margery jealous, and thereby force her to acknowledge their secret marriage) is told that the Baron and Margery have eloped together, and so rides off after them. In the manuscript version, once Margery and the Baron discover by enquiry that Jim and the widow have not after all made for London, the Baron delivers Margery a lecture about her stubborn pride in not living with Jim, deposits her at Jim's house, and returns to try to find him. The two men meet at a village called Letscombe Cross, and all is made clear between them—the Baron's honour vindicated, Jim's ruse explained. Jim and Margery settle down together and raise a family; the Baron is seen no more. There was no question at this stage of the Baron whisking Margery away.

The first move in this direction came in proof-additions for the *Graphic*, when Hardy deleted the Baron's sermon to Margery, and in its place had the Baron drive her to the coast where a yacht was awaiting him, and ask her if she would come with him 'steaming away all the world over'. Margery has a sudden enlightenment as to her predicament, and exclaims: 'Oh sir! . . . I once saved your life—save me now, for pity's sake!' The Baron does as he is told, and the sequel is the same as in the manuscript.

In the version that we read now, the 1913 text, there are further differences in the ending. Some of these derive from the moving of the setting of the story from the Froom valley near Dorchester to the Exe valley near Exeter, a move first pointed out by Purdy (p. 49). Others focus on the detour to the shore; having expressed in the *Graphic* a more plausible response to the situation on the Baron's part, in the book edition he turned his attention to Margery. When the Baron asks if she thinks she ought to be at her husband's house, in the *Graphic* she replies 'Yes, sir.' In 1913 this is replaced by 'She did not answer'. After the Baron's reiterated 'Of course you ought', Hardy further added 'Still she did not speak', and it is then that the Baron decides to turn the carriage towards his yacht.

When they have pulled up facing the yacht, and he asks her directly 'Will you come?', instead of replying 'I cannot', as she did in the magazine, her response in 1913 is 'I cannot decide'. She looks 'bewildered' rather than 'agonized', and, instead of bending to the Baron, she leans on him. The onus for decision is firmly on the Baron in the later version, and ultimately his conscience wins. However, when they reach Jim's home the Baron asked in the *Graphic* 'can you forgive a bad impulse'; in 1913 'bad' becomes 'lover's'—the first time in the story that he openly acknowledges his feeling towards Margery. In the last pages of the text Jim and Margery hear a report that the Baron has succeeded in killing himself, and in 1913 Hardy added a comment by Margery: 'Now that he's dead I'll make a confession, Jim, that I have never made to a soul. If he had pressed me—which he did not—to go with him when I was in the carriage that night beside his yacht, I would have gone. And I was disappointed that he did not press me.' Another addition stresses the reason why the Baron would not now succeed in an attempt to persuade her to leave with him: 'It would be so unfair to baby.' But Jim is still content with a wife who cares much less for him than he does for her.

Thus, to return to Hardy's 1927 note on the end of the story, the surviving evidence suggests that the reunion with Jim was of the essence of the story at first, and that the hints of desire for the Baron and the approach towards the abandonment of Jim were gradually added to the story as Hardy's view of probabilities evolved. There would have been nothing to hinder Hardy from rewriting the end of the story in 1913 to include the disappearance over the horizon of Margery and the Baron, and yet he stopped short of doing so. Such was the power over him of an established plot. And yet all this does not remove the possibility that in 1882 he had had some form of communication with the editorial board of the *Graphic* that dictated the conventional ending.

The last time that Hardy handled the story was when he prepared a dramatic scenario from it, probably for the consideration of the Dorchester Hardy players. At first he provided alternative last scenes—one in which Margery absconds with the Baron, the other in which she settles down with Jim (to which he appended the note 'But this is not so good an ending'), and then later deleted the second version altogether. The scenario is undated.

Though Hardy published 'The Romantic Adventures of a Milkmaid' and some other stories in 1883, as well as the essay 'The Dorsetshire Labourer', he did not commit himself to writing another novel until the spring of 1884, and it seems as if he were taking during that period a second 'sabbatical' from serious writing.

1883 was the year that Hardy moved back to Dorchester for the first time since his marriage, and most critics and biographers have sensed something symbolic about the move, as if Hardy were at last prepared to face his roots—a confrontation that would inevitably take some time to resolve. He began another concentrated bout of note-taking at about the same period, notes which were recorded in a commonplace-book with the self-explanatory title 'Facts, from Newspapers, Histories, Biographies, & other Chronicles—(mainly Local)'. He also set about purchasing the land for the house he planned that his father and brother should build for him, and he began himself to design the house, (his permanent commitment to Dorchester), Max Gate.

It is difficult to know whether Hardy's desire to write about his home town was a contributory factor to the move, or whether residence in the heart of Dorchester stimulated in him the need to embody the place in fiction. He would not, I think, have committed himself at this stage in his career to making Dorchester the centre of a novel as lightly as he committed himself to using Stinsford, the parish of his birth, in *Under the Greenwood Tree*—his conception of Wessex, and its implications, was by this time becoming clearer to him. When he did begin to write, he set the novel in approximately the same period as *Under the Greenwood Tree*; during the time of this childhood in the 1840s and 1850s. Just before he began writing *The Mayor of Casterbridge*, he also began a systematic reading through the early files (from 1826 onwards) of the local newspaper, the *Dorset County Chronicle*. Notes from this reading also found their way into the 'Facts' notebook and subsequently formed the basis for episodes in the novel.[3]

As is the case with 'The Romantic Adventures of a Milkmaid', there is

[3] See e.g. Christine Winfield, 'Factual Sources for Two Episodes in *The Mayor of Casterbridge*', *Nineteenth-Century Fiction*, 25 (1970), 224–31, and William Greenslade, 'Hardy's "Facts" Notebook: A Further Factual Source for *The Mayor of Casterbridge*', *The Thomas Hardy Journal*, 2.1 (Jan. 1986), 33–5.

very little external evidence in the form of letters or notes in Hardy's autobiography or publisher's records concerning either the early development of *The Mayor of Casterbridge* or arrangements with the *Graphic* for its publication.

It seems, though, that Hardy must have agreed terms with the *Graphic* well before the completion of the novel, since the manuscript shows that he designed the story at this stage to suit the requirements of a weekly magazine. In particular, he came to terms in the manuscript with the need for more and shorter episodes, and thus for a greater number of striking incidents in the plot, so that each episode would catch the reader's attention. Hardy wrote in old age, commenting on the novel's first book-publication, that he felt he had spoilt it more than any other by this superfluity of event,[4] but his comment is much less true of the novel as he had revised it for Smith, Elder's two volumes than it would have been of the serial of the manuscript. In fact, he removed many of the less well-integrated fragments of action in the *Graphic* version from the first-edition text, and it seems likely that he had intended from the first that they should be removed. The serial issue of his novels begins to have no relevance to anything but financial considerations in Hardy's mind.

The ascertainable timetable of events from conception to serialization of *The Mayor of Casterbridge* has a leisurely air about it: a note in *The Early Life* (p. 223) says that Hardy wrote the last page of the novel on 17 April 1885 and had taken more than a year over the composition. The serializations in England and America did not begin until January 1886, so there must have been almost two years between the preliminary work on the novel and its first appearance in print. We do not know for sure when Hardy sent the manuscript to Locker, the *Graphic*'s editor, but, as Purdy notes (p. 53), a letter from Locker to Hardy of 20 October (DCM) reports that proofs have already been despatched to America, so Hardy must have delivered copy well before then.

In fact, a little research shows that when writing for the *Graphic* Hardy worked to a timetable quite different from that he used in his writing for other journals. We know that his three other major contributions to the paper were submitted complete to Locker well in advance of publication: 'The Romantic Adventures of a Milkmaid' four months ahead, *A Group of Noble Dames* six and a half months ahead, and *Tess of the d'Urbervilles* eight months ahead of their appearance in print.[5]

---

[4] *Early Life*, p. 235.
[5] See Purdy, pp. 48, 63–5 and 68–73; *Letters*, i. 229.

These figures encourage the inference that Hardy sent off the manuscript of *The Mayor of Casterbridge* to the *Graphic* soon after finishing it, eight months or so before publication was scheduled.

We also know that Hardy received the first proofs of *Tess of the d'Urbervilles* about two months after sending the manuscript to the *Graphic*, and that he had not returned them six weeks later; it seems probable that it was similarly about two months before proofs of *A Group of Noble Dames* were ready.[6] It would therefore be reasonable to suggest that Hardy saw the galleys of *The Mayor of Casterbridge* also about two months after sending off the manuscript; some time, that is, in late June or early July 1885.

There is a striking contrast in tempo of composition and publication between these *Graphic* commitments and the only novel that intervened. Hardy probably began serious work on *The Woodlanders* in November 1885; publication began in *Macmillan's Magazine* in May 1886; he did not finish the manuscript until 4 February 1887 (see Purdy, pp. 55–7). This stressful pattern in which he was still at work on the last serial episodes well after the opening ones were in print is familiar from Hardy's earlier novels, and was also followed in *Jude the Obscure*.

It seems likely, then, that Locker or Thomas (the proprietor and publisher of the *Graphic*) made it a requirement of their serial contributors that their completed manuscript be submitted well in advance of the publication date. In part this may have been in order to give time for satisfactory illustration, an important feature of the *Graphic*, but it is also the case that a reading of the whole text long before it appeared in public would have given the editor and publisher more security about the nature of what they were purchasing, and a more relaxed opportunity to impose whatever censorship they felt was necessary.[7]

The story of their response to *A Group of Noble Dames* is told in the next section; Hardy's preparation of the manuscript of *Tess of the d'Urbervilles* for *Graphic* publication is well known, and is glanced at briefly in Chapter 6. It seems from evidence in the manuscript and the published serializations of *The Mayor of Casterbridge* that a certain

---

[6] *Letters*, i. 225–6, 229, 215.

[7] It is certainly true that Arthur Hopkins had some trouble with his illustrations to *The Return of the Native* because he did not have the whole story before him when making drawings for the first few episodes. Hardy sent Hopkins a summary of the character-relationships in the story, and expressed at Hopkins's invitation some criticisms of the first portrait of Eustacia (*Letters*, i. 52–3). Leon Edel, in his biography of Henry James, points out that the publication of some of James's stories was delayed because of difficulties with the illustrations (*Henry James: A Life* (New York: Harper and Row, 1985), 346).

amount of editorial interference may have been made in the development of the plot, similar to that which has been postulated earlier in this chapter for 'The Romantic Adventures of a Milkmaid'.

Christine Winfield, in her essay 'The Manuscript of Hardy's *The Mayor of Casterbridge*,[8] shows that Hardy's original conception of the Jersey relationship between Michael Henchard and Lucetta LeSueur was one of a six-year affair, euphemistically called by Lucetta an 'engagement'. This was replaced at a late stage, and in a certain amount of haste, in the manuscript by a story of her admiration of him, her rescue of him from drowning, and their marriage, the details of which were pencilled on the verso of a leaf and never inked over—something that occurs nowhere else in Hardy's manuscripts with substantial material that is ultimately intended for incorporation in the subsequent serialization. Winfield quite rightly feels that the change was probably made as a direct result of pressure from the *Graphic*, but she does not consider why the pressure should have resulted in changes to the manuscript itself rather than in proof-changes for the serial. Locker might have read the manuscript in April or May 1885 and sent it back to Hardy with a note of disapproval, but the editor would have been much more likely to wait for proofs before looking at the text, as he did with *A Group of Noble Dames*.

There are, however, two features of the manuscript that suggest a different scenario. Some leaves have a particularly faded appearance, as if they had at one time formed the opening or closing leaves of a separate batch of text (fos. 165, 249, 250, 283, 418, 419), and some have the notation 'The Mayor of Casterbridge' at the top in Hardy's hand (fos. 80, 165, 419). The fact that two leaves have both features makes it possible to suggest with some confidence that at some stage the manuscript was divided into sections. It would answer both questions if Hardy in fact sent off the manuscript to Locker in batches, for it then becomes rather more likely that the editor would have read and commented on manuscript rather than proof, and makes it easier to understand why Hardy might have responded to Grundian criticism in the manuscript rather than himself waiting for proof.

To set against this hypothesis there is the undoubted fact that twenty or so swear-words were bowdlerized in the *Graphic* proofs, probably by Hardy at editorial request—something, it will be remembered, that he had done quite happily for *The Trumpet-Major*. These, however, may have been made at the prompting of a different editorial authority.

[8] *PBSA* 67 (1973), 33–58.

Another interesting aspect of the early development of *The Mayor of Casterbridge* is that, for the first time in the history of Hardy's fictional texts, there are authorially motivated differences between the British and American serializations and first editions. Essentially, the texts of the *Graphic* and *Harper's Weekly* are the same, and thus the letter from Locker to Hardy of 20 October must mean that clean revises of the English serial were sent to America. However, the bowdlerizations of swear-words mentioned earlier do not appear in *Harper's Weekly*, and there is a handful of further alterations of the *Graphic* text that can hardly be attributable to editorial intervention in New York. It seems then that either the dilution of the profane language was made at a late stage to the English serial text, or else that it was made in the revises sent to America, and that Hardy, aware that American editors would tolerate more honest writing than English, included a restoration of the original words and phrases amongst a brief list, sent to the American editor, of other revisions that his restless creative mind felt necessary.[9] That these other changes were not made in the *Graphic* also, may have been because by this time the type had been plated, or else because Hardy's irritation with the small-mindedness of the English editor made him decide not to send the list for the English serial, but to keep it for the book-edition.

Hardy was anxious to make sure that the over-stuffed serial text should not get into book form in England or in America, but this caused a problem. From November 1885 Hardy was deeply involved in the writing and serialization of *The Woodlanders*, and had little time to spare for thought about revising *The Mayor of Casterbridge*. He must have delayed the work for as long as possible, since Henry Holt, who was to publish the first American edition, (and was anxious, in order to forestall the pirates, to have it ready to go on to the stands before the serial finished on 15 May 1886), had only received revised copy of the first forty chapters by 11 May.[10] He either never got the last five chapters, or

---

[9] One of the bowdlerizations is particularly crass. Riesner, in his essay on the development of the text of the novel, 'Kunstprosa in der Werkstatt', draws eloquent attention to it in a footnote (p. 272). This is my translation: 'One of the most delightful passages of the entire book is robbed of its punch-line: the constable, who in his reproduction of profane speech in front of the court abbreviates all curses, is impatiently interrupted by Henchard: "Come—we don't want to hear any more of them cust d's" (MS fo. 287, *Harper's Weekly*, p. 198). In the *Graphic* (p. 342) "cust" is missing.' It is also worth noting that the continuation of Henchard's speech was a proof-addition for the serial: 'Say the word out like a man, and don't be so modest, Stubberd: or else leave it alone.' This might be taken as Hardy's comment on the previous enforced bowdlerization.

[10] See Seth Weiner, 'Thomas Hardy and his First American Publisher', *Princeton University Library Chronicle*, 39 (1978), 134–57.

else received them too late to use; as it was, the American 'authorized' first edition only appeared towards the end of the month.

The copy Hardy sent to America would probably have been unrevised proofs for Smith, Elder's English edition, since though there were more than 500 revisions in the first forty chapters of Holt's edition, there were 250 further changes to these chapters in the English edition, changes presumably made on the proofs and incorporated in revises that were never sent to America. Additional differences are the radical alterations that Hardy made to the ending of the novel in Smith, Elder's edition, including the cancellation of Henchard's return to Casterbridge for Elizabeth-Jane's wedding to Farfrae—an episode that he restored in the first collected edition in response to the suggestions of friends.[11]

A Group of Noble Dames: *The Dead Hand of Mrs Grundy*

Hardy's next connection with the *Graphic* was considerably more painful. During 1889 Hardy corresponded with Locker about the possibility of providing a Christmas piece for his magazine the 'same length as the "Romantic Adventures of a Milkmaid" ';[12] it seems that agreement for what was to be the short-story sequence *A Group of Noble Dames* was finally reached in November, for publication in the Christmas special number of 1890. At the same time Hardy was also arranging, after its rejection in three other places, to sell to the *Graphic* the novel that was to become *Tess of the d'Urbervilles*, and the reception by the periodical of the Christmas piece must directly have affected decisions that Hardy made about the shape of his greatest achievement in fiction.[13] In fact, *A Group of Noble Dames* may be taken to represent the third stage, after his experiences with Leslie Stephen and Donald Macleod, in the disintegration of Hardy's respect for the editors and readers of monthly and weekly serials, and well repays close attention.[14]

The serialization of the six stories that form the nucleus of *A Group of Noble Dames* is documented in letters that passed between Hardy and the

---

[11] I am grateful to Professor Dale Kramer, who has shared with me the results of his work on the text of *The Mayor of Casterbridge*, some of which appear in the introduction to his World's Classics edition of the novel.

[12] *Letters*, i. 189.

[13] More details will be found in the introduction to the Clarendon edition of the novel.

[14] The 1968 University of Notre Dame dissertation 'A Textual Study of Thomas Hardy's *A Group of Noble Dames*' by A. Macleod has aspects of interest, but is too often inaccurate and thus unreliable.

Lockers, father and son, and in notebook entries that Hardy preserved for inclusion in *The Early Life*. There is some discrepancy between these documents that makes the establishment of the precise sequence of events difficult.

The first of these is on p. 295 of *The Early Life*: '*May 9*. MS. of *A Group of Noble Dames* sent to The *Graphic* as promised.' This was in the spring of 1890. There is then nothing surviving that relates to the next six weeks. One question that bears on the discussion of the serialization that follows, as it does on the serialization of *The Mayor of Casterbridge*, is whether the manuscript was sent straight to the printer for proofing before the editors and directors of the magazine read it, or whether it simply lay in a drawer untouched until the time came in the schedule of the *Graphic* for it to be considered. In this case the manuscript was destined for a Christmas supplement, so the end of June might have been time enough to look at the stories, even if illustration were a factor.

The next stage was apparently a letter of 20 June from William Locker, the editor's son and assistant, to Hardy, which has not survived (see Hardy's letter to Arthur Locker of 30 July below), and then there is a note in *The Early Life* (p. 297): '*June 23*. Called on Arthur Locker [editor] at the *Graphic* office in answer to his letter. He says he does not object to the stories [*A Group of Noble Dames*] but the Directors do. Here's a pretty job! Must smooth down these Directors somehow I suppose.'

This note may be a dramatization by Hardy, when writing *The Early Life*, of a diary entry, for something in it cannot be squared with the evidence of the two surviving letters that are quoted below. It must be mistaken in its date, in the name of the Locker he visited, or in the ascription of the letter, for William Locker wrote to Hardy on 25 June outlining exactly what was required of him in terms of revision, and why:

I have now read 'A Group of Noble Dames' and am sorry to say that in the main I agree with our Directors' opinion. In the matter of tone they seem to me to be too much in keeping with the supposed circumstances of their narration—in other words to be very suitable and entirely harmless to the robust minds of a Club smoking-room; but not at all suitable for the more delicate imaginations of young girls. Many fathers are accustomed to read or have read in their family circles the stories in the *Graphic*; and I cannot think that they would approve for this purpose a series of tales almost every one of which turns upon questions of childbirth, and those relations between the sexes over which conventionality is accustomed (wisely or unwisely) to draw a veil. To go through them *seriatim*—

The Old Surgeon's story ['Barbara'] is, it is true, not the least what Mrs. Grundy would call "improper," but its main incident is very horrible—just the sort of story an old surgeon might be expected to tell, but none the less unpleasant for that.

The Rural Dean is, as is natural, a good deal milder ['The Lady Caroline']; but still insists rather more than is perhaps advisable upon the childbirth business.

The Colonel's yarn is, of course, a mere anecdote; and would not suffer at all if some other ending were substituted for the discovery by Lady Baxby of her husband's vulgar amour.

Similarly, all that wants cutting out in the Churchwarden's story is the suggestion at the end that Lady Icenway intended to raise up seed unto her second husband by means of her first.

But the tales of the Crimson Maltster ['Squire Petrick's Lady'], and of the Sentimental Member ['Lady Mottisfont'] seem to me to be hopeless—Frankly, do you think it advisable to put into the hands of the Young Person stories, one of which turns upon the hysterical confession by a wife of an imaginary adultery, and the other upon the manner in which a husband foists upon his wife the offspring of a former illicit connection?

I quite admit that if the stories were to be written they could not be better or more innocently done—But I still think it very unfortunate that they should have been written for a paper with the peculiar clientele of the *Graphic*; and I am sure we should not be justified in printing them as they stand.

Now, what do you propose to do? Will you write us an entirely fresh story, or will you take the 'Noble Dames' and alter them to suit our taste; which means slightly chastening 1, 2, 3 & 4; and substituting others for 5 & 6? Please let me have an answer at your earliest convenience; or, if you can call, I shall be in every day except Saturday from 11 to 1 & 3 till 5.[15]

The first sentence of this letter may imply that Locker was reading the stories for the first time, in which case he would hardly have said that he did not object to them; on the other hand he may be indicating a rereading of the stories with the objections of his directors in mind. The last sentence seems to suggest that Hardy's note in *The Early Life* may have been misdated. Anyway, Hardy evidently set about the alterations to the stories that this section chronicles; the *Graphic* must have had Hardy's new version by the middle of July, for there is a letter Hardy wrote to his wife, probably on 24 July, which contains the following passage: 'I think it is all right with the *Graphic*—as they really don't themselves know what it is I have written, apparently: one of the directors having read the lst proofs in mistake for the second.'

Arthur Locker wrote to Hardy on this matter, and Hardy's reply is dated 30 July:

---

[15] Letter in the Dorset County Museum.

I am glad to say that on comparing the copy of the unrevised proof read by Mr Thomas (in mistake for the revised one) his marks thereon of passages for revision correspond almost exactly with changes I had already carried out in the revise which Mr Thomas has not seen, & which was the result of your son's original suggestions in his letter of June 20. So that there was nothing left for me to do beyond making a few additional changes in the wording—as shown on the revise herewith returned.

When Mr Thomas, & your assistant editor, read this, they will both see that their wishes have been complied with to the letter—& more.[16]

But these letters do not tell the full story. It seems from an examination of the manuscript, and a comparison between it, the *Graphic*, and the American serialization in *Harper's Weekly*, that there were two or three different layers of bowdlerization, some made voluntarily, and others under pressure from the editorial staff of the English journal.

To take the manuscript first,[17] there are in three stories passages that have been cancelled in blue pencil in the way that is familiar to students of the manuscripts of *Tess* and *Jude*; the cancellations are subsequently marked for inclusion (presumably) in the book-edition. They are relatively minor in 'The Lady Icenway' and in 'Lady Mottisfont', and seem to be early attempts by Hardy to avoid censure from the *Graphic*'s editors, a pre-empting of the kind of unpleasantness that in fact ensued. In 'Squire Petrick's Lady', though, the blue-pencil cancellations are at once more extensive and more problematic in origin; and, though some of the deletions are of the same sort as those in the other stories, there are features surrounding one or two that demand a rather different explanation. It is, thus, worth looking at the passages a little more closely.

There are, to begin with, a few cancellations in blue that are not marked for reinstatement; the first of these, after telling us that the infant born to Timothy Petrick and his wife was called Robert, originally read:

and her husband had never thought of it as a name of any significance, till, now, he had learnt by accident that before her marriage Annetta had been desperately enamoured of the young Marquis of Chrisminster, son of the Duke of Hamptonshire. Robert was his name.

After the blue pencil has been at work it reads:

---

[16] *Letters*, i. 215–16.

[17] The manuscript of the *Graphic* stories is in the Library of Congress, Washington.

and it was the name of the young Marquis of Chrisminster, son of the Duke of Hamptonshire.[18]

Though the *Graphic* omits even this, it is instructive to note that the more or less simultaneous American serialization in *Harper's Weekly* preserves the abbreviated manuscript version. In the first edition, despite its not being marked for retention (with stet marks under it), Hardy reintroduced the earlier reading, but with interesting variations:

and her husband had never thought of it as a name of any significance, till, about this time, he learnt by accident that it was the name of the young Marquess of Christminster, son of the Duke of Southwesterland, for whom Annetta had cherished warm feelings before her marriage.

Thus the first-edition recasting of the earlier manuscript text was made with the *Harper's* version also in mind. This pattern of variation raises at once questions about what was copy for the American serial, and for the first edition, questions that need more data before they can be at all resolved.

As if to confirm that these blue cancellations were made before Hardy had any direct communication with the management of the *Graphic*, there is in between them in the manuscript a change that surely echoes the same impulse, though not this time made in blue: Robert is referred to by his father successively as 'the little bastard', 'the little wretch', and 'the little fellow'. In context, the first seems the most appropriate, as well as being accurate so far as he knows; and the final reading is really too weak for the situation in which it is made. But Hardy must have known that 'bastard' would not have gone down too well with any of the magazines in which he was likely to find a home for the stories. Why 'wretch' was turned into 'fellow' I cannot guess; it simply seems a misjudgement.

Such cancels unmarked for retention are the minority, and there follow in sequence several paragraphs which have blue-pencil cancels and black, dotted underlining marking them for retention. In addition three consecutive leaves (or rather one leaf and the versos of the next two) have an indignant notation, each a variant of: '[N.B. The above lines were

---

[18] Was Hardy's spelling here of the young nobleman's title an error, or his first version of what was to become a familiar name to his readers? That it was an interlined replacement in the manuscript for 'Trantridge' (from *Tess of the d'Urbervilles* to *Jude the Obscure* via *A Group of Noble Dames!*) is strong presumptive evidence that the spelling was deliberate. If it was, did Hardy then think of Christminster as being pronounced with a short 'i', as the manuscript version of the name must have been?

deleted against the author's wish, by compulsion of Mrs Grundy, as were all other passages marked in blue.]' (See Figure 6, p. 86.)

One feature that these larger deletions have in common is that all the cancelled passages appear in the American serialization, though there are occasional small variations; this suggests that they are of a different kind from those earlier examined.

One of the cancelled passages has a detail that further suggests that they were made after the shorter unstetted cancellations. Squire Petrick is reflecting upon the implications of his perception that his son is illegitimate but of noble stock; in the heart of a paragraph that is all deleted in blue pencil there is:

To choose as her lover the immediate successor in that ducal line

Harper's, however, does not reproduce this as it does the rest of the paragraph; instead it reads:

To fix her choice upon the immediate successor in that ducal line

The first edition follows the *Harper's* reading. A clue to this deviation from the normal relationship between the blue deletions and the American serialization can be found in a close inspection of the manuscript, which reveals that the differing words have been much more heavily scored through, implying that the removal of 'as her lover' was made at an earlier stage than the rest of the cancellation, presumably at the same time as the first set of blue-pencil cancellations described above.

Upon consideration of these points it is right to conclude that the briefer cancellations in blue ink that have no dotted underlining were made some time shortly before Hardy submitted the manuscript to the *Graphic*. Hence the passages were omitted by the printers from the first proofs, and hence also their absence from the *Harper's* version which would have been set from these first *Graphic* proofs. The fact that there are small variants between the manuscript and *Harper's* (more of which are examined on pp. 129–33 below) makes it likely that Hardy had revised the set of proofs he sent to America.

The more lengthy deletions were then made by Hardy in the manuscript after getting it back from the printers with his proof, and after receiving first notice from the directors and editor of the English magazine that they were unhappy with the stories. He perhaps regarded the cancellations as a preliminary attempt to meet their unease. On the other hand, it seems at least possible that these deletions, with their accompanying anguished notes about the tyranny of Mrs Grundy, were

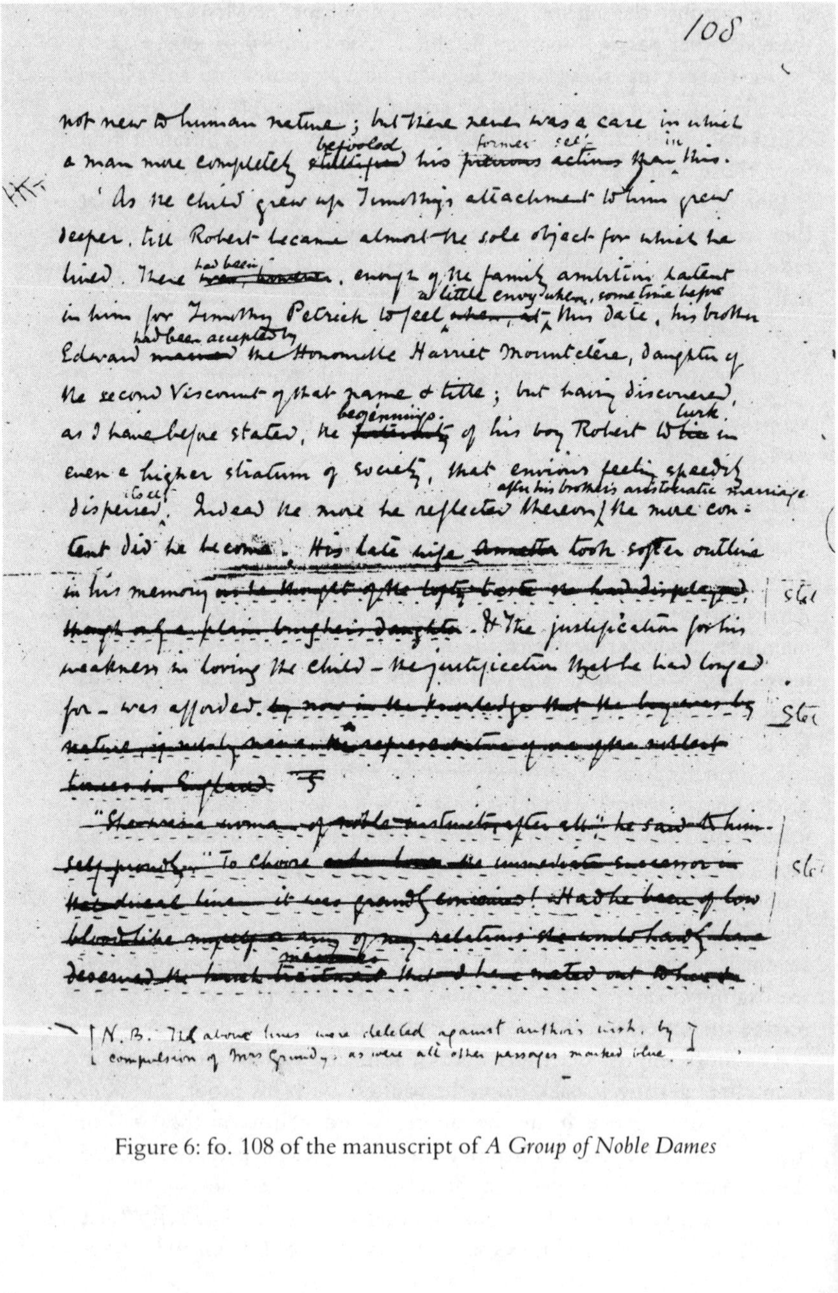

108

not new to human nature; but there never was a case in which a man more completely ~~stultified~~ befooled his ~~previous~~ former self ~~actions~~ in ~~than~~ this.

'As the child grew up Timothy's attachment to him grew deeper, till Robert became almost the sole object for which he lived. There ~~was, however,~~ had been enough of the family ambition latent in him for Timothy Petrick to feel ~~when, at~~ a little envy when, some time before this date, his brother Edward ~~married~~ had been accepted by the Honourable Harriet Mountclere, daughter of the second Viscount of that name & title; but having discovered, as I have before stated, the ~~potentiality~~ beginnings of his boy Robert to ~~be~~ lurk in even a higher stratum of society, that envious feeling speedily dispersed after his brother's aristocratic marriage. Indeed the more he reflected thereon the more content did he become. His late wife ~~Annetta~~ took softer outlines in his memory ~~as he thought of the lofty taste she had displayed, though of a plain burgher's daughter~~. & the justification for his weakness in loving the child – the justification that he had longed for – was afforded. ~~by now in the knowledge that the boy was by nature, if not by name, the representative of one of the noblest houses in England.~~

~~"Annetta was a woman of noble instincts, after all!" he said to himself proudly. "To choose [illegible] the immediate successor in that ducal line – it was grandly conceived! Had he been of low blood like myself or any of my relations she would have deserved the harsh treatment that I have meted out to her."~~

[N.B. The above lines were deleted against author's wish, by compulsion of Mrs Grundy, as were all other passages marked blue.]

Figure 6: fo. 108 of the manuscript of *A Group of Noble Dames*

made more as a physical reminder to himself, and anyone else who should see the manuscript, of the conditions under which the stories first saw print. In the introduction to the Clarendon edition of *Tess of the d'Urbervilles* I speculated that some of Hardy's dealings with editors over the serialization of the novel were deliberate attempts to provoke prudish or hostile responses that would provide further contemporary justification for the position he expressed in his essay 'Candour in English Fiction'; these cancellations and notes might be seen as directed to the same end.

Whatever Hardy may have expected in the way of trouble about the story, he cannot have imagined that the response would be so destructive; he cannot have conceived that he would have to ward off demands for a completely new narrative by altering the existing one out of all recognition. In the manuscript the story turns upon the claim of a wife dying in childbirth that her child was not fathered by her husband, with added hints that a young nobleman was the actual father. It explores the developing attitudes of the widower to the son thus left to him; at first he is outraged, then he is both attracted by the boy himself and seduced by the noble blood in him, and he becomes in time pleased by the child's irregular birth (until, that is, he learns first that his wife habitually suffered from delusions, and then that the nobleman in question was out of the country at the relevant time). Finally, the full development of the son's physiognomy as he grows into a man confirms that he is all too securely his own child, and Hardy observes with irony the father's dismay.

Extra-marital sex seems to have been the moral transgression that the editors of the *Graphic* would on no account accept; what Hardy did for the English serial was to make the deathbed confession one of substitution after the original child's death rather than of illegitimacy. This meant that all the material dealing with the connection with the noble family was irrelevant, and was excluded, thus at a stroke reducing the story by half. Hardy deleted the passage:

She thereupon related an incident concerning the baby's parentage, which was not as he supposed.

In its place the *Graphic* has:

She thereupon declared to him that the baby was not theirs. Her infant had died when a few hours old, and, knowing his desire for an heir, she had with the assistance of the nurse exchanged her child for a poor woman's living one, born about the same day.

Hardy is forced to be more explicit; he cannot now risk leaving anything to the reader's imagination. If the enforced change has a virture, it is that in making the wife's motive her husband's great desire for an heir he brings the story even more in line with those around it, in which the inability to engender a male successor haunts most of the male protagonists. After this fundamental change of direction there are occasional adjustments to phrases to accommodate the different version, but mostly there is in the *Graphic* just the straightforward omission of paragraph after paragraph.

It seems probable that Hardy made these wholesale changes on the proofs, since, where it was possible, he showed skilful economy in adapting phrasing from one version to another, something seen to even greater effect in his revision of *The Well-Beloved* (looked at in Chapter 8). In the light of this economy, it comes as a slight surprise to see that the ending of the story has been completely rewritten. Petrick's son in the new version tries to get money at school by fraud, and the father, instead of seeing ancestral features gradually fix themselves in his child's face, perceives 'in this deed of his son additional evidence of his being one of his own flesh and blood, but it was evidence of a terrifying kind.' So we have the dubious hypothesis advanced, that ability in forging documents is an inheritable faculty.

At its best, in the form in which it is now generally read, 'Squire Petrick's Lady' is not one of Hardy's greatest stories, but it does have a satisfying ironic pattern to set against its deficiencies in characterization and plot. From the version in the *Graphic* nothing can be salvaged; and if we turn to another of the stories most heavily and awkwardly bowdlerized for the English serialization, 'Lady Mottisfont', the changes Hardy was forced to make (though smaller in volume than for 'Squire Petrick's Lady') are even more destructive of the original idea of the story. Indeed the alteration bears comparison, on a different scale, with what Hardy was constrained to do a year later to the central theme of *Tess of the d'Urbervilles* by the prospect of publishing in the same magazine.

At the heart of the story is another illegitimate child; this time Dorothy, the daughter of Sir Ashley Mottisfont and a Contessa of no other name. Sir Ashley is widowed, and when he marries again he successfully interests his wife in the infant whom he 'found one day in a patch of wild thyme'—the more easily since it seems that they can have no children of their own. The Contessa, however, is anxious to have the child, to 'adopt' her; the noble lady's wealth and the perfection of her mind and person make it difficult to deny her. As Lady Mottisfont works out the real relationship between the girl, her husband, and the Contessa—calling herself rather nicely 'a walking piece of simplicity' for not having recognized it earlier—she agrees, with some anguish, to let Dorothy go. She attempts suicide, but is prevented by her husband. The twist in the story is that the Contessa eventually wishes to remarry, and so offers Dorothy back to the Mottisfonts again, only to find that Lady Mottisfont is at last pregnant and has no longer room in her affections for her husband's illegitimate daughter. The victim of the story has to return to the house of the peasant countrywoman who had taken care of her as an infant, where the hardships of life cause her pain for a while; eventually she marries an engineer, a man who does something useful in the world.

The most convincingly created character in the story is Sir Ashley Mottisfont, whose low-key gentleness, patience, kindness, and concern for his wife and his child are well-established in a series of details, speeches, and actions; his failure to tell his wife the whole story of Dorothy's parentage stems more, we believe, from desire to save her pain than from intent to deceive her.

The crucial enforced change in the *Graphic* is the cancellation of this passage narrating Lady Mottisfont's response to Dorothy and her probable parentage:

the baby whom her husband had so mysteriously lighted on during his ride home—concerning which remarkable discovery she had her own opinion; but being so extremely amiable and affectionate that she could have loved stocks and stones if there had been no living creatures to love, she uttered none of her thoughts.

It was replaced by a two-paragraph tale of secrecy, suicide, crime, and poltroonery:

Lady Mottisfont did not at this time guess her husband's true relation to the child, the circumstances of which were rather remarkable. Before knowing Philippa, he had secretly married a young woman of the metropolis, of no position, daughter of a dealer in East India Stock; and a short time after the marriage this man was convicted and hung for forgery. The disgrace thereof made Sir Ashley reluctant to avow his marriage, since he had not yet done so: his wife's hopes in her future were completely shattered; and soon after the birth of their child, in a moment of gloom at her husband's disgust with his alliance, she put an end to herself.

She had an only sister, who, more fortunate, had wedded an Italian nobleman and left England before her father's crime was known. On this account she was not available as protector of the baby, who was thus thrown entirely upon Sir Ashley's hands. But still he would not own her by reason of the said events; and thus it fell out that the child was handed over to the tender care of a villager as though she were a child of shame.

There are other omissions and alterations to take account of the fact that the Contessa is now Dorothy's aunt; but this is the significant one. It represents an almost total reversal of Sir Ashley Mottisfont's character; he becomes so heartless that he drives his first wife to suicide, and abandons his quite legitimate child to the (ironically expressed) 'tender care' of a villager. It is pleasant amidst all this self-centred cruelty to see Hardy getting in at least a reference to the original situation in 'as though she were a child of shame'. But the rather delicate touches that earlier defined Sir Ashley, above all his affection and care for Dorothy once his wife has finally rejected her, all now run counter to the powerful impression created by the addition in the *Graphic*, making a nonsense of the story.

It is not hard to imagine the cynicism with which Hardy undertook this kind of destruction of his central themes, his minimal regard for the seriousness or intelligence of the readers of the *Graphic* (he must have been writing tongue in cheek when he added 'whom the shrewd reader may guess to be Dorothy's aunt' in the serial).

'Barbara of the House of Grebe' ('Barbara' as it was called in the *Graphic*) also received the hostile attentions of the magazine's editorial board. The first thing that was thrown out is much of the horror that Barbara felt at the revelation of the face of her husband Edmond on his return from Italy; Barbara's terror, Willowes's demand that she look a second time, her shudder at the sight, are all omitted. What remains is: 'when it was done she shut her eyes at the spectacle that was revealed.' Even the adjective 'hideous' is removed from before 'spectacle'. When Uplandtowers prepares to mutilate the statue of Willowes, a similar restraint was imposed by the *Graphic*'s editors.

Other enforced changes were connected with the desire for an heir and with childbirth. In a characteristic pattern, Hardy was allowed to retain this:

he beheld the door of the private recess open, and Barbara within it, standing with her arms clasped tightly round the neck of her Edmond, and her mouth on his. The shawl which she had thrown round her nightclothes had slipped from her shoulders, and her long white robe and pale face lent her the blanched appearance of a second statue embracing the first.

He was not, however, allowed to include Lord Uplandtowers's response to this sight, his feeling that what the statue of her first husband was getting, he was not. He had to omit:

The heir presumptive to the title was a remote relative whom Lord Upland-towers did not exclude from the dislike he entertained towards many things and persons besides; and he had set his mind upon a lineal successor. He blamed her much that there was no promise of this, and asked her what she was good for.

Without experiencing Barbara's extreme distress at the frightening aspect of her first husband, it becomes very difficult for the reader to accept the complete transformation in her attitude to her second husband after his 'treatment'. That Hardy also felt this, is implied by a final omission from the manuscript which may have been made as a corollary of the enforced changes rather than as part of the sequence of alterations demanded of him:

How fright could have effected such a change of idiosyncracy learned physicians alone can say; but I believe such cases of reversional instinct are not unknown. The strange upshot was that the cure became so perfect as to be itself a new disease. She clung to him so slavishly that she would not willingly be out of his sight for a moment.

In 'The Lady Caroline (afterwards Marchioness of Stonehenge)' it is again childbirth that is the most objectionable element, even though the woman is quite properly (though secretly) married. Lady Caroline is anxious to pass off her as yet unborn child as that of a cottager who had also loved her now-dead husband; this coy introduction of the topic:

And Lady Caroline whispered a few words to the girl.
"O my lady!" said the thunderstruck Milly,
"What will you do?"

becomes in the *Graphic* the apparently inconsequential:

My heart reproaches me so for having been ashamed of him that I get no rest night or day.

And, later, 'How can I, when he is the father of the poor child that's coming to me?' is altered to 'How can I, honestly?'

The conclusion of the debate between Milly and Lady Caroline is that both go away, and, in the words of the manuscript, 'Milly came home with an infant in her arms'. We may well wonder how the whole point of the story is to be saved in the *Graphic*, which has made not even an indirect allusion to pregnancy as a motive for Lady Caroline's behaviour.

In fact, the editors bowed to the essential, and 'the child of the marriage of Lady Caroline' (not, it should be noted 'the child of Lady Caroline'; that would have been too direct) is added after 'arms'.

As noted earlier, the fact that the marriage in this story had taken place made no difference to the attitude of the editors of the *Graphic* towards pregnancy, and the same is true of their response to the details surrounding the secret visits that Lady Caroline's secretly wedded husband made to her: all the mechanism of his entry to the house of her parents is omitted, as is the idea of his staying there an hour, and the lateness of that particular hour ('the hour of one' is reduced to 'the hour'); it is no longer possible to imagine that they have been sleeping together. In fact, the *Graphic*'s 'hatchet men' seem to have disliked the whole concept of the story, and may have suggested to Hardy that he change the reaction of the just-married couple to their situation from 'both being supremely happy and content' to 'both being presumably happy and content' (though, the implication is, they should be utterly miserable if they had any right feeling). It is, on the other hand, just possible that the substitution of 'presumably' for 'supremely' was a compositorial error in the magazine; if so it was a pleasant piece of serendipity which Hardy saw no reason to change.

At least with 'Anna, Lady Baxby' the meddling of the *Graphic* is straightforwardly concerned to remove a loose woman. In the manuscript Hardy introduces a girl from Sherton with whom Lord Baxby has made an assignation at the entrance to his castle. For the *Graphic* he replaces her with some characters who are plotting to remove Lord Baxby's wife Anna from the castle so that her brother, who is in charge of the parliamentary troops besieging the castle, will find himself able to storm it. This change alters the whole fabric of the climax of the story, but for once does not completely destory the story's credibility, simply makes it something else. In both cases Anna discovers the outsiders, and the result is the same: instead of leaving the castle to join her brother as she had planned, she returns and remains faithful to her husband and the royalist cause. That in one version she is sent back by jealousy and an awakened sense of the sexual value of her husband, and in the other by patriotism and family feeling, might be seen to represent two facets inherent in Anna in any case. But it would have been sad to lose permanently the detail of Anna tying her husband's hair to the bed to make sure that he did not get up and go out after she managed to get back to sleep again; it was, naturally enough, omitted in the *Graphic* version.

The imposed changes made in 'The Lady Icenway', the last of the *Graphic*'s six stories to be looked at, resemble quite closely those made in 'Barbara'. There are several substantial passages omitted from the *Graphic* or altered in it; the first is an omission which is very reminiscent of Lord Uplandtowers's attitude to his heir:

> It was a matter of great anxiety to him that there should be a lineal successor to the barony, yet no sign of that successor had as yet appeared. One day he complained to her quite roughly of his fate. "All will go to that dolt of a cousin!" he cried. "I'd sooner see my name and place at the bottom of the sea!"

The second is a passage cancelled in blue pencil in the manuscript, in which it is implied that Lady Icenway might have a son by her bigamous husband and pass it off as the child of Icenway. Without this possibility the story loses much of its point; and the ending has to be altered so that Lady Icenway simply regrets not waiting for her first love to be in a position to marry her, instead of wishing she had thought of her plan for getting Icenway an heir before that first love died.

The kinds of change forced upon Hardy, thus brought together for scrutiny, reveal the extent to which the stories in *A Group of Noble Dames* dramatize the dynastic sense of the ruling class, and rejoice in showing the twists by which the desire for an acceptable heir is thwarted or perverted. Examination of the alterations also highlights the thoughtful psychological understanding of relations between men and women over marriage and children which is for the most part destroyed in the *Graphic*'s versions of the stories. That Hardy felt that these interferences were more unwarranted than any in his fictional career to date is suggested by the fact that all bar one of the excised passages reappear in the first edition of the collection, sometimes in a revised form. This cannot be said of those equally mutilated serializations *Tess of the d'Urbervilles* and *Jude the Obscure*.

It has already been hinted that the magazine issue of the stories in America was substantially different from its appearance in the *Graphic*. And, in fact, while these violences were being done to the story sequence in England, the American serialization in *Harper's Weekly* remained more or less inviolate; the only bowdlerizations that it suffered were those marked in blue on the manuscript, already discussed. However, this is not the whole story of the *Harper's* text; there are other independent and unique differences. One example is in the first paragraph of 'Lady Mottisfont'; in talking of the interior of Wintoncester Cathedral the phrase 'three hundred steps westward' occurs in the manuscript; in the *Graphic* 'amid those magnificent tombs' was added to it, and the first edition also has the addition, as does every subsequent text. There is, however, a further expanded version in *Harper's*: 'amid those magnificent ecclesiastical tombs and royal monuments', suggested by the subsequent reference in the story to the dust of kings and bishops. There are four similar instances of independent *Harper's* additions in the early part of the story.

These revisions are not of the kind that might have been made by the American editor, and so must have appeared on the copy that Hardy sent to *Harper's*; there is no reason to suspect that he saw proof of the American printing. It is virtually certain that copy for *Harper's* was a duplicate of the first set of proofs that he received from the *Graphic*. It is also probable that it would have been marked with approximately the same revisions that appeared on this first set of English proofs (though we have sufficient evidence, from the manuscript of *Two on a Tower* for instance, that Hardy found it very difficult to revise identically two copies of the same text). Thus the likelihood is that these unique readings in *Harper's* represent Hardy's earlier intentions for the magazine issue, which were lost sight of in the face of frantic messages about other aspects of the stories from prudish gentlemen.

A somewhat different pattern occurs in 'The Lady Caroline' where in one sentence, for instance, the manuscript and the *Graphic* have 'walked' and 'a lake' and *Harper's* has the characteristically Hardyan 'trudged afoot' and 'fish-ponds'. The first edition in this case follows the American serial (though with what must be a compositorial error in 'trudged about'). The implication of this example and others like it is that Hardy must have retained a copy of the first *Graphic* proofs and consulted them as well as the manuscript and the published *Graphic* version when reconstituting the stories for the first book-edition.

It has already been suggested that Hardy was aware that some details in his stories might provoke an alarmed response from those in charge at the *Graphic*, and that as a result he blue-pencilled a few passages in the manuscript. Evidence from the American serial shows that Hardy still felt uneasy at the proof stage. In 'Barbara of the House of Grebe' for instance, after her marriage to Lord Uplandtowers (in the manuscript and the first edition) Barbara seems to show no sign of producing an heir: 'He blamed her much that there was no promise of this, and asked her what she was good for.' The *Graphic* excludes the whole thing, as it does all those passages relating to childbirth; in *Harper's* the first part of the sentence stands, but the insult is omitted and it ends at 'this'. The American version seems to be another voluntary attempt by Hardy to pre-empt the foolish pruderies of the *Graphic* through self-bowdleri-zation, and as such the cancellation would also probably have been made in the early *Graphic* proofs. There are similar instances in this and other stories.

There are thus stranded in *Harper's* a number of authorial revisions, and an editor of *A Group of Noble Dames* would have to decide what to do with them. Though the self-censorship should be rejected, there is an adequate argument for retaining in an edited text other independent revisions in *Harper's*. Although Hardy almost certainly had a copy of the first *Graphic* proofs to refer to when making the first-edition text, it has also been pointed out that he may have made further revisions on the set he sent to America. Any decision about stranded variants will necessarily depend upon the priorities and principles of the individual editor.

The reader who is interested in considering in detail the effect that Hardy's experiences over the serialization of *A Group of Noble Dames* may have had upon the development of *Tess*, once he knew that it also was to appear in the *Graphic*, will find all the necessary material in the Clarendon edition of the novel. In general terms it may be said that the cynicism with which Hardy treated the readers of the periodical version of the short-story sequence was equalled in his handling of the novel. The substitution in the serial of a mock-marriage for Tess's violation in the Chase was made with no regard to probability and thematic integrity; what the readership of the *Graphic* thought of a story in which the whole of a girl's future happiness is made to depend upon her inability to tell a real registrar from a man dressed up as one is hard to say. At this moment in his career Hardy probably imagined that they were incapable of thinking about it at all.

It is of some interest that when the proof-sheets of *Tess* in the *Graphic* were sent to America for *Harper's Weekly*, Hardy felt sufficiently certain of the capacity of American audience to tolerate a greater degree of realism in sexual matters to omit the episode with the fake registrar, and replace it with the following:

He said it must be private, even from you, on account of his mother, and by special licence. However it came to nothing, and then he pestered me and persecuted me—and I was in his power—and you may guess the rest . . . Since then I have been staying on at Trantridge. But at last I felt it was wrong, and would do so no longer, though he wished me to stay; and here I am.

Although he was unable to restore for Americans the episodes he had left out for the English, he contrived with his customary economy to ensure that for part of his serial audience at least he would tell the truth about Tess.[19]

---

[19] By the time Hardy came to serialize his last novel, *Jude the Obscure* (an eventually painful process well outlined by Patricia Ingham in her 'The Evolution of *Jude the Obscure*', *Review of English Studies*, NS 27 (1976)), he was clear about the nature of this version of his work. In a telling fragment from a letter of 16 February 1895 to Grant Allen he wrote: 'I wish I could send you the real copy of the story I have written for Harpers', as the form in which it is appearing there is a conventionalized one, in several points' (*Letters*, ii, 68–9). It is indeed the unreality of the serializations of *Tess* and *Jude* that most directly strikes a reader familiar with the first editions.

6

From Tess *to* Jude

1892–1894

Tess of the d'Urbervilles: *One-Volume Editions*

Tess of the d'Urbervilles was the second of Hardy's books to be published by J.R. Osgood and Clarence McIlvaine, two Americans based in London, and the only one appearing under their imprint that had its first edition in three volumes. *Jude the Obscure* and *The Well-Beloved* first appeared in one volume; they were issued as part of the publishers' collected edition of Hardy's work in 1895 and 1897, and by then the period of the dominance of the three-decker novel had passed.

Before 1890, the issue of Hardy's novels in a cheaper one-volume form after their initial appearance in two or three volumes was dependent upon the publisher's perception of his own interests in the matter. It will be recalled that Hardy was anxious in 1876, during his first 'sabbatical' from writing, to persuade Smith, Elder to publish cheap editions of *Far from the Madding Crowd* and *A Pair of Blue Eyes*, and he derived a steady modest income from the sale of these one-volume texts. In the eighties, Sampson Low acquired the rights to publish most of the single-volume editions, and they issued eight of Hardy's novels in uniform bindings. This was the nearest he came to a collected edition of his works until 1895.

Of all of the printed texts of Hardy's novels examined in this book, the first one-volume edition of each is perhaps the most neglected by textual and literary critics; and yet it was potentially an important step in the development of all the novels. It was the first time that the novel had been reset after the first edition—after, that is, the reviewers had had their say about it, and Hardy always took the opportunity to revise, to a greater or lesser degree.

It is possible, to some extent, to generalize about the kinds of revision that Hardy made at this stage in the creation of each text. The most important or lengthy alterations are almost without exception cancellations of material, often whole paragraphs, sometimes whole chapters, as in *The Hand of Ethelberta*.[1] His attention to the text was intermittent:

---

[1] See Purdy, p. 23.

there will be half a dozen revisions on one page, often sparked off by a single important change; and these will be followed by half a dozen pages with no revisions at all. In several of the novels there is also a falling off in the number of alterations as the novel progresses. To a degree, this may have been because the early parts of the novel, often published before Hardy had the feel of the whole, still required some correction; but it must also indicate a gradual weariness of the business of reading attentively the same text—in the case of *The Woodlanders* for the fourth or fifth time in a year.

If there was no reimpression of the first edition (there was of *Far from the Madding Crowd*, *Two on a Tower*, and *Tess of the d'Urbervilles*), then it is in the cheap edition that the revisions made in response to the cavillings of critics are most likely to be found. Hardy was always sensitive to such suggestions, and it is quite likely that a number of the one-volume revisions other than those that can be directly traced were the result of critical prompting from friends or acquaintances.

Beyond these common factors, the revision of each novel has its particular emphasis, and there is one novel in particular, *Tess of the d'Urbervilles*, that breaks the mould in most interesting ways. I want to look first at a few examples to illustrate the patterns I have outlined, and then to look in more detail at the major exception.

One substantial example of cancellation in *The Mayor of Casterbridge* is at the beginning of chapter XV: Elizabeth-Jane Newson's beauty is in question, and the following two passages are left out in the one-volume edition:

This particular virgin was just a shade too far the other way; and she paid the penalty. Sober and discreet, she was yet so hearty, that her homespun simplicity afforded none of those piquant problems which are afforded by the simplicity that is carefully constructed by art.

In short, it was obvious to real philosophers that Casterbridge young-manhood of the deep-seeing sort ought to have had a solicitous regard for her. So they took no notice of her at all.

If the news got abroad that she was unwell, Henchard's door was not haunted by young fellows with cigars, making some excuse for inquiring indirectly about her. But to set against this, at inn gatherings of the rollicking sort, where discussions of the female world were apt to take a turn irreverent to the sex, the criticism was stopped when it came to Elizabeth with, 'I say, now, we'll leave *her* alone.'

Perhaps the young men were penetrating enough to see that she was too honest to be a woman of correct education.

It is the tone here that is wrong, and the passages also give an altogether alien impression of Casterbridge, one that is far from skimmity-rides and from all the other associations that Hardy was trying to build up around the town: its Roman past, and its intimate involvement with the agricultural landscape that enclosed it. On the other hand, that this sort of thing was a part of Dorchester in the 1850s and 60s, when Hardy was a young man, seems also true; it is just that he was no longer interested in re-creating that aspect of Dorchester life when refining his ideas about Casterbridge in 1887.

Hardy relatively rarely emends his characterization in the one-volume texts, though occasionally there is a small, telling change. In *The Mayor of Casterbridge*, at this stage, his purpose is to undermine Farfrae a little. This might be the motive behind the omission of 'honest' from: 'The town was small, but the corn and hay-trade was proportionately large, and with his native sagacity he saw honest opportunity for a share of it.' But the chief stroke is to add what is the meanest of all of Farfrae's commercial calculations to the deliberations of Elizabeth-Jane and her husband during the search for Henchard at the end of the novel. To the passage: 'by resting the horse for a couple of hours at a village they had just traversed, it would be possible to get back to Casterbridge that same day; while to go much further afield would reduce them to the necessity of camping out for the night' Hardy added: ' "and that will make a hole in a sovereign," said Farfrae.'

One group of substantial deletions in *A Pair of Blue Eyes* occurs in chapter XXXVI, which contains the response made to the new-won celebrity of Stephen Smith by the residents of his small Cornish home town of St Kirrs. Alan Manford, in his World's Classics edition of the novel, details some of the omissions and adds that they were made 'as a result of *The Spectator*'s comment that the chapter was "forced and caricatured without any compensating humour" ' (p. 392).

Hardy was also affected by a notice of *A Pair of Blue Eyes* in the *Saturday Review* of 2 August 1873:

He occasionally uses cumbrous words, like 'synthetized' and 'filamentous', where simpler ones would have served the purpose; and the word 'empirically' occurs in a passage where it cannot be said accurately to retain its own meaning or to convey the author's. He puts the phrase 'sweetheart' into a position which it does not really hold among the social class which he is describing

In the one-volume edition he altered each of these words, replacing the first three with 'cried', 'stringy', and 'practically', and, for 'sweetheart', using a variety of phrases according to the context. Such ready responsiveness to criticism is characteristic of most of the one-volume texts.

It is naturally the case that in the one-volume editions, as in all others, Hardy revised sentences and phrases that are at the heart of the thematic structure of the particular novel. For instance, two of the central narratorial statements in the first chapters of *The Woodlanders* were also emended at this stage; the first describes Little Hintock as a place 'where, from time to time, no less than in other places, dramas of a grandeur and unity truly Sophoclean are enacted in the real' (p. 8). In the one-volume edition, Hardy deleted 'no less than in other places', removing a detail that might distract the reader's attention from the concentration on the village. The second has the narrator saying of Giles and Marty: 'And yet, looked at in a certain way, their lonely courses formed no detached design at all, but were part of the pattern in the great web of human doings then weaving in both hemispheres, from the White Sea to Cape Horn' (p. 24). Hardy decided that his narrator should commit himself wholeheartedly to this perception, and removed 'looked at in a certain way'.[2]

These few examples give an idea of how the revision runs in the majority of the novels, but *The Trumpet-Major* at this stage takes matters to an extreme. It has already been suggested that Hardy tended to grow tired of this particular stage of revision towards the end of most novels—with *The Trumpet-Major* he gave up entirely at the end of the sixth chapter. It is not clear why this should have been so, though it seems a reasonable guess to associate it in some way with the illness that Hardy suffered during the winter and spring of 1880–1. It is also interesting that of the fourteen changes that he did make, the majority are the simple deletion of redundant phrasing—just as one might expect.

The one-volume edition that rewards attention most liberally is that of *Tess of the d'Urbervilles*, called by the publishers the 'fifth edition' because there were four impressions (though only three have been identified) of the three-volume first edition; it marks a somewhat different stage in the development of the novel from the other one-volume texts already glanced at.

When the novel was serialized in the *Graphic* Hardy split off two episodes and published them separately, and made many other temporary revisions; this well-known history is important here because the work

---

[2] Page-references are to the Clarendon edition of the novel (Oxford, 1981).

needed to restore (for the most part, though not entirely) the manuscript version for the first book-edition meant that he had less energy, and perhaps less time, than usual for fresh considerations of character and theme. Most of this energy he expended on developing Tess herself and themes directly associated with her. That is not to say that in the very large number of alterations made for the first edition there were no reworkings of other aspects of the novel; but it did mean that when, a year later, Hardy was able to revise freely for a reset edition, the novel had still not become a stable text in his mind, and that as a result his creative engagement with it was of a different order from that in the other novels at this stage; in each of them, he was altering details in a text that he chose to think of as established (almost fixed), whereas in the one-volume edition of *Tess*, concepts and characters in the novel were still being worked out.

Two other factors may have contributed to this sense that in 1892 the novel was still growing: once Hardy knew he was going to publish *Tess* in the *Graphic* (with whose editorial board he was about to tangle over *A Group of Noble Dames*—see Chapter 5), he may well not only have excised material from the earlier part already written, but also have felt unable to make revisions as he would have liked at that stage; more significantly, he must have written the second half of the novel, from Tess's confession to Angel onwards, with the *Graphic*'s sensibilities in mind. The first edition would then have been the place to introduce the different tone or incident; but, as I have already said, there was so much to do to the text at that time that he would hardly have felt happy that he had even got (not everything right, because Hardy never felt that) most things more or less right. Hence the extra attention that he had to pay to this next resetting of the novel. His intense commitment to the novel and its heroine must also have made it hard for him to accept that they had finished growing in a substantial way. However, the plates of this edition were also used for the Osgood collected edition and for Macmillan's 1902 Uniform edition, making it inevitable that the one-volume issue was the stage at which the novel became to all intents and purposes fixed—at which the creative umbilical was cut.

It is one of the most noticeable features of *Tess* that the narratorial tone is not homogeneous, that it is split into two voices, which may, in a simplified way, be defined as detached and engaged. Quite a large number of changes in this edition are made in the distanced authorial narrative voice, as if Hardy was only beginning to realize in one or two areas exactly what it was that his novel meant to him personally and what he was saying through it to the world (what one might call the manifesto aspect of the novel). An example of this is the rewriting of a paragraph in chapter V. It occurs at a place where the manuscript folio is lacking, so the first witness is the serial version:

As Tess grew older, and began to see how matters stood, she felt somewhat vexed with her mother for thoughtlessly giving her so many little sisters and brothers. Her mother's intelligence was that of a happy child: Joan Durbeyfield was simply an additional one, and that not the eldest, to her own long family of seven. (p. 49. Page references are to the Clarendon edition.)

For the first edition Hardy introduced into this simple mixture of Tess's and the engaged narrator's perception something that could only belong to the distanced narratorial voice, replacing 'she felt somewhat vexed with her mother' with 'she felt Malthusian vexation with her mother'. He also added, 'when it was such a trouble to nurse those that had already come' after 'brothers', and altered 'seven' to 'nine when all were living'.

When he came to the paragraph again a year later for the one-volume text it was with these three already revised details that Hardy was concerned. The first change was an attempt to integrate the apparently alien idea from political economy more closely into the engaged fabric of the novel; the phrase became 'she felt quite Malthusian towards her mother'. The economic motif was also intensified in the other two passages: 'those that had already come' was changed to 'and provide for them'; but more significantly the number of the family, suggesting a large but finite problem, was removed, and in its place Hardy added an outsider's view of their socio-economic position while leaving the family indefinitely large: 'nine when all were living' became 'waiters on Providence'. It cannot be a coincidence that Hardy thus linked the ideas of 'Providence' and 'provide':

As Tess grew older, and began to see how matters stood, she felt quite Malthusian towards their mother for thoughtlessly giving her so many little sisters and brothers, when it was such a trouble to nurse and provide for them. Her mother's intelligence was that of a happy child: Joan Durbeyfield was simply an additional one, and that not the eldest, to her own long family of waiters on Providence.

And so the paragraph remains, with one exception: in 1895, for the Osgood edition, (though it meant a little plate alteration), Hardy added 'a' before 'Malthusian', subtly increasing the strength of the inference that Tess herself might know what it is to be a Malthusian.

Of all these changes, it is the last one made in the one-volume text that reverberates longest through the novel. That the Durbeyfields are a 'long family of waiters on Providence' is one of Hardy's chief accusations against them, one indeed that Tess herself does not escape; and the phrase gathers force as the crucial events of Tess's life are enacted. Though a small change it has a disproportionately large significance, and this might equally well be said of the whole revision undertaken for the one-volume text.

There are one or two other places where Hardy's concern for the economics of rural life surfaces in one-volume changes, changes expressed also through the distanced narrative voice. One of these suggests that Hardy had done a little research between the first edition and this revision, or else that someone had told him something. It occurs at the beginning of chapter X, in a narratorial aside explaining why so many of Tess's contemporaries at Trantridge were married; previously the passage read: 'marriage before means was the rule here as elsewhere'. This generalized sententious comment of the superficial moralist was replaced in 1892 by an adequate economic motivation: ' a field-man's wages being as high at twenty-one as at forty, marriage was early here' (p. 84). This informed and concerned perception comes from the same sector of Hardy's interests as that which had stimulated him to write his essay, 'The Dorsetshire Labourer' (some of which is incorporated into chapter LI of *Tess*). In reviewing in 1892 the role of 'cottagers who were not directly employed upon the land', in the relevant passage at the beginning of chapter LI, Hardy felt the need to add that they 'had formed the backbone of the village life in the past,' and that they 'were the depositories of the village traditions' (p. 478). This is his own class that he is writing about, and it is as if it took until the one-volume edition for Hardy to figure out the crucial role with which he wanted to invest that class. In a sense this is a definitive statement of the finally established concern in Hardy which led directly to the revisions made in the two great collected editions that followed. Though it is not exactly a 'village tradition' that field men were paid the same wage whatever their age and experience, the motivation that caused Hardy to register this fact as a reason for early marriages is very much that of the village historian.

A change in chapter XXXIII is also worth considering in this context: where the narrator describes the peal of bells rung from the church in which Angel and Tess are married, the passage has been considerably revised. In the manuscript's first version 'a modest peal of four notes broke forth'; later, still in the manuscript, 'a modest peal of three bells broke forth—the limited expression of the small tower ranging no further'. In the serial, 'tower' was altered to 'parish', which transferred the sense of limitation from building to people. This distinction was taken up and further refined in the first edition, when the passage after the dash was altered to 'the power of expressing joy in such a small parish ranging no further', suggesting perhaps a financial connection between the smallness of the parish and the paucity of bells. But the crucial change in emphasis came only in the one-volume edition—the fifth time the description had been revised—when the passage became: 'a modest peal of three bells broke forth—that limited amount of expression having been deemed sufficient for the joys of such a small parish' (p. 302). At once, the meanness of the carillon is the responsibility of some agency superior to the parish and the parishioners, and class and authority have become factors; at the same time the irony is considerably sharpened. That the identity of those who have made the decision is left vague only increases the scope for suspicion—vicar? lord of the manor? church commissioners? Whoever it is, the decision is made outside the community. The final changes to the passage partially remove this ambiguity, by adding 'by the church builders' after 'sufficient'; both the paperback edition of 1900 and the Wessex edition of 1912 have this. Ambiguity still remains, since the narrator does not say who was responsible for building the church, but even more clearly it is not the folk who worship, or who get married, or christened, there.

Again it is Hardy's aligning himself with his class that stimulates the 1892 change. But *Tess* is a curious novel; I have used the terms detached and engaged narrator to distinguish between the primary voices that can be heard attempting to direct a path through events and introducing states of mind. I want now to suggest that there are contradictions within the detached narrator. I am not claiming that it was in this one-volume edition that Hardy *first* embodied in his narrator the representative of his class; what does seem to be true is that at this time something about this novel in particular, and his perception of his own fiction in general, was clarified, and stimulated the revisions I have been looking at and others like them. The 'Dorsetshire Labourer' borrowings, though lamenting, at times angrily, the decline of the artisan-craftsman class in rural areas, are written from the point of view of one who has escaped from that class-destruction into middle-class celebrity as a writer; the change to the bell-passage is made from a different point of view, that of a displaced and oppressed craftsman. And these two facets of Hardy's writing coexist uneasily in *Tess*, though driven far into the background for most readers by the power of the personal history that the novel enacts, the conduct of which is substantially the business of the engaged narrative voice.

In part, this distinction might be defined by the characters of Angel and Tess, and Hardy recognized that he had a problem in the presentation of Angel (one that he thought about carefully during the revision for the one-volume edition), especially in his relation to Tess. For instance, when Angel's harp is first introduced it is simply 'an old harp which he had bought at a sale'. We are given a fresh insight into Angel's nature by the addition to this, in 1892, of 'saying when in a bitter humour that he might have to get his living by it in the streets some day'. We hardly get a glimpse of this bitterness during his time at Talbothays, and the added detail here prepares us in a very small way for what comes at Wellbridge (p. 168).

There are changes made to every aspect of Angel's sense of his relationship with Tess, changes to his thoughts of her, to his physical sense of her, to his conversation with her. One of the most memorable sentences in Angel's unspoken response to Tess was only added at this stage of the novel's development: his naive and rather priggish 'what a fresh and virginal daughter of Nature' (p. 172) was until the one-volume edition the more down-to-earth 'what a genuine daughter of nature'. The reader is, of course, aware of the ironic significance of 'virginal' at the moment that the thought passes through Angel's mind, but the irony becomes more powerful and poignant when the truth is also revealed to Angel. The capitalization of 'Nature' is significant too, in that it reflects accurately the tendency in Angel to abstraction and idealization, and thus helps to make his seduction by 'nature' at Talbothays more ironically effective.

Hardy was unsure how far Angel should be physically aware of Tess. In earlier revised texts the tendency had been towards emphasizing Angel's asceticism at the expense of his capacity for sensuous perception, but in 1892 Hardy felt that the balance needed readjusting. Thus, for example, to a fragment of observation: 'Clare, regarding for a moment the wave-like curl of her lashes as they dropped with her bent gaze, lingeringly went away', Hardy added 'on her soft cheek' after 'lashes', registering more fully the impact of Tess on Angel's senses.

It is in particular during the terrible days at Wellbridge that Hardy uses revisions to dialogue to modify the reader's perception of Angel. Soon after Tess's narration of her experience with Alec, Angel proposes that she is out of her mind, and then answers himself:

'Yet you are not. I see nothing in you to warrant such a supposition as that.' He stopped to resume sharply, 'Why didn't you tell me before'

So it is in the first edition, harsh and apparently without feeling; it becomes quite different in the one-volume edition:

'Yet you are not . . . My wife, my Tess—nothing in you warrants such a supposition as that?'
    'I am not out of my mind,' she said.
    'And yet—' He looked vacantly at her, to resume with dazed senses: 'Why didn't you tell me before' (p. 324)

Here, instead of a secure assertion it becomes an agonized question, and instead of being sharply self-possessed he is bewildered.

We also see Angel differently through the narrator's commentary. To Tess's perception—'She was awestricken to discover such determination under such apparent flexibility'—Hardy added a narratorial view, this time directly engaged with the character, as if it were only now that he felt fully the force of the character he had created: 'His consistency was, indeed, too cruel' (p. 341). On the other hand there is the addition a few pages later of: 'Some might risk the odd paradox that with more animalism he would have been the nobler man. We do not say it' (p. 344). The second sentence is Hardy's narrator at the height of evasiveness, and the plural pronoun, the characteristic note of the reviewer, is quite remarkably out of place. Furthermore Hardy *does*, of course, 'say it'. The 'odd' is so clearly ironical that it ensures the reader's disbelief of the narrator's denial, and encourages the reader to see in the word 'Some' Hardy himself separating himself still further from the text that has proceeded from his pen into print.

There are more engaged narratorial comments, though, and that one of these occurs in the same paragraph as that just considered points yet again to the remarkable flexibility of the narrative voice in *Tess*. As if to remind the reader of Angel's claim that he had not married the Tess before him but another woman in her shape, in the first edition the paragraph ends: 'The figurative phrase was true: she was another woman than the one he had desired.' This was an addition in the first edition; a year later Hardy felt that this put the matter too actively, and altered the last phrase to read 'the one who had excited his desire', which puts the primary onus on Tess; here is more evidence that Hardy has been thinking closely about the relationship between the two characters.

A second example is of a change to the summary of the couple's situation at Bramshurst Court; it is a moment that provides some interest. Tess says, 'looking through the shutter chink':

'All is trouble outside there: inside here content.'

He peeped out also. It was quite true: within was affection, pity, error forgiven: outside was the inexorable. (p. 531)

This is the first-edition version, holding subtly in balance the three voices of Tess, Angel, and the narrator. There is a carefully managed contrast between Tess's perception and the second, which is Angel's mediated by the narrator and uses vocabulary that could not, despite her education, ever be Tess's. And in particular it is the word 'pity' that distances Angel from Tess; however selfless the pity, it is necessarily the emotion of one in happy and superior circumstances towards one in sad and distressed. As Meredith saw in the 44th section of *Modern Love*, when the lover feels pity he knows that he has left love behind. Hardy too saw this in 1892, and altered 'pity' to 'union', transforming the effect, giving authority to the reader's sense that in these few days there is an intensity of emotion which is in its way satisfying to the lovers reunited, remembering the earlier contention that 'experience is as to intensity, and not as to duration' (p. 177).

It is not only in his relationship with Tess that Hardy alters the way that the reader is enabled to see Angel; when he meets with Izz Huett at Wellbridge Hardy reshapes a number of Angel's speeches, making him less patronizing, less priggish, more aware of the implications of what he asks Izz to do, and more aware of the pain he causes her by his withdrawal.

One of the revisions is to the central question itself; Angel reveals that he has parted from Tess: "I have separated from my wife for personal, not voyaging, reasons. I may never live with her again. Will you go with me instead of her?" (p. 374). The middle sentence was an addition to the first-edition text, but Hardy was not satisfied with the simple proposal, and a year later he gave to Angel a piece of honesty deriving from self-knowledge, amending the last sentence to read: "I may not be able to love you; but—will you go with me instead of her?"

Besides these and similar changes to aspects of Angel, there is a wide range of other facets of the novel that attracts Hardy's attention during this revision. Both of the other central characters, Tess and Alec d'Urberville, are refocused in small ways. The effect of the revisions to aspects of Tess is to make her more aware of what she is doing and feeling, and to make her slightly less immature; they might be taken as a pattern for the general direction of all the revisions that were made to her role in the novel from the first edition onwards. In the one-volume version almost all of the changes that relate to her are made to the three crisis-points in her life; her violation, her confession, and the murder of

Alec—and their surrounding prefigurings and consequences. Laird has detailed the most important ways that the violation is altered:[3] the removal of the 'cordial' that Alec forced Tess to take before laying her in the leaves; the addition of 'succumbed to a cruel advantage he took of her helplessness; then, temporarily blinded by his flash manners, had been stirred to confused surrender awhile: had suddenly despised and disliked him, and had run away' (p. 117) to the narratorial summary of her life after that night; and the addition of a reference to her child that looks backward to that night: 'A little more than persuading had to do wi' the coming o't, I reckon' (p. 127).

I have already looked at many of the changes to the confession, but there is a further point worth mentioning: as Tess is preparing to match Angel's confession, Hardy decided in 1892 to make the most important feature of the whole episode more explicit for the reader, ensuring, as elsewhere in revision for one-volume editions, that the significance of the moment for his argument about Tess will not be missed. To Tess's 'No, it cannot be more serious, certainly' he added 'because 'tis just the same!' (p. 318).

It was at this time that Hardy added what in isolation seems the most important single sentence in the narratorial voice that helps the reader to understand the events surrounding the murder of Alec. As Tess leaves him on the doorstep of The Herons, Angel has an insight into her state of being, which illuminates all that has preceded and all that follows— another of those passages of crucial clarification in which Hardy the faithful presenter of Tess recognizes for the first time precisely the implications of the character he has created through three successive revisions: 'But he had a vague consciousness of one thing, though it was not clear to him till later; that his original Tess had spiritually ceased to recognize the body before him as hers—allowing it to drift, like a corpse upon the current, in a direction dissociated from its living will' (p. 515). It seems possible that another addition slightly earlier provided the hint that stimulates Angel's insight into Tess's state of mind. It comes in Tess's explanation of how it is that she is with Alec again: 'These clothes are what he's put upon me: I didn't care what he did wi' me!' (p. 514).

It is in this edition also that the first tentative steps are taken towards the reconsideration of Alec d'Urberville's conversion, which is completed in the paperback edition of 1900 and the Wessex edition of 1912. At this stage in the transformation from sincerity to hypocrisy the

---

[3] J.T. Laird, *The Shaping of Tess of the d'Urbervilles* (Oxford: Oxford University Press, 1975), 176–9.

motivation is not the criticism of reviewers concerning the probability of
the conversion but rather Hardy's deeper penetration into Alec's response to the sight of Tess again after a number of years and in such a role.
Hence the addition (p. 422) to Alec's first words to Tess: 'Of course . . .
there is something of the ridiculous to your eyes in seeing me like this.
But—I must put up with that.'

Similarly, to his second speech (p. 423) Hardy adds: 'though perhaps
you think me a humbug for saying it' and to his third (p. 423) the
comment: 'Well, it is a strange story; believe it or not'. The strangeness
of the story was the subject of some comment, and in the later editions
Hardy went much further (see pp. 170–1 below).

Finally, there is a good example of Hardy rethinking his attitude to a
fundamental idea within the narrative. It is at the end of chapter V that
his narrator analyses the implications of the first meeting between Alec
and Tess:

Tess Durbeyfield did not divine . . . that there behind the blue narcotic haze was
the "tragic mischief" of her drama—he who was the blood-red ray in the spectrum of her young life.

And further:

she might have asked why she was doomed to be seen, and marked, and coveted
that day by the wrong man, and not by a certain other man, the exact and true
one in all respects—as nearly as human mutuality can be exact and true; yet to
him at this time she was but a transient impression half-forgotten. (pp. 56–7)

There is a certainty about these passages that amounts to determinism,
suggesting both that Tess's life is pre-ordained, and that the fiction in
which the narrative is conducted is leading to already previsioned ends.
In 1892 Hardy altered both, so that they now read:

Tess Durbeyfield did not divine . . . that there behind the blue narcotic haze was
potentially the "tragic mischief" of her drama—one who stood fair to be the
blood-red ray in the spectrum of her young life.

and

she might have asked why she was doomed to be seen and coveted that day by
the wrong man, and not by some other man, the right and desired one in all
respects—as nearly as humanity can supply the right and desired; yet to him who
amongst her acquaintance might have approximated to this kind, she was but a
transient impression half-forgotten.

Thus, Alec is only potentially the tragic event, and Angel 'might have approximated' to the 'right and desired' lover of Tess. When looked at in isolation this change seems significant and, even when reintegrated into the continuous fabric of the novel, the reverberative effect felt is quite different in the second version. We can no longer rest comfortable on the narrator's authoritative statement which implied that if Angel and Tess had come together before she met Alec, all would have been well in their relationship; there is now room for doubt whether the two would ever have found the basis for a lasting and satisfying relationship in marriage or out of it. In the end Hardy is giving both his narrator and his reader more freedom.

There may be a good case for choosing as a favoured version of a much-revised novel the one where it can first be suggested that the writer's sense of it became established. With most novels, that is likely to be its first appearance in book form, and with Hardy too this is so for most of his novels. With *Tess*, though, I have argued that this one-volume edition represents, with one quite important exception, Hardy's first final version of the novel. That exception, the way in which Alec's conversion is vulgarized and trivialized, might be the subject of some debate—to what degree was it forced upon him by critical comment? But, in any case, that is a narrow area of concern; and it is the feature of the one-volume edition of *Tess*, as it is not of any other of Hardy's novels, that the revisions range widely throughout the text, and are in many cases of the first importance in understanding the ideas or characters that they touch.

'Wessex Folk' and the Preface to Jude the Obscure

At about the same time as Hardy was making this revision to *Tess*, and a year or so after the publication of *A Group of Noble Dames*, he tried his hand again at a linked story-sequence. This time the narratives concerned lower-class rural life of the kind that readers by now associated with Hardy's name. 'Wessex Folk', as the group of stories was called for its 1892 appearance in *Harper's New Monthly Magazine*, is of particular interest not because it was mangled in serialization, but because parts of the surviving manuscript (in the Berg Collection of the New York Public Library) are in an early draft form; the only fragments of Hardy's published fiction for which we have such an early stage of development. It provides, then, a unique opportunity to look at the very early stages in the genesis of one of Hardy's works.

The most extensive account of the early history of one of his texts is to be found in the preface to the first edition of *Jude the Obscure*, the novel that followed the composition of 'Wessex Folk', and this account provides a context within which to study the short-story manuscript. Hardy wrote of *Jude*: 'The scheme was jotted down in 1890 from notes made in 1887 and onwards . . . the narrative was written in outline in 1892 and the spring of 1893, and at full length, as it now appears, from August 1893 onwards into the next year.' As far as the first stage outlined in this programme is concerned, there are no notes that are relevant to 'Wessex Folk', but we can see, preserved in *The Early Life* and elsewhere, plenty of notes that furnished the seed for elements in novels. *Tess of the d'Urbervilles* offers a good example from nearly the same time. The following entries in *The Early Life* are presented as extracts from Hardy's notebooks:

[1888]   "*September* 30. "The Valley of the Great Dairies"—Froom."
         " 'The Valley of the Little Dairies'—Blackmoor."
         "In the afternoon by train to Evershot. . . . The decline and fall of the Hardys much in evidence hereabout." (p. 281)
[1889]   "*May* 5. . . . That which, socially, is a great tragedy, may be in Nature no alarming circumstance." (p. 286)
         "When a married woman who has a lover kills her husband, she does not really wish to kill her husband; she wishes to kill the situation." (p. 289)

To them may be added an entry from the 'Facts' notebook Hardy began in the early 1880s: 'Waggoner asleep in his waggon—night—Bridport Rd.—meets coach—shaft of waggon enters breast of leader' (fo. 117). This was paraphrased from a report in the *Dorset County Chronicle* of 15 October 1829.

These notes are undoubtedly significant; they contain embryonic suggestions of one of the important environmental contrasts of the novel, two of its major themes, two of its most startling incidents, and the motivation behind one of them. It is not unreasonable to imagine that similar series of notes existed for earlier novels and stories.

The manuscript of 'Wessex Folk' indicates that such random but suggestive notes would probably have formed the groundwork for the next stage of development: a more detailed narrative scheme, though still in note form—'jotted down', as Hardy puts it in the *Jude* preface. The opening of the story-sequence shows how this 'scheme' would be moved on into a 'narrative written in outline'. At first it read:

It is a quarter to 4 on Sat^y afternoon, & the scene is the high street of a market town. /As the hour draws near/ a van standing in front of the Black Hart Inn: no horse in: no sign of the carrier. Timed to leave at 4. At half past 3, packages arrive.

Once he had got the framework down, with its abbreviation, instant cancellation, numerals, and monochromatic punctuation, Hardy began thinking about it, expanding the references, changing his mind, offering himself alternatives:

It is Sat^y afternoon winter or summer? & the scene is the high street of county town. a large carriers van standing in front of the White Hart Inn: market Black on the side of the tilt: Burden—Carrier to Upper < Trentripple > Joggingford < ton >. Timed to leave at 4. At half past 3, packages arrive.

The most striking element in the new matter is the local detail, the alterations always tending towards identity with the observable reality. Dorchester is the 'market' town he has in mind, hence the 'county' alternative; the inn in Dorchester outside which the carriers for places east of the town left their vans was the White Hart, and in 1890, when Hardy was writing the sequence, there was really a carrier called Burden who left from the White Hart every day for Troy Town and Puddle-town. The name of the fictional carrier's destination is the subject of uncertainty not only here, but also on the verso of the final leaf of the extant manuscript, where there is a gaggle of possible names:

Liddlington, Joggington, Fiddlington, Hide Trent, Trudginton, Middle-hinton, Trentingdale, Puddle-cum-quack, Fudley-cum-Pipes, Puddle-cum-Ales, Trentpuddle, Longpuddle, Hidehinton, Hidepuddle, Trentington, Hintonhide, Hinton, Hintonhyde, Plyntonhyde, Piddinghide and Middle-trenton.

The majority of these names shows that Hardy had in mind a combination of Piddletrenthide and Piddlehinton, the villages in the Piddle valley above Puddletown, though some stress the labour of getting there, and others the inhabitants' love of drinking and smoking. It is typical of Hardy's early drafts that he chooses in the end a name for the village without any associations with a real place.

The manuscript was left in this state, descriptively richer than at first, but full of indecision and still essentially in note form; we now have to imagine Hardy making at least one fair copy of this text in which the alternatives would be resolved, and which itself would certainly be altered before it was submitted to the printers. Purdy (p. 84) suggests on the basis of a page reproduced in *Harper's Monthly Magazine* of 1925, that this fair-copy manuscript existed in that year, though he was unable to trace it thirty years later. Unfortunately, the reproduced page contains the beginning of 'An Incident in the Life of Mr. George Crookhill' which is on a leaf missing from the extant draft manuscript, so no comparisons can be made between the two. There are, however, no significant differences between the text on the page reproduced in 1925 and the serial version of the same passage.

After the second manuscript which perhaps no longer survives, there would be proofs and revises on which Hardy might make further changes, before the next state of the text that does survive, the serialization in *Harper's New Monthly Magazine*. The opening lines we have been looking at appeared in the issue of March 1891 on page 587:

It is a Saturday afternoon of blue and yellow autumn-time, and the scene is the high street of a well-known market-town. A large carrier's van stands in the quadrangular fore-court of the White Hart Inn, upon the sides of its spacious tilt being painted, in weather-beaten letters, 'Burthen, Carrier to Longpuddle.' These vans, so numerous hereabout, are a respectable if somewhat lumbering class of conveyance, much resorted to by decent travellers not overstocked with money, the better among them roughly corresponding to the old French *diligences*.

The present one is timed to leave the town at four o'clock precisely, and it is now half past three by the ancient dial face in the church tower at the top of the street. In a few seconds errand-boys from the shops begin to arrive with packages, which they deposit in the vehicle, and then they turn away whistling, and care for the packages no more.

The notes have now been fully developed, the inert indications of time and place have become an active narrative in a manner recognizably Hardy's. The sentence comparing the carriers' vans with French *diligences* establishes by its tone and frame of reference what is essential in almost any Hardyan fiction, the distance between the narrator and what he is about to relate. Once we accept him as a well-travelled, urbane man, used to travelling by a form of transport several degrees superior to the van, and not concerned about the cost, Hardy can allow the narrator to perform for him one of those actions which are most characteristically his speciality as an artist, worming his way into the consciousness or subconsciousness of evidently unknown characters by intuitive imagination—here the object is the collective unconscious of the errand-boys.[4]

---

[4] For further discussion of this characteristic, see S. Gatrell, 'Travelling Man' in *The Poetry of Thomas Hardy*, ed. Patricia Clements and Juliet Grindle (London: Vision Press, 1980), 167–8; see also *Early Life* pp. 151, 173–4 for other isolated examples, and pp. 183–4, 190, where Hardy explains the method.

And, as they turn away whistling, the scene has been jerked into life. The village's name has been changed to the familiar Longpuddle, Hardy in the end choosing one of his trial series which is more closely identifiable with the real location he has in mind. The alteration of the carrier's name shows the same tendency.

In this connection, the history of this passage may be traced a little further, to its appearance in the first edition of *Life's Little Ironies* (1894), where 'Wessex Folk', retitled 'A Few Crusted Characters', was first collected. Here Hardy made his last alterations to this fragment of the text, and they may well have been a response to Alfred Parsons' head-piece-illustration in *Harper's*, which showed High East Street in Dorchester, with carriers' vans parked along the side of the road. It also showed quite clearly that the clock visible from that point is in the thin-spired tower of the town hall and not the solid, square church-tower of St Peter's; Hardy changed 'the ancient dial face in the church tower' to 'the clock in the turret', yet again revealing his anxiety to secure accuracy of topographical description wherever possible.

Only one, or perhaps two, of the stories that appear in the Berg manu-script might be considered intermediate between outline and a settled state. The most interesting story from this point of view is the one that now appears first, though from a cancelled pagination of the MS it was originally to have come second—'Tony Kytes, the Arch-Deceiver'. It is mildly comic, and tells how Tony, driving home from market in a cart, has to deal successively, and eventually together, with three girls who would each like to marry him.

Even though the narrative line is relatively simple, unresolved alterna-tives for details of its development exist in the manuscript; characteriza-tion is rudimentary, and Hardy has not really considered whether the story has any point beyond its comic resolution. It is reasonable to think of it as only partially completed; it has gone beyond the note stage, but is certainly not in a form that Hardy might think of as publishable.

It is not surprising, then, that there are substantial differences between the story as it appears in this manuscript and its printing in *Harper's*, the next surviving text for comparison. His most important task in develop-ing the skeleton-manuscript was to give the three girls in the tale some individuality; there was no space for rounded characterization, but they had to become more than the female ciphers they are in the manuscript. The first girl Tony picks up on his way home is Unity Sallet; she asks him for a ride, after which their dialogue is represented in the manuscript at first by: 'T:she s^d. Why did you desert me for that other one. I sh^d. have made you a more loving wife than she. . . . Well they talked on,

when what sh^d. T. see over the hedge'. Later he adds 'You deceived me
T &c' after 'she. . . .' as a shorthand indication that the conversation is
to be developed; and, when it reaches *Harper's*, it has become twenty-six
lines long, giving us a much more vivid sense of Unity's independent
existence. In fact, the idea of Tony's deceiving her, despite the story's
title, is not followed up; instead Unity tries to seduce him with their
long acquaintance and the rather bold 'And—can you say I'm not pretty,
Tony? Now look at me!' The forwardness of this suggestion presumably
stems from her dismay at Tony's engagement to Milly Richards, and
need not be seen as contradicting her earlier assertion of herself that
''Tisn't girls that are so easily won at first that are the best.'

What Tony sees over the hedge while speaking with Unity is the
feather in Milly's hat; she has come out because she was asked to by
Tony, and in *Harper's* this is stressed. Her first speech in the manuscript
reads:

My dear T. says Milly, looking up with a pout at him when he got near, how
long you've been coming home: & I've come to meet you as you asked me, to
ride home with ye: & talk over our future home.

By the time it appears in print it has become:

'My dear Tony!' cries Milly, looking up with a little pout at him as he came
near; 'how long you've been coming home! Just as if I didn't live at Upper
Longpuddle at all! And I've come to meet you as you asked me to do, and to ride
back with you, and talk over our future home—since you asked me, and I promised. But I shouldn't have come else, Mr. Tony!'

The third girl Tony gives a lift to (having persuaded the other two to
hide in the back of the waggon) is Anna Jolliver. In the manuscript she,
like the other two, accosts him from the roadside; in the serial, in order
to provide a certain amount of variety, she calls down to him from a
window of her aunt's house overlooking the road. Anna too sets out to
convince Tony that she is the one he ought to marry, and with some
success; the manuscript is quite clear about this, but in the magazine the
narrator of the story adds that Tony was won over 'by this pretty offering mood of a girl who had been quite the reverse (Anna had a backward
way with her at times, if you can mind)'.

It is striking that Hardy should, in the period between writing the
manuscript that survives and the publication of the serial, have decided
to show that though the girls were being forward, not to say bold, in
their approaches to Tony, in the light of his engagement to Milly, this
was not at all their normal behaviour. It is not clear whether this is a

generalization about the nature of girls when faced by the exigences of securing a husband, or whether some editorial hand, perhaps at Harper's, or perhaps Hardy pre-empting such interference, decided that such a coming-on disposition in three girls had somehow to be qualified.

Eventually, in an accident, all three girls are thrown out of the cart into the road, and the climax of the story comes as Tony tries to find one of them who will marry him after all. He rather rashly assumes that Anna will still be willing, and in the manuscript he is telling the other girls this when she interrupts with: 'She is *not* willing, Sir, says Anna hot & strong, for she was the one of the three that had most spirit.' In the serial the scene proceeds differently, and at the point of interruption there is the following passage:

Tony had not noticed that Anna's father was coming up behind, nor had he noticed that Anna's face was beginning to bleed from the scratch of a bramble. Anna had seen her father, and had run to him, crying.

'My daughter is *not* willing, sir,' says Mr. Jolliver hot and strong. 'Be you willing, Anna? I ask ye to have spirit enough to refuse him.'

'That I have, and I do refuse him,' says Anna, partly because her father was there, and, partly, too, in a tantrum because of the discovery and the scratch on her face.

This new material, marked as usual by economy in using the earlier phrasing, is partly prefigured by a late addition to the manuscript in the same place; 'Now T. hadn't seen that A's father come up behind . . . hated T . . . 's father. (registrar Mr Cox)),' though the suggestion about Mr Jolliver hating Tony's father (Tony was Toby in the manuscript, hence I suppose the uncertainty over his name) is not taken up in the serial, because Hardy has by that time the different reason for introducing him. In the manuscript Anna walks disdainfully away from Tony with her head in the clouds; but Hardy evidently had second thoughts about the probability of this, as by the time it appears in *Harper's* he adds to her rejection of Tony: 'she would not have refused Tony if he had asked her quietly, and her father had not been there, and her face had not been scratched by the bramble . . . away she walked, upon her father's arm, thinking and hoping he would ask her again.' These few lines show an attempt again to understand the motivation of a character who in the manuscript is more a puppet than an individual; action based on parental pressure, vanity, and the awkward situation, conflicting with inner hope and desire. In a brief space Hardy has opened Anna out, made her for a moment the subject of the reader's involved interest.

When we notice the serial addition made to Unity's similarly scornful manuscript rejection: 'And away walks Unity Sallet likewise, though she looked back when she'd gone some way, to see if he was following her,' it becomes clear that Hardy is also altering his view of the probable response of girls in general to such a situation, deciding that they would be incapable of sustaining the proud and dismissive reactions of the manuscript.

It is not only the girls whose personalities are clarified in the new ending; in the manuscript Milly has nothing to say to Tony's unenthusiastic 'What must be must be, I suppose'. She presumably acquiesces, as their banns are put up the following Sunday. In *Harper's*, however, Hardy adds a brief exchange between them after Tony has outlined fate's apparent plan:

'If you like, Tony. You didn't really mean what you said to them?'
'Not a word of it,' declares Tony, bringing down his fist upon his palm.

The question makes Milly's placidity easier to accept, and his reply justifies quite neatly for the reader the story's title.

This analysis of the first parts of the 'Wessex Folk' manuscript shows how it fits neatly into the outline Hardy made of his work on *Jude the Obscure*. It seems more than likely that many of his novels went through analogous stages, and that before he reached the printer's-copy manuscripts that have been examined earlier in this book, Hardy would have had similar rough working-drafts of individual chapters and episodes outlined in note form, filled out to some degree with alternatives and brief indications of character and incident.

One detail in the version of the first two paragraphs of the story-sequence as it appeared in *Life's Little Ironies* in 1894 is an indication of an aspect of his work that was engaging Hardy more and more thoroughly as the nineties progressed; it will be recalled that the name of the destination of the carrier's van was finally fixed as Longpuddle (a name representing with topographical accuracy the conflation of the two Dorset villages along the river Piddle that Hardy had in mind), and that a detail of his description of Casterbridge was altered to fit more closely the observable reality of Dorchester. This desire to diminish as far as possible the element of disguise over the settings of his novels, while retaining the last veil of fictionality, achieved a partial fulfilment when his fiction was published for the first time in a complete collected edition.

7

A First Collected Edition
1895–1897

The Issue of Wessex

Although to have published a collected edition of his work was a milestone for Hardy, a material assurance of his importance as a writer, this was not the most powerful motive that led him to agree to the proposal of James Ripley Osgood and his partner Clarence McIlvaine. What Hardy looked forward to most keenly was the opportunity to revise all of his fiction from a common standpoint, the standpoint of Thomas Hardy, delineator of Wessex. The collected edition offered him the chance to see his work as a whole thing, to place each text in the pattern of existence that Wessex had become for him. It is the single most important publishing event in Hardy's career as a writer of fiction, and marks a point of significance in the development of almost every book; in order to understand its influence upon the reader's experience of Hardy's work, it is necessary first to trace the growth of Wessex in the novelist's creative imagination.

Several writers have discussed Hardy's Wessex and its relationship in topographic and social terms with the historical counties of south-western England,[1] but none has fully considered the gradual nature of the development of Wessex, or the implications of the process of revision for the Osgood, McIlvaine edition. It is also important, in this respect, to take into account the further refinement of Wessex that Hardy made for the second collected edition of his work (published by Macmillan in 1912), and to try to distinguish between the two.

The clearest of Hardy's statements, though not necessarily the most reliable, about the birth and growth of his conception of Wessex are to be found in the prefaces that he wrote for his novels in 1895–7 and 1912. In the preface to *Far from the Madding Crowd* there is this:

In reprinting this story for a new edition I am reminded that it was in the

---

[1] See e.g. W.J. Keith, 'Hardy and the Literary Pilgrims', *Nineteenth-Century Fiction*, 24 (1969), 80–92; Michael Millgate, *Thomas Hardy: His Career as a Novelist* (London: Bodley Head, 1971), 235–48; Merryn Williams, *Thomas Hardy and Rural England* (London and Basingstoke: Macmillan, 1972); Andrew Enstice, *Landscapes of the Mind* (London and Basingstoke: Macmillan, 1979).

chapters of 'Far from the Madding Crowd' . . . that I first ventured to adopt the word 'Wessex' from the pages of early English history, and give it a fictitious significance as the existing name of the district once included in that extinct kingdom. The series of novels I projected being mainly of the kind called local, they seemed to require a territorial definition of some sort to lend unity to their scene. Finding that the area of a single county did not afford a canvas large enough for this purpose, and that there were objections to an invented name, I disinterred the old one.

And in the 1895 preface to *Tess* he wrote:

In the present edition it may be well to state, in response to inquiries from readers interested in landscape, pre-historic antiquities, and especially old English architecture, that the description of these backgrounds in this and its companion novels has been done from the real.

After mentioning natural and prehistoric features that are present in his work under their existing names, he goes on to add that

in planning the stories the idea was that large towns and points tending to mark the outline of Wessex—such as Bath, Plymouth, The Start, Portland Bill, Southampton, &c.—should be named outright. The scheme was not greatly elaborated, but, whatever its value, the names remain still.

In respect of places described under fictitious or ancient names—for reasons that seemed good at the time of writing—discerning persons have affirmed in print that they clearly recognize the originals. . . . I shall not be the one to contradict them.

The implication of these passages is that almost from the first Hardy was aware of the significance that 'Wessex' was to have for him; that in 1873, while writing *Far from the Madding Crowd*, he already had a plan for a series of novels that would embody the environment and society of south-western England, using an easily penetrable disguise over real places and buildings, and a less easily penetrable disguise over the people.

This is a rationalization of a process with several stages. W.J. Keith writes of the influence that the 'literary pilgrims' of the 1890s (when the tourists began to take up Hardy's works as guidebooks) may have had in forcing Hardy to reconsider his topographical descriptions; but it is necessary to go back much earlier than the 1890s.

Far from the Madding Crowd is, as Hardy said, the starting-point. Not only is the first edition of the novel the first time that 'Wessex' appeared in book form, it is also the first time that Hardy reused place-names first appearing in an earlier novel; thus Budmouth, Casterbridge, Mellstock, and Yalbury, from the first edition of *Under the Greenwood Tree* (1872), are either locations of scenes or are mentioned in the later novel. It is also the first time that a character from an earlier novel appears in a later; Joseph Poorgrass responds to the story in chapter VIII about his encounter with an owl: ' "Joseph Poorgrass of Weatherbury,"—that's every word I said, and I shouldn't ha' said that if 't hadn't been for Keeper Day's metheglin.'

Though Hardy had Yellowham in mind when mentioning Yalbury, Dorchester when describing Casterbridge, as much in *Far from the Madding Crowd* as in *Under the Greenwood Tree*, they are so imprecisely delineated that no reader not a native of those places would have realized the fact.

If Hardy's representation of Mellstock in the 1872 version of *Under the Greenwood Tree*, or his representation of Casterbridge in the 1874 edition of *Far from the Madding Crowd*, is considered in any detail, then it is evident that he based the one on Stinsford and the other on Dorchester. The division of the fictional parish into East Mellstock, 'the main village'; West Mellstock 'the church and vicarage . . . originally the most thickly populated portion'; and Lewgate, 'a mile to the north-east . . . where the tranter lived', corresponds precisely to the fragmentation of Stinsford parish into settlements at Lower Bockhampton, Stinsford, and Higher Bockhampton. But it would have been impossible to use (as has been done for the 1912 revised version) an Ordnance Survey map to illustrate the topography of the novel.

In the fictional Casterbridge there is a Union, and there is a prison, but the one is at the opposite end of the town from the Dorchester Union, and the other looks quite different from Dorchester Gaol. It might have been that, though he needed to use the reality that was so familiar to him, Hardy thought that fiction should be as fictional as possible, or else that he did not want anyone at home to imagine that he had put them into a novel. For whatever reason, he chose to include distances, directions, and descriptions that bore no relation to the reality.

That this was a deliberate act rather than carelessness or indifference is suggested by one detail from *Far from the Madding Crowd*:[2] Hardy was well aware that Joseph Poorgrass, returning from Casterbridge to Weatherbury with the coffin of Fanny Robin, would have had the sea on his right hand were he in fact driving from Dorchester to Puddletown. The first edition, though, has 'left', which was emended to 'right' in the Osgood edition; it is possible to show Hardy consciously at work on the

---

[2] Norton Critical edition, ed. R. Schweik (New York, 1986) p. 216.

disguise of the landscape detail here, because the manuscript at this point originally read 'right', and he altered it above the line to 'left'.

Thus, on the one hand, Hardy in 1873 felt the first promptings of an idea that he might use a landscape familiar to him to link together his novels; on the other, it was still the case for almost all his readers that Weatherbury had no more 'real' existence than Snoodly-under-Drool—another of Hardy's invented place names in *Far from the Madding Crowd*. *Under the Greenwood Tree* and *Far from the Madding Crowd* spring from a common source in Hardy's creative imagination, and so it is unsurprising that he should have found it right to merge slightly the worlds of the two novels. His next work, *The Hand of Ethelberta*, is quite different; yet it has many scenes that take place in what we now recognize as Dorset equivalents, and it contains four names that eventually became fixed on the map of Wessex: Anglebury, Knollsea, Melchester, and Sandbourne. There are no connections with earlier novels, but it seems probable that by this time discerning and enthusiastic readers of Hardy's novels had realized the extent to which he based his rural creations upon Dorset realities. In 1876, the year of *The Hand of Ethelberta*'s publication, an article was published in *The Examiner* entitled 'The Wessex Labourer', which was largely a review of Hardy's work; he had already been identified as a 'regional' novelist, and his region was being pinned down. Writing five years later, in *The British Quarterly Review* for 1881, Kegan Paul, himself a Dorset man, noted of *The Hand of Ethelberta*:

Though the scene is laid partly in London, the whole country portion of it is pure Dorset; but in his treatment of the scenery we could wish that Mr. Hardy had either been less minute or more accurate. To a non-native it does not matter, but to those who know it is perplexing to find Swanage made forty miles instead of twenty by road from Bournemouth, and that the trees of Lulworth can be seen in a gap of the hills from Corfe Castle.[3]

The question of the relationship between fiction and reality in the creation of environments came to a head for Hardy in the next novel, *The Return of the Native* (1878). The manuscript shows that he found it difficult to decide exactly how to treat the heath in relation to the country that surrounded it, and in relation to those earlier novels that had, as the real basis of their fiction, landscapes that adjoined the area Hardy had in mind when creating the heath. At first he thought to include no names from the earlier novel, then two or three, and finally settled for one—the

[3] *Thomas Hardy: The Critical Heritage*, ed. R.G. Cox (London: Routledge, 1970), 89.

slightly exotic watering-place, Budmouth. This indecision is bound up with the importance of the heath in the structure of the novel; Hardy wanted somehow to link the novel to *Under the Greenwood Tree* and *Far from the Madding Crowd*, and yet to preserve the heath as a place apart, mysteriously powerful, outside the boundaries of the normal everyday life, that was one of the dominant motifs of those earlier novels. Apart from Budmouth, the heath has only one urban contact with the outside world, the anonymous Southerton, where anyone with business that cannot be performed on the heath has to travel; but no action in the novel. ever takes place there, we only hear of things happening there, and have no sense of it as a community or as a group of buildings.

In *The Trumpet-Major* (1880) Hardy faced a different problem: what is the proper attitude to take towards the environment of an historical novel? This time he was much more certain of the right answer; the carefully balanced mixture of half-disguised reality and fictional creation is abandoned as far as is practicable. The only considerable exception is the centre of the action, the village of Overcombe, which was a composite fabrication, made of fragments drawn from three or four neighbouring locations, and thus had also to have a fictional name. Otherwise Dorset and other south-western places are given their real names; Weymouth is of almost equal prominence with Overcombe, and for the first time is described in some detail—though it is the Weymouth of several decades before any of the other novels in which it or Budmouth occurs. There is also a scene in Dorchester, in which existing features of the town were used and named accurately—All-Saints' church, and Grey's Bridge, for instance. It was, evidently, Hardy's feeling that though the characters are to a degree imaginary, the war they are living through and some of the events related are real enough, and an authentic environmental context is an essential part of the historical nature of the novel. This is not Wessex at all, but southern Dorset; and any reader of Hardy who was until this novel unaware of Hardy's 'region' now had unmistakable evidence.

It is interesting to see that in 'The Distracted Young Preacher', a story written at about the same time as *The Trumpet-Major*, the same pattern is adhered to. Hardy is retelling an actual event—using for instance the real name of the customs officer involved—as it had been told to him by those who had experienced it. The village which is the centre of the smuggling is called Nether-Mynton—a more or less transparent fictionalization of the Dorset village Owermoigne—but every other name, from Swanage to Weymouth, Warm'ell Cross to Lulworth Cove, is that of an existing Dorset place. On the other hand, 'Fellow-Townsmen', written a year or so later, preserves scrupulously the anonymity of the environment, so that only a Dorset man like Kegan Paul would guess the existing place used as the basis of the story's site; but 'Fellow-Townsmen' is a purely invented story.

It is with Hardy's return to live in Dorchester, and the writing of *The Mayor of Casterbridge*, that the first stage of a new development in the idea of Wessex begins. Casterbridge is connected along the filaments of the routes of carriers' vans to surrounding areas, carriers 'who hailed from Mellstock, Weatherbury, Hintock, Sherton Abbas, Stickleford, Overcombe, and many other villages round'.[4] Thus, in one sentence, connection is established with *Under the Greenwood Tree*, *Far from the Madding Crowd*, 'Interlopers at the Knap', 'The Romantic Adventures of a Milkmaid', and *The Trumpet-Major*. Henchard, at the end of the novel, is tracked across Egdon by Mr and Mrs Farfrae to his death-place—an appropriate connection with *The Return of the Native*. Caster-bridge is the centre, the focus of Wessex, and for the first time Hardy wants to offer it to the reader as a whole thing, rather than a series of indistinctly joined fragments. To this end he is also more free in the introduction of characters from other novels and stories: Bathsheba Everdene's uncle James, and Boldwood from *Far from the Madding Crowd*, are in the manuscript, and Lawyer Long, who makes a brief appearance in the earlier novel, was added to this one in the first edition. Darton, from the story 'The Interlopers at the Knap', was added to the manuscript, and 'old dame Ledlow', a female relation of *Under the Greenwood Tree*'s Farmer Ledlow of Mellstock, is mentioned. This comes close to the community of action that Hardy may have been searching for, though whether he would have expected his readers to notice this common element in 1886 is doubtful.

In his presentation of the novel's focal point, the town of Caster-bridge, Hardy still follows his practice in *Far from the Madding Crowd* of deliberately ensuring that the fictional town is not an exact re-creation of the Dorset one; as Christine Winfield and Dieter Riesner have pointed out, three prominent features of Dorchester—the King's Arms, the Antelope hotel, and St Peter's church—were in the manuscript ori-ginally introduced by their existing names, but in revision before the manuscript was sent to the *Graphic* these were altered to The Golden Crown, the Stag, and to St Jude's. Riesner also notes that there are ano-malies in the detail of Casterbridge; that, for instance, when the royal

[4] *The Mayor of Casterbridge* chapter IX, Wessex edition, p. 68.

visitor leaves the town he goes 'up the straight High Street . . . in continuation of the journey coastward', something a visitor to Dorchester then as now would not have done.[5]

The stage that Hardy reached between 1881 and 1885 can best be summarized by saying that Wessex as a region had come to be a very powerful concept for him, for his imagination as a writer of fiction, something that had to be taken into account whenever he began a story or a novel. It has a life that is quite separate from Victorian Dorset, and by using fictional names, and by ensuring that fictional places deviated in clear ways from their existing originals he made certain that it remained separate. Wessex society is not yet Dorset society.

The Return of the Native and *The Woodlanders* (1887) have many things in common; in this context, the striking point of similarity is that, as there is virtually only one town—Southerton—to which Egdon dwellers go to obtain what they lack, so there is almost only one journey's end for the inhabitants of Little Hintock and the woodlands; all business is conducted in Sherton Abbas. The great difference between the two towns, though, is a measure of the increasing power that Wessex has in Hardy's creative thinking as an equivalent of Dorset and the surrounding area. Whereas Southerton has no existence beyond the novel, and indeed hardly any within it, Sherton Abbas (a name, it will be remembered, that first appeared in *The Mayor of Casterbridge*) is transparently named after the Dorset town Sherborne, and, thus, is lent a solidity of existence beyond that which it gains through the narrative. Both heath and woodlands are formed by Hardy into environments that isolate and insulate, in which the dwellers hold minimal contacts with outsiders. Yet, in *The Woodlanders*, there is the sense of a small thriving metropolis without which the Hintock folk would be hard pressed to exist; the same is not at all true of *The Return of the Native*, where the economy of the heath is only passingly of significance.

Two years after *The Woodlanders* was brought out, there were two small publishing events which are of some significance in the picture of development I am trying to build up. One of these was a reissue of Hardy's first novel, *Desperate Remedies*, with revisions and a preface. Two changes are worth considering: the county town that in the first edition had been called Froominster, taking its name from the river that

---

[5] Riesner, 'Kunstprosa in der Werkstatt: Hardy's *The Mayor of Casterbridge* 1884–1912', in Dieter Riesner and Helmut Gneuss (edd.), Festschrift für Walter Hubner (Berlin: Erich Schmidt, 1964), esp. pp. 317–19; Winfield, 'Thomas Hardy's Revisions of *The Mayor of Casterbridge*' (Univ. of London Ph.D. thesis, 1971).

flows through Dorchester, was renamed; but instead, as might have been expected, of becoming Casterbridge, the name was altered to Troominster. It seems that Hardy's sense of Wessex and its importance to him as an idea that could unite all his work had reached just the stage that a new edition of *Desperate Remedies* might have undermined; he had neither the time nor the energy to rewrite the topography of the novel to accord with other novels that have their action in approximately the same area; so he decided to push it further away, and to disguise the county town more effectively, so that no casual reader might make the identification with Dorchester. That this was the case is further indicated by the change of Lewborne Bay to Darborne Chine, as different as possible from the Lulworth Cove that Hardy had in mind when writing the novel.

This rejection of *Desperate Remedies* from Wessex was made at roughly the same time that J.M. Barrie was writing 'Thomas Hardy: The Historian of Wessex', which appeared in the *Contemporary Review* for 1889; it is worth quoting at some length from one paragraph:

The closing years of the nineteenth century see the end of many things in country parts, of the peasantry who never go beyond their own parish, of quaint manners and customs, of local modes of speech and ways of looking at existence . . . Thus, the shepherds and thatchers and farmers and villagers, who were, will soon be no more, and if their likeness is not taken now it will be lost forever. Mr. Hardy has given much of his life to showing who these rustics were and how they lived, and his contemporaries have two reasons for believing his pictures true. One is that Billy Smallbury, Poorgrass, Grandfather William, and the others are still to be met with, though their days are numbered. Posterity will not have them to measure the rustics of Mr. Hardy by, but it will have the other and lasting test. The truth lives on in literature, because it is felt to be true, and one knows that whoever reads of Dick Dewy in 1989 will feel as sure of him as we are of the Vicar of Wakefield.[6]

It seems possible that this essay may have had some effect on Hardy's own understanding of what it was that he was writing; it often takes a perceptive outsider to express precisely an essential tendency of a writer's whole work. It is striking that the phrase 'Hardy has given much of his life to showing who these rustics were and how they lived' finds an echo in the General Preface that Hardy wrote for his work in 1912: 'At the dates represented in the various narrations things were like that in Wessex: the inhabitants lived in certain ways, engaged in certain

[6] *Critical Heritage*, pp. 158–9.

occupations, kept alive certain customs, just as they are shown doing in these pages.'[7] It is too facile to believe that there was a single decisive moment that fundamentally altered Hardy's attitude to the Wessex that he was creating; but reading this essay by Barrie may well have clarified for Hardy something that he had been feeling for some time. That Barrie took hints from Hardy's own essay 'The Dorsetshire Labourer' may be guessed, and that Hardy was already aware of the decline of his childhood's social order, and that he was concerned to preserve some of it in his fiction, seems obvious. But to see another man reading his work and expressing this so clearly and sensitively must have been an encouragement and, as I have suggested, a clarification of purpose.

I do not want to suggest either that *Tess of the d'Urbervilles* (1891) has the shape it has because of Barrie's essay—that too would be manifest nonsense; but, as many critics have pointed out, in *Tess* the relationship between the character at the heart of the novel and the landscapes she inhabits is fundamental to our understanding of the novel. At each stage of her progress through life she moves to a place that echoes her experiences, intensifies them, in part forms them, so that Talbothays and joy seem synonymous, Sandbourne and seedy finery, Chaseborough and corruption, Stonehenge and murder and sacrifice, and so on. This is the most important aspect of the change that has taken place in Hardy's use of Wessex, but it is not all; many of the names on the Wessex map originate with this novel, and almost all are of the transparent variety that allow the reader (compel him) to make the instantaneous transference to an existing Dorset name; also, because hills and rivers and other configurations of the landscape are given their existing names, and because the novel covers so much of the county, we get a feeling for Dorset within the feeling for Wessex. Things, one might say, when compared with *The Woodlanders*, have come much further out into the open; not, like *The Trumpet-Major*, into actual Dorset names, but into equivalences such as Marlott for Marnhull, Evershead for Evershot, Emminster for Beaminster. For the first time there are almost no place-names in the novel that Hardy needs to alter at any stage later than the first edition. It is also the case that in *Tess* there appear characters from earlier tales: William Dewy from *Under the Greenwood Tree*, Conjuror Fall from *The Mayor of Casterbridge*, and Conjuror Trendle from 'The Withered Arm'. It seems reasonable to hypothesize that between 1889 and 1891 there began in Hardy's imagination the creative process that led

[7] The General Preface appeared in *Tess of the d'Urbervilles*, vol. i of the Wessex edition, pp. vii–xiii.

to the all-pervading topographical and socio-historical revisions for Osgood, McIlvaine's collected edition of 1895–7, which it is now time to consider in more detail.

Keith's suggestion—that the increasingly frequent identification of Hardy's place-names with existing ones in south-western England, and the publication of maps with such corresponding identifications, put a pressure on Hardy that he could not resist to provide these identifications himself—almost certainly isolates one of the influences behind the Osgood revisions, but, as has been seen, there were powerful developing forces at work within Hardy himself that tended in the same direction.

When Hardy came to review his fiction for this first collected edition (to review it, that is, as a series of books, a whole thing) there were two impulses conflicting within him (a not unfamiliar experience for Hardy): on the one hand, this relatively recently formulated sense that he was indeed a historian of Wessex, that he had a duty to record accurately and lovingly what was being destroyed; and, on the other, the long-established feeling, intimately connected with the early growth of each novel, that though Wessex was important, often essential, to the fabric and structure of individual novels, it remained something only related to the reality from which the fictions drew their roots—a delicate balance between the necessary land that Hardy had trodden, and the imagined world that he had created for other than topographical effects.

What has to be reported is that the later and more immediately present sense dominated the revision. One way of epitomizing the difference that this makes to the reading experience of Hardy's work is to consider the effect of dividing Wessex into areas corresponding precisely to English county boundaries, something which first happens in this edition. Confronted, as the reader is in each volume, by a map of part of England divided into the familiar shapes of Devon, Hampshire, Wiltshire, and the other counties, which are, however, labelled Lower Wessex, Upper Wessex, Mid Wessex, and so on, there is no way to avoid the one-for-one relationship. It becomes compulsory to think that South Wessex is Dorset, even though Hardy is at pains in many places to disown such unqualified identity between fiction and life.

This map imposes its authority and its pattern of equivalent identities on novels that are not suited to it and are thereby distorted, and upon novels that were created before the name Wessex had even occurred to Hardy.

To see how this new tendency in Hardy's ideas works in practice, consider the transformation in the environment of an early novel, *Under the*

Greenwood Tree, over the two revised editions. What happens is that there is hardly a path trodden or a road driven over, a house visited or a building described, that does not have some change made to it in either 1896 or 1912, or frequently in both. Take the description of the characters' movements in the first chapter of the novel as an example; every reference to the lanes is altered, and there is a pattern to these revisions. What was topographically undefined in the first edition—'a lane'—becomes located, in the Osgood version, but the location is vague—'a lane near Mellstock Cross'. By the time the whole chapter is read in the Wessex edition in 1912 (where 'near Mellstock Cross' became 'towards Mellstock Cross'), it is possible for a reader to take a large-scale map of the parish of Stinsford and lay his finger on a particular spot on a particular lane there represented, and to be sure that the point on the map is a sign of the objective reality that Hardy was re-creating in the final version. It is too much of a generalization to say that this pattern can be applied to the environmental revisions as a whole in either edition, but it does provide a model for many such revisions; when Hardy left room for doubt as to the exact correspondence between fiction and life in 1895–6, that doubt was for the most part removed in 1912. Thus, still in the first chapter of *Under the Greenwood Tree*, the first edition's 'I have just been for a run to warm my feet' passes without a change in 1896, but in 1912 becomes: 'I have just been for a run round by Ewelease Stile and Hollow Hill to warm my feet'. If readers care to look at the same large-scale map, they will find Hollow Hill, and the footpath Dick Dewy followed; and if they are particularly enthusiastic, they can run the same course, and enter more fully into Dick's experience; re-create the novel physically as well as imaginatively. And they can be fairly sure that they are also doing something that the author frequently did, forging another layer of intimacy with the text.

There are, in the novel, two set pieces of revision: the description of the tranter's house, and the presentation of the town of Budmouth. The fundamental transformations from an anonymous cottage to a close approximation to Hardy's birthplace, and from an unidentifiable seaside resort to a detailed re-creation of Weymouth, take place in 1896, but in both cases further refinements in 1912 make the correspondences more unmistakable. And there are some fifty or so other places where this kind of process of revision has left its mark.

The relocation of the novel in what is the Ordnance Survey's Stinsford, with a diaphanous veil cast across it, removes one of the elements that made *Under the Greenwood Tree* seem to reviewers before

1896 a perfectly constructed idyll—the feeling that Mellstock represented any rural village. On the other hand, the geographical and topographical precision is in harmony with the kind of approach to parish history that stimulated the changes in 1896 of the name of a clockmaker from 'Ezekiel Sparrowgrass' to 'Ezekiel Saunders' and the name of an alehouse from 'the Old Souls' to 'Morrs's': Thomas Saunders, a watch and clockmaker, was living in High Street, Dorchester, in 1842, and Jeanne Howard points out that James Morrs 'master blacksmith . . . kept a beershop on his premises' at about the same time in Stinsford.[8]

It is always easy to get a distorted picture of the effect that a relatively small number of changes can have in the reading-experience of the novel as a whole; but *Under the Greenwood Tree* in the version of 1912 is in some ways a substantially different novel from the one that a few hundred people read in 1872. The difference is only partly to be found within the individual text. The cumulative effect of similar changes to all the novels and stories is overwhelming.

In *Under the Greenwood Tree*, it is possible to see that the seeds of the 1912 landscape were present in the first edition; but this is not the case with *The Return of the Native*, in which the transformation is fundamental. Whereas previously the heath was only connected with the surrounding world by a single identifiable thread to Budmouth, when Hardy had finished revising the novel in 1895 the heath is, as it were, pinned down. The town Southerton, which might have been in any direction and at any distance from the centre of the heath as far as the reader of the first edition knew, has entirely disappeared, and in the places where that name occurred are, variously, Casterbridge, Anglebury, and Weatherbury. A place 'about two miles to the right of Alderworth', unnamed in the first edition, is now defined as Stickleford. Thus, the extent of the heath is measured, from Casterbridge in the west to Anglebury in the east, from Weatherbury in the north to Stickleford in the south; the limitless intensity which characterized the impact that the heath makes in many passages and on several characters in the first edition is now vitiated by the known boundaries—the more so in that the reader cannot help but make the translations from Anglebury to Wareham, Stickleford to Tincleton, Weatherbury to Puddletown, and Casterbridge to Dorchester. What was once of mysterious extent and of shifting definition is now a limited tract of land any tourist can tramp over.

[8] Howard, 'Thomas Hardy's "Mellstock" and the Registrar General's Stinsford', *Literature and History*, 6 (Autumn, 1977), 179–202.

The Trumpet-Major undergoes just as radical a transformation in 1895; very nearly all the real names that were used in the first edition are altered to their by now established Wessex equivalents: thus Dorchester becomes Casterbridge, Salisbury becomes Melchester, Exeter becomes Exonbury, and Weymouth becomes Budmouth. By making these alterations Hardy has quite changed the character of his story; what was once a historical romance, with its base in real happenings and places, now becomes more than half fictionalized. Where an inhabitant of Dorset in 1808 might have said that the king's coach 'only reaches Andover by suppertime', only a dweller in the fictional Wessex could say that it 'is timed to change horses at Woodyates Inn—between Mid and South Wessex—at twelve o'clock.' So two extremes—the novel whose created environment was once closest to observable reality, and the novel whose landscape had been the most deeply imagined—suffer in the Osgood edition from a half-way compromise that distorts Hardy's original conception of both for the sake of creating a uniform, consistent, only part-imagined country.

The effects explored in these three novels can be duplicated to a greater or lesser degree in each of the books published before 1890; often the revisions are referred to in revealing passages of the prefaces that Hardy wrote. He found *A Laodicean* ultimately impossible to incorporate: 'Looking over the novel . . . I hazard the conjecture that its sites, mileages, and architectural details can hardly seem satisfactory to the investigating topographist, so appreciable a portion of these features being but the baseless fabric of a vision.' Hardy struck a similar note in the preface to *The Woodlanders*:

I have been honoured by so many enquiries for the true name and exact locality of the hamlet 'Little Hintock', in which the greater part of the action of this story goes on, that I may as well confess here once for all that I do not know myself where the hamlet is more precisely than as explained above [in the 1895 preface] and in the pages of the narrative.

He does his best with both of these novels, but his intentions when he first created them were so thoroughly other that, despite much revision, it remains impossible to be certain of correspondence between Wessex and real locations.

There is a phrase in the *Far from the Madding Crowd* preface that has been much quoted in studies of Wessex, but usually in its 1912 version, and the difference between the two is instructive. In 1895 Hardy described Wessex as 'a merely realistic dream-country'; this might be paraphrased 'only a dream-country presented realistically', but by 1912 the phrase was altered to 'a partly real, partly dream-country' (the change was actually made in the reset preface for the Uniform edition of 1902), and Hardy has acknowledged that the topographical changes have transformed Wessex into the hybrid thing that now so powerfully confronts the reader.

I have already shown how revision in 1912 takes the definition of the relationship between Wessex and south-western England a stage further; one of the reasons for this was that by 1912 many of the places that were decaying in 1895 had decayed, many of the customs that were passing had passed, many of the objects that were going out of use had disappeared. This is the culmination of a process that Hardy had foreseen, and it prompts a slightly different kind of addition to the text, the historical footnote: 'The reader will scarcely need to be reminded that time and progress have obliterated from the town that suggested these descriptions many or most of the old-fashioned features here enumerated.' This characteristic example is from chapter IX of *The Mayor of Casterbridge*.

There are also notes that seek to explain Dorset expressions, like this from chapter VIII of *Far from the Madding Crowd*, relating to Mark Clark's speech 'A queer Christian, like the Devil's head in a cowl': 'This phrase is a conjectural emendation of the unintelligible expression, "as the Devil said to the Owl," used by the natives.' There are others in chapter XXXII of *Tess of the d'Urbervilles* and chapter IV of Spring in *Under the Greenwood Tree*.

Other Aspects of the Osgood Edition

The whole tendency of this analysis has been to suggest that to reinterpret a central element of a novel of the 1870s by the light of ideas of the 1890s or the 1910s will make it a different thing. And it is further true that other characteristic aspects of earlier novels are eroded in a common pattern of revision for the collected editions.

The most significant of these is the greater freedom that Hardy felt in 1895 than even ten years earlier to be more explicit about sexual encounters and related matters.[9] This loosening of the Grundian shackles

---

[9] It is interesting in this context to note the degree to which a fellow novelist considered that Hardy was primarily responsible for a general relaxation in late Victorian attitudes in these areas. In a letter to his friend Eduard Bertz of 17 March 1892 George Gissing wrote: 'Remarkable, by the way, how English opinion is progressing in the matter of subject for fiction . . . Indeed, after Hardy's "Tess," one can scarcely see the limits of artistic freedom.' (*The Letters of George Gissing to Eduard Bertz*, ed. Arthur C. Young (New Brunswick: Rutgers University Press, 1961), 149.)

did not result in the invention of completely new actions. Rather, Hardy made clearer at certain places in some novels what he had always intended, what, that is, had been in his imagination as he conceived the incident, though he had been forced by contemporary attitudes to disguise or omit it. Thus, for the most part, these changes may best be seen as a return to an original conception. Some novels, like *The Trumpet-Major*, *A Pair of Blue Eyes*, or *Under the Greenwood Tree* have very few such changes, since Hardy at no stage intended them to have any sexual incident beyond the occasional kiss. In others, though, there are quite substantial alterations in this area: in 1877, for instance, Hardy felt himself unable to make it clear in *The Return of the Native* that Eustacia and Wildeve made love before Wildeve married Thomasin, or that if Eustacia went to Budmouth or Paris with Wildeve it would be as his lover. Similarly, it was only in the Osgood edition of *The Mayor of Casterbridge* that Hardy felt able to put in print the sexual nature of the early relationship between Michael Henchard and Lucetta LeSueur that had evidently been part of his earliest conception of the plot (see above, ch. 5), or to change the definition of skimmity-ride as something that is done 'when a man's wife is—well, a bad bargain in any way' to something that is done 'when a man's wife is—well, not too particularly his own' (Osgood edition, p. 314).

The largest number of revisions like these occurs in *The Woodlanders*, and they are also thematically the most important. In particular, the sexual awareness of Grace Melbury is significantly increased: she recognizes more clearly the implications of Suke Damson's early morning visit to Fitzpiers, she encapsulates her sudden perception of the relationship between her husband and Felice Charmond in the exclamation 'He's had you!', and she is able wryly to suggest that Suke, Felice, and she are equally Fitzpiers's wives. The embrace that she shares with Giles Winterborne while she thinks her divorce from Fitzpiers a possibility is more intense, and she is more insistent both that Giles should, after all, share with her the hut he has given up to her, and, after his death, that she has made love with him. Her sexual vitality had always been vaguely felt in the novel, but now it is unmistakable.[10]

Hardy's correspondence shows that from the first he did not believe that the reconciliation of Grace and Fitzpiers would be long-lasting; the impermanence of Fitzpiers's love was a settled thing by the end of the novel. He must have hoped that his readers would have felt the same way but, to emphasize the point, in the Osgood edition he gave a speech to

[10] *The Woodlanders* (Oxford: Clarendon Press, 1981), 228, 242, 287, 298, 300.

Mr Melbury in which he predicts that Fitzpiers will soon find another Felice Charmond: 'let [Grace] bear in mind that the woman walks and laughs somewhere at this very moment whose neck he'll be coling next year as he does hers tonight' (p. 335).

Pregnancy and childbirth were also subjects that editors and publishers (and many readers) in the 1870s and 1880s thought should not be mentioned in fiction, and many of the direct and indirect references to them were added to the texts of the novels only in the Osgood edition. It was not until 1895, for instance, that readers of *A Pair of Blue Eyes* could learn that Elfride Luxellian died of a miscarriage, and only in the same year was it apparent in *The Mayor of Casterbridge* that Lucetta Farfrae died from a similar cause. Even *Under the Greenwood Tree* did not escape entirely: in the Osgood edition Mr Penny says of his married daughter, who has just had her fourth child, 'She do know the multiplication table onmistakable well.' These examples contrast with the changes that Hardy was invited by Leslie Stephen to make to his description of Fanny Robin's child, and by those responsible for the *Graphic* to the stories in *A Group of Noble Dames*.[11]

Hardy, it will be remembered, was involved with *Jude the Obscure* at the same time as he was making the revision for the Osgood edition, and it is not surprising that occasional touches of the heavy irony found throughout that novel find their way also into earlier ones. In *The Trumpet-Major*, for example, when a list of the dead and wounded at the battle of Trafalgar was issued, it only contained the names of the officers, 'the friends of ordinary seamen and marines being on that occasion left to discover their losses as best they might.' In 1895 Hardy altered 'on that occasion' to 'in those good old days', changing the specific to the general and thus the whole tone of the sentence. Characters too are sometimes the target of this kind of change: in *The Mayor of Casterbridge*, Farfrae sings a 'song of his native country'. In 1895 this becomes a 'song of his dear native country, that he loved so well as never to have revisited it.'[12]

There were also considerable changes to the style of some of the earliest novels. In *Under the Greenwood Tree*, for instance, there was often a jocularity in the narratorial voice which the maturer Hardy felt he had to neutralize. This fragment, for example, is from Winter chapter II of

[11] *A Pair of Blue Eyes*, World's Classics edition (Oxford: Oxford University Press, 1985), 370. *The Mayor of Casterbridge*, World's Classics edition (Oxford: Oxford University Press, 1987), 288. *Under the Greenwood Tree*, World's Classics edition (Oxford: Oxford University Press, 1985), 18. See above pp. 17–18 and 80–93.
[12] *The Trumpet-Major*, Wessex edition, p. 316. *The Mayor of Casterbridge*, World's Classics edition p. 324.

the first edition: 'their eyes meditatively seeking out with excruciating precision any small speck or knot in the table'. In 1896 Hardy removed from it 'with excruciating precision', and in 1912 'small'. In *A Pair of Blue Eyes* it is a sometimes exaggerated formality that marks out the relative immaturity of the novel, and again it disappears in the revised editions; a speech like 'I am compelled to leave for Oxford' becomes 'I've got to run up to Oxford'.[13] Similar examples might have been drawn from both *Far from the Madding Crowd* and *The Hand of Ethelberta*, and while most readers would accept that such changes are for the better, yet something distinctive has been lost from the early novels.

In the end, the reader and editor of Hardy, particularly of the novels written before 1885, have to make a choice between a Wessex or a pre-Wessex text. They have to decide, for instance, whether *The Trumpet-Major* is better read as a novel set in Dorset or in South Wessex, or whether *A Pair of Blue Eyes* is enhanced by the knowledge that Elfride Swancourt died in childbirth—whether to abide by Hardy's original version of the novel, or to accept the transformation that he made to aspects of it in the light of later ideas and convictions. There are arguments on both sides, and, indeed, the best solution would be to have both versions of the novel available in accurately and sensitively edited texts.

Some of the arguments in favour of the first editions of these novels have been expressed in the preceding discussion. One strong argument in favour of the last revised version is that successive generations of readers have experienced the homogeneity of Wessex, have shared this aspect of Hardy's maturer vision. To reject the revisions of 1895-6 and 1912 would be to reject this idea of Wessex, and Hardy's attempt to preserve it for us in his fiction, and maybe some distortion of original intention is a small enough price to pay for the perpetual fascination that Hardy's Wessex exercises over us.

Aspects of the Illustration of Hardy's Novels: Macbeth Raeburn and the 1895 Etchings; Hermann Lea and the Wessex Edition Photographs

The drawings that accompanied the first appearance of many of Hardy's novels when they were serialized in magazines have been reproduced and discussed in a book by Arlene Jackson. However, as far as I am aware, no one has remarked, other than in passing, upon the etchings by Macbeth Raeburn which accompanied the Osgood, McIlvaine collected edition. There were only seventeen of them, but they represent as well as anything else that happened in 1895-6 the development in Hardy's attitude

---

[13] *Under the Greenwood Tree*, p. 20. *A Pair of Blue Eyes*, p. 142.

to his texts. More attention has been paid to Hermann Lea's photographs in illustration of Hardy's novels, but this has been predominately directed towards Lea's *Thomas Hardy's Wessex*, published in 1913 in a format which matched the Macmillan Wessex edition rather than the handful of his photographs which were reproduced as frontispieces for the volumes of the Wessex edition.[14]

There is no substantial discussion in Hardy's own writing of the question of the illustration of fiction; the nearest we have is in a letter to Arthur Hopkins, the illustrator of *The Return of the Native* in *Belgravia*, where Hardy says: 'My opinion, & I believe that of most novelists, is that the writer & illustrator of a story can hardly ever be in thorough accord unless they live in constant communication during its progress, & in these days that is almost impossible' (*Letters*, i. 52). The nearest that Hardy came to the kind of collaboration hinted at in this letter was with George Du Maurier over the first few illustrations for *A Laodicean*. Hardy had chosen the artist, and wrote to him: 'The first number of the story is now written (roughly), & if you are willing to begin at once I can call on you any day & hour you name (except Thursday) with the MS. in my hand, read it over to you, & finish our talk about the first picture' (*Letters*, i. 76). The lengthy illness that spoiled the novel must also have cut short this close co-operation between author and artist.

There is no evidence to show why, some years later, Macbeth Raeburn was chosen by McIlvaine to provide the illustrations for the new collected edition of Hardy's work in 1895. Henry Raeburn Macbeth was the son of a well-known Scottish painter, and, by the time he started to show his work at the Royal Academy, an elder brother was also making a name as an artist; so, in order to prevent confusion and assure himself of independent consideration, in 1882, soon after he had moved to London, he changed his name to Henry Macbeth Raeburn. He had begun painting at the age of eighteen, studying in the life-school of

---

[14] Arlene Jackson, *Illustration and the Novels of Thomas Hardy*, (Totowa, NJ: Rowman and Littlefield, 1981). *Thomas Hardy Through the Camera's Eye*, ed. J. Stevens Cox (Beaminster, Dorset: Toucan Press, 1964); David Baron's 'Landscape Convention—Thomas Hardy & John Pouncy' *The Thomas Hardy Year Book*, 13 (1986), 35–49, throws some light on earlier attention that Hardy may have paid to both drawing and photography of topographical subjects. Baron draws attention to Hardy's 1906 Preface to Henry Moule's *Dorchester Antiquities*, in which Hardy recalls discussions in 1881 about the possibility of Moule providing illustrations for some of Hardy's writing (whether past or future is unspecified), quoting a letter from Moule in which he writes: 'If, as you think, landscape with smallish figures will do, I trust that I should be able to do you justice.' Baron also makes a reasonable case for Hardy's knowledge of Pouncy's *Dorsetshire Photographically Illustrated* (1857), though his discussion of ways in which Hardy's handling of landscape in his fiction may have been indebted to Pouncy's photographs is unconvincing.

the Royal Scottish Academy, and had his first picture hung at the Royal Academy in 1880. He took up etching at the beginning of 1884, and three years later his work in this medium was also on display at the Royal Academy.

The only other original work of his in the field of book-illustration that I have come across is a handful of the more than four hundred etchings that were prepared for Andrew Lang's Border edition of Scott's novels in 1892. The evidence of these is that he had a strong dramatic sense, and that he was much happier when drawing landscape than figures, though there is one fine portrait in *Waverley* in the manner of his Scottish predecessor Sir Henry Raeburn. He was also employed to etch the drawings of others, notably two by Millais that were frontispieces to *The Heart of Midlothian*. His being chosen may have depended on no more than the fact that he was available at the time, or that he was an acquaintance of McIlvaine.

The etchings themselves are sometimes very fine—I particularly like the cottage in torrential rain that illustrates 'The Three Strangers' in the *Wessex Tales* volume—and are always very lively and worth consideration; but what is more interesting in this context than their quality is the note that is appended to the letterpress description of each of them: 'Drawn on the spot'. Macbeth Raeburn made at least two trips to Dorchester; the first in December 1894, which may have lasted for ten days or so, and another in March 1895. That the relationship between artist and author grew cordial may be inferred from the form of address that Hardy used in writing to him. At the end of November 1894 Hardy wrote to advise Macbeth Raeburn of trains to Dorchester, and to explain that improvements to Max Gate made it impossible for him to offer accommodation, beginning the letter 'My dear Sir'. Macbeth Raeburn planned to arrive on 3 December and put up at the King's Arms; the next we hear is that on 16 December Hardy was glad that he had arrived home without trouble, this time beginning the letter 'Dear Raeburn'. In this letter he also encouraged the artist to make the trip to Boscastle to do a drawing for *A Pair of Blue Eyes*, since 'the coast there is so very picturesque, & has such changing aspects of light and shade that you ought to see it. Photographs, being taken always in fine weather, miss all that is most striking in the scenery there' (*Letters*, ii. 65). It seems that Macbeth Raeburn took the hint and made the trip (the etching of the harbour is another of his successes), since the third surviving letter from Hardy, undated but attributed by the editors of Hardy's letters to March 1895, refers to it:

If you have not read The Woodlanders, and as I cannot very well go to Sherborne Monday . . . would it not be better to come straight on here from Boscastle: & do the Woodlanders after The Return of the Native, Trumpet-Major
&c? Moreover, unless you do Sherborne Abbey itself (which comes into the tale)
the woodland scenery of the story is as accessible from here as from Sherborne—it lying half way between this town & S.

You will excuse cramped accommodation I am sure. My wife is quite well
now—& will be glad to see you. (*Letters*, ii. 70)

It will be noted that the artist has been invited to stay at Max Gate, and it
is further evidence of Hardy's pleasure in his company that he addresses
him at the start of the letter as 'My dear Raeburn'.

The editors of the letters comment that 'Raeburn's notes on this letter
indicate that Hardy had suggested for possible subjects to draw for *The
Woodlanders* "Mintern—Devil's Kitchen or Lion's gate—or Hermitage
under High Stoy" '.

In *The Later Years* Hardy describes this visit, presumably the second
that Macbeth Raeburn had made to Dorchester:

In March of the next year (1895) Hardy was going about the neighbourhood
of Dorchester and other places in Wessex with Mr. Macbeth Raeburn, the well-
known etcher, who had been commissioned by the publishers to make sketches
on the spot for frontispieces to the Wessex Novels. To those scenes which
Hardy could not visit himself he sent the artist alone

There follows Hardy's relation of Macbeth Raeburn's problems in drawing in Charborough Park for *Two on a Tower*.

This evidence has been presented to show how far Hardy had come in
his attitude towards the illustration of his fiction. Only occasionally,
when his novels were serialized, did Hardy have control over what scenes
from his novel were to be illustrated; and, though he sent drawings of
details of costume and equipment to various artists, the magazine
illustrations were almost entirely concerned with the characters in his
work rather than the environment. For the Osgood, McIlvaine edition it
was decided, probably by Hardy, that the frontispieces should be purely
landscape drawings, and he directly involved himself in the choice of
scene to be illustrated, more or less setting up Macbeth Raeburn's stool
and saying, 'there before you is what I had in mind when I wrote of
Rainbarrow, draw that', or else giving him fairly detailed directions as
to what was the appropriate landscape to take.

All this is utterly in keeping with the developed concept of Wessex
that pervades the freshly revised texts, Hardy announcing with clarity
through the frontispieces that there was a spot in the real world from

which the fictional landscape or building could be drawn. And, what is more, the change in the form of illustration in 1912–13 from etching to photograph can also be seen as emblematic of the further development that took place in Hardy's view of Wessex, as embodied in the second collected edition. Whereas an etched drawing is an interpretation of a landscape or a building made through the eyes of a creative artist, who may suppress or invent details to assist the composition of his picture, a photograph is a reproduction of what can be contained within a camera lens, and, though work on the negative can falsify the mechanically obtained image, in Hermann Lea's work used for the Wessex edition the pictures remain objective records of the scene. It was towards such historically accurate objectivity that Hardy often seemed to be working in his revisions of environmental details in the Wessex edition.

It was a few years earlier, in 1908–9, that Henry James had used photographs by A.L. Cobùrn as frontispieces for the New York edition of his novels and tales, and in some ways they might be thought a half-way house between the Macbeth Raeburn and the Lea illustrations in Hardy's collected editions. Ralph Bogardus, in his excellent study of Coburn and James,[15] discusses the close collaboration between novelist and photographer, showing how James gave Coburn detailed shooting-scripts to take with him to Paris and Rome and Venice, but also making it clear that Coburn's contribution as artist to the enterprise was vital. The relationship between Hardy and Macbeth Raeburn seems to have been very similar, but there remains the difference between the graphic artist and the photographer.

James addresses himself in the preface that he wrote for *The Golden Bowl* in the New York edition to the question of the frontispieces. He begins by expressing his sense of the danger to fiction of illustration that seeks to abrogate a part of what the narrative itself should perform—the presentation to the reader's imagination of sufficiently vivid pictures of character or scene or action embodied in the text. He then explains why he decided, in spite of this, that illustrative photographs should form a part of this new and important edition of his work: 'the proposed photographic studies were to seek the way, which they have happily found, I think, not to keep, or to pretend to keep, anything like dramatic step with their suggestive matter.' They were to be 'expressions of no particular thing in the text, but only of the type or idea of this or that thing'. As a practical example of what he meant, James discussed the two

[15] *Pictures and Texts: Henry James, A.L. Coburn, and New Ways of Seeing in Literary Culture* (Ann Arbor: UMI Research Press, 1984).

illustrations to *The Golden Bowl*; this is what he said of the second, a misty and more or less unidentifiable view of Portland Place, dominated by the rear of a cab that has just passed the camera placed in the middle of the roadway:

it was equally obvious that for the second volume . . . nothing would so nobly serve as some generalized vision of Portland Place. Both our limit and the very extent of our occasion, however, lay in the fact that, unlike wanton designers, we had, not to 'create' but simply to recognize—recognize, that is, with the last fineness. The thing was to induce the vision of Portland Place *to* generalize itself.

James took the objective nature of photography and turned it into something symbolic; Lea's photographs have none of this deliberate indirectness. They proclaim what they are, the real version of a half-imaginary scene in the novel or story.

Lea made three separate attempts at illustrating Hardy's work, each more ambitious. The first (in collaboration with the Revd Thomas Perkins, another keen photographer and acquaintance of Hardy), was a series of sets of postcards, the second a modest guide book, and the third the companion to the Wessex edition, already mentioned. On each occasion it seems, from Lea's notes and Hardy's letters, that Hardy was not especially enthusiastic about the idea, but that when he began to see the photographs his interest was sparked and he began to make suggestions. On 1 March 1904, for instance, when the postcard project was in full swing, Hardy wrote to Lea: 'The view of Henchard's house which you propose to take will, I fear, make a prosaic picture, being a flat front elevation; unless you cd do it aslant from some upper window on the other side of the street' (*Letters*, iii. 109). Once Hardy had said that he did not object to the various proposals for publication, Lea always consulted him about the photographs, and it was inevitable that, though he never used a camera himself, Hardy's acute visual sense ensured that he developed an eye for what made a successful photographic image. When it came to illustrations for the Wessex edition, it is not surprising that Hardy should have turned to Lea, who by 1911 would have accumulated a large stock of suitable negatives. In a note that Lea wrote for the Hardy collector, E.N. Sanders, in 1944, he recalled that Hardy 'himself arranged with the publishers that the frontispieces to the Wessex Edition (1912) should be from photographs taken by me, and he spent much time in choosing the viewpoints he wanted'.[16] The extent of Hardy's active

---

[16] *Thomas Hardy Through the Camera's Eye*, p. 49.

involvement is hard to gauge. The only letters to Lea concerning the frontispieces that survive deal with *A Group of Noble Dames* and *A Changed Man*. On 7 June 1912 he wrote:

The view of Winchester would do, though it is a little injured in its effect by the mass of chairs, & by being so mathematically central. But it is not worthwhile to go to take another. If, however, you should be going, please take one rather aslant, giving a glimpse of an aisle, & of some of the very fine monuments. However, perhaps such a view is not possible. (*Letters*, iv. 220)

The picture that appears in the published volume is taken slightly to the right of centre, though neither aisle nor monuments are visible. It is interesting to note that Hardy's own drawing of the cathedral, which appeared in *Wessex Poems* as an illustration to 'The Impercipient' (p. 183), is very similar, though the chairs are filled with people rather than empty as in Lea's photograph.

In 1913 Hardy collected his last volume of short stories together, and wrote to Lea on 6 September: 'The Publishers say the new vol: should have a frontispiece & I have told them it must be M. Castle. Can you, therefore, prepare to take it as soon as convenient' (*Letters*, iv. 302). Hardy expressed here no opinion as to angle or viewpoint, but when he had examined the alternative prints that Lea offered him he had more to say:

I think the view I have marked A gives the best idea of a castle artificially constructed. The others might be natural hills. . . . Height and darkness are the effects required. For this I imagine a strong sunlight is necessary; but you know best. . . . What is required is that the Castle shd stand high up in the picture so that there may be not much sky. (*Letters*, iv. 304)

The published frontispiece is taken from the highest rampart of the castle, and has both height and darkness; but the effect is still to make the remainder of the earthwork seem natural rather than artificial.

It is just possible to sense in these directions that Hardy is anxious to get a photograph that will embody atmospherically the tone of 'A Tryst at an Ancient Earthwork', a story that appears in the collection. On the whole, though, the impression given by the frontispieces is that they have little of the effect that James was after in his collaboration with Coburn, but rather that they are straightforward objective representations of scenes from the novels.

It is, in the end, characteristic of the two novelists that James uses and names real places, but chooses not to illustrate them realistically, whereas Hardy disguises his places under false names, creates his own world, and yet chooses to explode that disguise through his frontispieces.

8

The Last Novels

1895–1897

The Pursuit of the Well-Beloved *(1892)* and The Well-Beloved *(1897)*

The transformation of *The Pursuit of the Well-Beloved*, the serial story that appeared in the *Illustrated London News*, into the text that formed *The Well-Beloved*, the last published novel in the Osgood, McIlvaine collected edition, offers the most substantial evidence of Hardy at work on a large-scale revision. Indeed, his alterations were so extensive that they give rise to the question of whether in making them he was revising the story or was turning it into another story. It is possible, of course, to claim that as soon as one word is changed in a novel it becomes a different novel, and in certain special circumstances that position might be tenable practically as well as theoretically (see chapter 11 below). For most readers, in most cases, however, there would have to be substantial changes to plot, theme, and character before a revising author could be considered to have made a different work from the fabric of the old.

The definition of the line beyond which alteration to a text constitutes producing a new work would probably depend ultimately upon subjective judgements, and in order to be even sure of that much, study would have to be made of a very wide range of altered texts—a study that I have not made. Hence, I do not propose to try to formulate such a definition for Hardy's novel, though I think the question is an important one and deserves consideration. What I intend to do is to present some of the evidence that might be used by a reader to help decide the question.

The major changes Hardy made have recently received a substantial amount of critical attention,[1] and may be summarized here, though one or two will also be elaborated a little in what follows. The essence of the narrative remained unchanged, the search of a man for an ideal well-beloved, and his involvement with a female member of successive generations of the same family. Perhaps the most important alteration was to

---

[1] See e.g. J. Hillis Miller's edition of *The Well-Beloved* (London: Macmillan, 1975), and the essay on the novel in his *Fiction and Repetition* (Oxford: Blackwell, 1982), 147–75; Tom Hetherington's introduction to the World's Classics edition of the novel (Oxford: Oxford University Press, 1986); and Richard Taylor's chapter on the novel in *The Neglected Hardy* (London and Basingstoke: Macmillan, 1982), 147–73.

the way the reader is invited to understand the concept of the well-beloved, but Hardy had several other ends in view. In part, he aimed to make the narrative more naturalistically convincing, and the removal of the hero Pearston's two marriages and his suicide attempt is the most substantial change in that direction. In part, criticism of *Jude the Obscure* led him to reduce the acerbic attack on marriage embodied in the serial. He also wanted to modify the environmental fabric of the story in the light of the coherent view of Wessex that had emerged from his work on the Osgood, McIlvaine edition. All these motives for Hardy's extensive revision have been examined, but something that underlies them has not much been considered—the fact that a large part of what Hardy discarded or altered was inadequately conceived and insufficiently imagined.

Hardy might simply have abandoned these unacceptable passages and rewritten from scratch, but his pride in his craft, and, perhaps, his embarrassment at the poor quality of his workmanship in the serial, led him instead to reimagine them. Thus, throughout the novel sentences are radically altered, while substantially retaining the detailed framework of the original. In what follows I want to look in some detail at how Hardy rewrote the beginning and the ending of the novel, and to glance, in passing from one to the other, at some significant intervening fragments of change.

The Opening of the Novel

That the first difference to strike any reader comparing *The Pursuit* with *The Well-Beloved* is the disappearance of the serial's first chapter might seem at once to undermine the thesis just enunciated concerning the essential conservatism of Hardy's rewriting—but this first chapter is an irretrievable disaster. In it Hardy shows himself quite uncertain about the kind of story he was setting out to write. It begins in the fairy-tale mode ('Once—and that not long ago—there was a young sculptor . . .'), moves through sentimentality ('They all [love-letters] showed affection which once had lived, though now it was all past and gone. No, he could not burn them here and alone'), and ends in satire ('he took his summer raincoat . . . rolled it hastily round the lumps of undying affection'). When he came to reflect upon it, four years later, Hardy would have recognized the lack of control in the tone of the chapter, but what dictated the omission of the whole, I think, must have been his sense that it would be much better to have the reader first encounter the central character of the novel in the landscape where his well-beloved has its beginning and its end, rather than in a London sitting-room.

By way of replacement for this chapter, Hardy added for the first edition an epigraph from Crashaw's 'Wishes. To his (supposed) Mistresse' that stands opposite to what is now the first page of the text:

> Now, if Time knows
> That Her, whose radiant brows
> Weave them a garland of my vows;
> Her that dares be
> What these lines wish to see:
> I seek no further, it is She.

In this poem Crashaw imagines at some length the qualities possessed by his ideal woman—'That not impossible she / That shall command my heart and me'. The lines Hardy quotes begin Crashaw's conclusion that a woman may exist who will aspire to meet his conditions, who will dare to be 'what these lines wish to see'. Thus, instead of an uncertain attempt to indicate Pearston's propensity for brief love-affairs through the letters that he tries to burn in his London home, we have a first allusive hint of the Platonic ideal or essence of female, in the form of the well-beloved, that drives Pierston from woman to woman.

The text that this quotation now faces, the start of the first chapter of *The Well-Beloved*, is unmistakably a version of the beginning of the second chapter of *The Pursuit*, and yet it has been utterly changed. To examine the details of the revisions Hardy made to the first two paragraphs of the serial chapter in order to produce what is now the opening of the novel is to approach at once an understanding of the magnitude of his enterprise.

Chapter II of *The Pursuit* begins thus:

About two o'clock the next day he was ascending the steep roadway which led from the village of Slopeway Well to the summit of the rocky peninsula, called an island, that juts out like the head of a flamingo into the English Channel, and is connected with the mainland of Wessex by a long, thin beach of pebbles, representing the neck of the bird.

What follows is a close analysis of the way in which this and subsequent sentences were transformed for the book version of the story.

It was impossible for Hardy to retain the pronoun 'he' for the beginning of *The Well-Beloved*. In the discarded first chapter of the serial we learned that 'he' was a sculptor and that his father was a commercial

man, and Hardy might have reused this information. Instead, the first
thing we now learn about him is that he is different. The book version
begins:

> A person who differed from the local wayfarers was climbing the steep road
> which leads through the sea-skirted townlet definable as the Street of Wells

Most readers would agree by the end of the novel that the man is indeed
different from most other men.

After the first few words the relationship of the two versions is closer,
and yet almost every word is altered. The name-change and the addition
of the descriptive phrase 'sea-skirted townlet' are characteristic of the
spate of topographical revision Hardy made to his fiction in 1895–6 that
this novel concluded; but the striking difference is that between 'led' and
'leads'. The change of tense at once transfers the environment from one
that is past and possibly imaginary to one that is present and eminently
visitable—an alteration emblematic of Hardy's new sense of the place of
Wessex in his fiction.

The sentence in *The Well-Beloved* proceeds to take up the simile in *The
Pursuit* that likens the shape of Portland to a flamingo, and mould it into
something at once less whimsical and richer in association:

> . . . and forms a pass into that Gibraltar of Wessex, the singular peninsula once
> an island, and still called such, that stretches out like the head of a bird into the
> English Channel. It is connected with the mainland by a long thin neck of
> pebbles 'cast up by rages of the se', and unparalleled in its kind in Europe.

The addition of the European dimension is important. The 'person', as
we will learn in the next sentence, has himself connections with the
Continent, and soon thereafter we discover that the 'Gibraltar of
Wessex' is his parental home. The quotation from Leland provides the
beginning of a historical context for the island. But Hardy's handling of
the flamingo simile which he took from the serial is more fully representative of the imaginative power that he brought to the task of
vitalizing his inert prose. He decided that, however close the similarity
between the head of a flamingo and the shape of Portland on the map, the
associations of 'flamingo' were inappropriate in the context—exotic and
Alice-in-Wonderlandish. In his new version the bird simile is retained
unspecified, and part of it is integrated metaphorically into his description—'a long thin neck of pebbles'—by simply replacing 'beach' with
'neck'.[2] It is such economy of effort combined with thoroughness of

---

[2] It is interesting, in this context, to note that in the 19th edition of *Black's Guide to Dorset*, ed.
A.R. Hope Moncrieff (London: A. & C. Black, 1926), the entry on the Isle of Portland begins with

transformation that will be noticed time and time again in the work of reimagining his text.

The second paragraph in *The Pursuit* begins:

He recollected that it was two years and eight months since he had paid his last visit to his father, at this, his birthplace, the intervening time having been spent amid many contrasting scenes at home and abroad.

In *The Well-Beloved*, this straightforwardly factual sentence is expanded into a paragraph that opens with another insight into the nature of the central character:

The pedestrian was what he looked like—a young man from London and the cities of the Continent. Nobody could see at present that his urbanism sat upon him only as a garment. He was just recollecting with something of self-reproach that a whole three years and eight months had flown since he paid his last visit to his father at this lonely rock of his birthplace, the intervening time having been spent amid many contrasting societies, peoples, manners, and scenes.

The first sentence of this new version is doubly ambiguous, ambiguity deriving from the uncertain meaning of 'was' and 'from'. The unidentified traveller 'was what he looked like'. The reader, pausing at the dash, might well wonder what it means to be what you look like. It might mean that your profession or something else relatively superficial is revealed by your manner and appearance, or alternatively it might mean that your exterior is an accurate guide to your essential qualities. And the reader, hesitating momentarily between these two, finds no security in the remainder of the sentence. The wayfarer is young, that much is clear, but how can one tell whether the statement that he is 'from London and the cities of the Continent' signifies (as is perhaps more commonly the case in such a construction) that he would in some sense accept these sophisticated urban centres as his home, or whether it implies no more than that he has just arrived from these places.

Though the subsequent sentence clarifies the matter, the ambiguity is deliberate. Hardy might easily have written 'He looked like a young man who had just journeyed from London and the cities of the Continent, and indeed such was the case.' By choosing, so early in the novel, to leave the reader doubting for a moment, Hardy is sowing seeds that will bear fruit later, when we realize that Pierston is at heart in the same

---

a reference to a description of the island by Victor Hugo: 'Victor Hugo . . . rightly enough compares this "rude sea mountain" to a bird's head, its beak turned towards the ocean, its occiput towards Weymouth, and the Chesil Bank for its neck' (p. 82). I have been unable to trace the reference, though in support of the argument for a possible borrowing it must be said that Hardy was familiar with Hugo's works.

uncertainty himself. He is unsure whether the city clothes he wears are the truth about himself, or just a covering for the quarrier beneath. As a successful artist he does belong to London—London is his natural home. As a native of the Isle of Slingers though—an inheritance that he cannot shed—he belongs to the rock in its isolation and inwardness. Though the narrator claims in the second sentence of the paragraph that the pedestrian's 'urbanism sat upon him only as a garment', I do not think that by the end of the novel we are convinced of the unqualified truth of the claim. He lives out the remainder of his days on the Island, it is true, but he also imports to the ancient village modern ideas of urban development, still restlessly oscillating between the two cultures.

When Avice the third says to the elderly Pierston near the end of the novel 'What you looked I thought you were' (p. 177),[3] she is only commenting on another variant of the ambiguity within his life: Which is the truth about him, the tally of years or the freshness of spirit? In fact, these two sentences inaugurate a questioning that goes on throughout the novel: what *is* Pierston, which is the real Pierston? Pierston himself is searching for himself, a search represented most acutely in his pursuit of the well-beloved. Can he love another person, or only an image projected by himself?

However, for the time being at least, the rest of the second paragraph of *The Well-Beloved* eases the reader's mind as the narrator makes it clear that the journeying man is returning to his birthplace (though in retrospect it might be noticed that the narrator carefully does not say that he is returning home). The relationship with the serial text is also closer. The man has been away for a year longer in the first edition, and this might be considered to account for the self-reproach with which he now reflects upon his absence. The narrator here omnisciently reports the man's thoughts, and it is not clear whether the newly added and rather coy 'had flown' represents accurately a certain archness in the man's thought, or whether it is the narrator imposing his characteristic diction upon the character. Something of the same question arises when the man's thought that he has re-entered the place of his birth is given a strong emotional charge by the addition of 'lonely rock': is it the character or the narrator who sees the place as isolated and barren?

The rest of the second paragraph in *The Pursuit*:

What had seemed natural in the isle when he left it now looked quaint and odd amid these later impressions. The houses above houses, one man's doorstep

---

[3] Page-references are to the World's Classics edition.

rising behind his neighbour's chimney, the gardens hung up by one hedge to the sky, the unity of the whole island as a solid and single block of stone four miles long, were no longer familiar and commonplace ideas. All now stood dazzlingly clean and white against the blue sea, the sun flashing on the stratified facades of rock—

> The melancholy ruins
> Of cancelled cycles . . . Prodigious shapes
> Huddled in grey annihilation.

is turned into a third paragraph for the first edition:

What had seemed usual in the isle when he lived there always looked quaint and odd after his later impressions. More than ever the spot seemed what it was said once to have been, the ancient Vindilia Island, and the Home of the Slingers. The towering rock, the houses above houses, one man's doorstep rising behind his neighbour's chimney, the gardens hung up by one edge to the sky, the vegetables growing on apparently almost vertical planes, the unity of the whole island as a solid and single block of limestone four miles long, were no longer familiar and commonplace ideas. All now stood dazzlingly unique and white against the tinted sea, and the sun flashed on infinitely stratified walls of oolite,

> The melancholy ruins
> Of cancelled cycles, . . .

with a distinctiveness that called the eyes to it as strongly as any spectacle he had beheld afar.

To begin with, Hardy recognized that what seems natural may also seem quaint and odd—hence the change to 'usual'. The alteration from 'when he left it' to 'when he lived there always' is an attempt to reinforce the reader's awareness of the roots the man has in the 'lonely rock'. After this, in the serial there follow the man's fresh impressions of the isle after absence, but in *The Well-Beloved* Hardy interposed another sentence: 'More than ever the spot seemed what it was said once to have been, the ancient Vindilia Island, and the Home of the Slingers.' This interpolation has an affinity with the new description of the man from the beginning of the second paragraph, since it too has to do with things being, or not being, what they seem. Unless a reader is very well versed in the pre-Roman history of the south-west of England, both references in the sentences are likely to be opaque. There is a clue in 'ancient', but, presented only with the preceding sentences and knowing little of the author and his probable subject-matter, a reader might well be led for a moment to anticipate some early science-fiction story after the manner of H.G. Wells, in which the lonely rock is about to enter a different time-warp (and in a way this would be a sympathetic response, since the relativity of time does become a significant theme in the novel). A whimsical reader might be encouraged by the capitalization of 'Home' into wondering, further, whether the time-traveller will find himself in an Institution for compulsive stone-throwers.

It is easy to mock this sentence, because at the best the response elicited by the references within it is a suspense of judgement on the question it raises: how is the Gibraltar of Wessex like the ancient Vindilia Island, whatever that was? or, more precisely, by what process is the Gibraltar of Wessex transformed in the man's consciousness into the likeness of Vindilia? 'More than ever' suggests that there had always been for him (and possibly for the narrator) a resemblance between the two, but the reader is not at present let into the secret. The following description, though picturesque, is of no direct assistance, being either civilized and contemporary, or geological.

As the narrative progresses over the following chapters the signification of Vindilia and Slingers is clarified, and the retrospective reader has to assume that the landscape is like the man, that the environment is both what it seems to the eye that takes in the topography of houses and gardens, and what it seems to the inner eye of imagination that senses beneath the surface the signs of past histories and customs.

In revising the subsequent narration of what the traveller sees, Hardy is at pains to emphasize the otherness of the place—the 'towering rock' and its 'almost vertical planes', as the sun flashes on their 'distinctiveness', are to be thought of as 'unique'. He was also anxious to point out the geological formation of the rock, adding 'limestone' and 'oolite'. The reasons for these changes are bound up with Hardy's new view of the whole novel. That the Isle of Slingers is a place apart where the past mingles uneasily at times with the present, that its surface appearance and its sedimentary substructure can be matched nowhere else in Europe, become important instruments in rendering more probable the strange nature and experiences of the returning man.

Thus, taking stock, there is relatively little completely new material in Hardy's rewriting of what is now the opening of the novel, but what has been changed is of considerable significance. In these first three paragraphs there are now embedded two important fresh ideas—uncertainty about the essential qualities of the journeying man, and the ambiguity of the environment to which he is returning. Prose that was essentially without an informing personality—either of narrator or character—has now, with considerable economy of effort, been filled with life.

The Island, the Well-Beloved, and Marriage

It soon becomes evident, in comparing the serial with the first edition, that the attention Hardy paid to reworking his account of the topography and history of the Isle of Slingers had a purpose beyond that accounted for by the developments in his conception of Wessex between 1892 and 1896, developments that have been charted earlier in this study (chapter 7). The isolation and the uniqueness of the place, established at the very beginning of *The Well-Beloved*, are rapidly exploited in additions Hardy made to the second chapter of the novel. Pierston, the returned native, stands in a churchyard by the sea, and the narrator now explains that the church 'had long been a ruin. It seemed to say that in this last local stronghold of the Pagan divinities, where Pagan customs lingered yet, Christianity had established itself precariously at best' (p. 12). On the same page the narrator also reports Pierston's interpretation of the 'evening and night winds' that blow over the island; they were, to his mind,

charged with a something that did not burden them elsewhere . . . It was a presence—an imaginary shape or essence from the human multitude lying below: those who had gone down in vessels of war, East Indiamen . . . There could almost be felt the brush of their huge composite ghost as it ran a shapeless figure over the isle, shrieking for some good god who would disunite it again.

The harmony between the Pagan place and the quality of the mind of the man born and brought up in it is gradually established in additions like these, so that both might seem fitting homes for the well-beloved (itself sometimes seen as 'an imaginary shape or essence').

Indeed, to the first occasion on which the narrator approaches an explanation of the concept of the well-beloved Hardy added for the first edition that 'she was a subjective phenomenon vivified by the weird influences of his descent and birthplace' (p. 11), and a little later he gives Pierston an extra sentence in a speech to his London artist-friend Somers—'We are a strange visionary race down where I come from' (p. 33). This last addition combines well the idea that Pierston's ancestry and nurture are responsible for the power of the well-beloved over him, with the increase in references to the supernatural that accompany the appearances of the well-beloved in the first edition.

Alongside the establishment in the first edition of a uniquely weird and receptive environment, full of ancient survivals, there is also perceptible a radical change in the conception of the well-beloved itself. There is an early example of this on pp. 9–10: in *The Pursuit* the narrator says of Pearston: 'he had quite disabused his mind of the old-fashioned assumption that the idol of a man's fancy was an integral part of the personality in which it might be located for a long time or a short while.' The crucial alteration is very simple—the replacement of 'a man's' by 'his'. Through this single brief change the perception itself, and by implication the whole analysis of the perception that follows in the novel, becomes personal to Pierston, and possibly subjective, rather than being proposed as a general rule, possibly objective, to which all men conform. Naturally, the 'old-fashioned' was removed as well, since what is only pertinent to one individual cannot be said to derive from any kind of fashion.

Associated with this fundamental change is another of similar importance, also on p. 10, that further redefines the well-beloved. Pierston is uncertain whether his elusive idol/ideal well-beloved has fixed itself in the first Avice. In the serial the question is phrased thus: 'But did he love Avice—see the Well-Beloved made manifest in Avice at all?' Throughout the revision for the first edition the question of loving and the question of the location of the well-beloved are separated, and in this instance the first part of the sentence is simply abandoned, and the second part is altered so that the question reads 'But did he see the Well-Beloved in Avice at all?' The problem of whether he loves the woman or the phantasm is one that haunts Pierston all through the novel.

The effect of a sequence of similar changes through the novel is to make the well-beloved more subjective (personal to Pierston), to provide through Portland inbreeding and tradition a naturalistic reason for its appearance in him (and in one of the Avices), and, further, to suggest that it is impossible for Pierston to maintain for long an emotional relationship with a woman once he suspects that the well-beloved has taken up its abode in her. It remains unclear to what extent the narrator implies that the well-beloved is a figment of Pierston's imagination, but it does seem certain from the revised ending that it disappears when Pierston's artistic sense also vanishes. He becomes meanly utilitarian—this is what it is to be without the well-beloved.

In removing one of Pierston's marriages, and delaying the other by forty years, Hardy brings about a considerable reduction of the material in the story which might be construed as a deliberate attack on marriage—a reduction which may well be the consequence of writing *The Pursuit* before *Jude the Obscure*, and coming to rewrite *The Well-Beloved* only after he had assimilated the critical response to the more cele-

brated novel. There are many instances of places where such comment
has disappeared from *The Pursuit* text, and the reader has no cause for
regret. Occasionally, though, a passage, now removed, was at least as
effective in its critique of marriage as anything on the subject in the
greater novel. The following example is embodied in natural and
unforced speech, unlike, for instance, some of Sue Bridehead's
comments on marriage, and the point is not rammed home by character
or narrator, as so often in *Jude the Obscure*. The dialogue is between
Pearston and a chance passer-by who is struck by Pearston's gaze
towards his wife, the third Avice, who appears in the distance:

> "A tidy little figure-of-fun that, Sir," said the man.
> "Yes. A dainty little creature, like a fairy . . . Now, would you assert, my
> friend, that a man has a right to force himself into her presence at all times and
> seasons, to sit down at her table, to take her hither and thither—all against her
> liking?"
> "No, sure."
> "I thought so. And yet a man does it; for he has married her."
> "Oh! She's his wife! That's a hoss of another colour. Ha, ha, ha!"
> "I don't think it is," said Pearston.[4]

Pearston's quiet restraint, contrasted with the conventionally vulgar
attitude of the wayfarer, is very moving.

The Last Chapters

The last part of the novel is that which was most thoroughly altered in its
impact, and it is also there that we see most dramatically the way in
which Hardy was anxious not to rewrite completely, but to refine his
first ideas.

In *The Pursuit* Pearston has married the third Avice, in *The Well-
Beloved* Pierston is about to marry her; he then realizes that she would
rather be with someone else. In the serial he decides to 'disappear from
England' and writes a letter to his friend Somers to explain why; in the
book Avice writes a letter to her mother, saying that she plans to go
'away to get the ceremony solemnised' (her marriage to the Channel
Islander Leverre). Hardy has both Pearston and Avice III use the same
method to achieve their ends: Pearston takes a boat without oars and tries
to drown himself in the Race; Avice and Leverre take the same boat,

---

[4] *Illustrated London News*, 10 December 1892, 741.

forgetting oars, and nearly drown in the Race; both boatloads are saved by men from a lightship. The serial version in the following parallel texts is on the left:[5]

This he followed as it wound down the narrow defile spanned by the castle arch, a portion of which defile was, doubtless the original fosse of the fortress.	they wound down the defile spanned further on by the old castle arch, and forming the original fosse of the fortress.
The sound of his own footsteps flapped back to him from the	The stroke of their own footsteps, lightly as they fell, was flapped back to them with impertinent gratuitousness by the
vertical faces of the rock.	vertical faces of the rock, so still was everything around.
A little farther and he emerged upon the open summit of the lower cliffs, to his right being the sloping pathway leading down to the little	A little further, and they emerged upon the open ledge of the lower tier of cliffs, to the right being the sloping pathway leading down to the secluded
creek at their base.	creek at their base—the single practicable spot of exit from or entrance to the isle on this side by a seagoing craft; once an active wharf, whence many a fine public building had sailed—including Saint Paul's Cathedral.
Pearston descended, knowing the place so well that he found it scarcely necessary to guide himself down by touching the vertical face of stone on his right hand.	The timorous shadowy shapes descended the footway, one at least of them knowing the place so well that she found it scarcely necessary to guide herself down by touching the natural wall of stone on her right hand, as her companion did.
Thus proceeding he arrived at the bottom, and trod the few yards of shingle which here alone could be found on this side	Thus, with quick suspensive breathings they arrived at the bottom, and trod the few yards of shingle which, on the forbidding shore hereabout, could be found at this

---

[5] This passage will be found in the World's Classics edition, pp. 187–9, 251–2.

of the island.	spot alone. It was so solitary as to be unvisited often for four-and-twenty hours by a living soul.
Upon this confined beach there were drawn up two or three fishing-boats and a few skiffs,	Upon the confined beach were drawn up two or three fishing-lerrets, and a couple of smaller ones,
beside them being a rough slipway for launching.	beside them being a rough slipway for launching, and a boathouse of tarred boards. The two lovers united their strength to push the smallest of the boats down the slope, and floating it they scrambled in.
One of the latter he pushed down the slope, floated it,	
and jumped into it without an oar.	The girl broke the silence by asking, 'Where are the oars?' He felt about the boat, but could find none. 'I forgot to look for the oars!' he said. 'They are locked up in the boathouse, I suppose. Now we can only steer and trust to the current!'
The currents here were strong and complicated.	The currents here were of a complicated kind. It was true, as the girl had said that the tide ran round to the north, but
At a specific moment in every flood there set in along the shore a reflux contrary to the outer flow, called 'The Southern'	at a special moment every flood there set in along the shore a narrow reflux contrary to the general outer flow, called 'The Southern'
by the local sailors. It was produced	by the local sailors. It was produced

There follows, in both, a sentence describing the effects of this current in which there is only one change, 'isle' in *The Pursuit* becomes 'peninsula' in *The Well-Beloved*.

	The disturbed area, as is well-known, is called the Race.
It is called the Race.	
Although the outer tide, therefore, was now running towards the mainland,	Thus although the outer sea was now running northward to the roadstead and the mainland of Wessex,
'The Southern' ran in full force	'The Southern' ran in full force

towards the Beal and the Race
beyond.
Pearston's boat was caught by it
in a few moments, as he had known
it
would be;
and thereupon the grey rocks rising
near him, and the grim stone
forehead of the isle above,
just discernible against the sky
slid away from Pearston northwards.

  He lay down in the bottom of
the frail craft, gazing at the sky
above.
The undulations increased in
magnitude, and swung him higher
and lower. The boat rocked, received

a smart slap of the waves now and
then,
gyrated;
so that the lightship which stolidly
winked at him from the quicksand—
the single object which told him of
his bearings—was sometimes on his
right hand and sometimes on his left.

Nevertheless, he could always discern

from it that his course, whether
stemwards or sternwards, was
steadily south, towards the Race.

towards the Beal and the Race
beyond.
It caught the lovers' hapless boat
in a few moments, and, unable to
row
across it—mere river's width that it
was—they beheld the grey rocks near
them, and the grim wrinkled
forehead of the isle above,

sliding away northwards.

  They gazed helplessly at each
other, though, in the long-living
faith of youth, without distinct fear.
The undulations increased in
magnitude, and swung them higher
and lower. The boat rocked,
received
a smart slap of the waves now and
then,
and wheeled round,
so that the lightship which stolidly
winked at them from the quicksand,
the single object which told them of
their bearings, was sometimes on
their right hand and sometimes on
their left.

Nevertheless they could always
discern
from it that their course, whether
stemwards or sternwards, was
steadily south.

The rest of the chapter is quite different in the two versions. Pearston is
swept against the lightship and thus rescued, becoming unconscious
after uttering a cry of 'fierce resentment at the interruption of his
design'. The lovers, on the other hand, set light to handkerchieves,
attract the attention of the lightship, and are rescued, thus justifying
their confidence in their immortality.

  Two somewhat conflicting suggestions might be made about what a
comparison of the two versions implies. The first is that Hardy was
imaginatively too lazy to rethink the now untenable climax of his story,

and so took a copy of the *Illustrated London News* and tinkered around with it to produce the lovers' escape out of the old man's suicide-attempt with the minimum of effort. A different way of putting this first view would be to say that even when the original and the projected revision are as far opposed as suicide and elopement, the appearance of the text in print had a hypnotizing effect upon Hardy's imagination from which he could hardly escape. The alternative view, and the one that I prefer, is that Hardy used his original material in a thoroughly conscious way, aware that the earlier version was insufficiently thought out and carelessly written; that he deliberately set himself the task of turning a scrappily worked-out, melodramatic episode into something more fully imagined and more positive in its contribution to the structures of the novel.

One sentence shows most clearly what the effect of Hardy's reconsideration is. In *The Pursuit* he wrote 'The sound of his own footsteps flapped back to him from the vertical faces of the rock.' In *The Well-Beloved* this became: 'The stroke of their own footsteps, lightly as they fell, was flapped back to them with impertinent gratuitousness by the vertical faces of the rock, so still was everything around.' The underlying difference is that in the later version Hardy entered into the consciousness of his characters, rather than simply recording the moment from the outside, so that there is an intermingling of narrator and character, of objective and subjective. The lightness of their footfall and the stillness of the night are details observed by the narrator which enrich the reader's experience of the scene, but the most prominent change, of 'from' to 'with impertinent gratuitousness by', originates in the perception of the eloping lovers, trying to get away undiscovered. The narrator has made it clear by the addition of 'still' that even light steps are bound to echo loudly, hence it is only to the anxious minds of Avice and Leverre that the noise can appear gratuitous; it is their sense that the noise is impertinent, and it is they who give the rock agency in this rude and unwarranted behaviour—in the difference between 'from' and 'by'. It seems not too strong to say that the passage has been transformed by these alterations.

The narrator continues to envisage the action more clearly and in more detail: for instance, 'the open summit of the lower cliffs' is considerably less easily visualized by the reader than 'the open ledge of the lower tier of cliffs'. Then there are added several indications of the remoteness of the spot: the creek is 'secluded' rather than 'little', the shore is 'forbidding hereabout' and 'so solitary as to be unvisited'. On the other hand, there is a boat-house on the beach. The lovers, too, are seen more fully than was Pearston: they are ironically, but vividly, 'timorous shadowy shapes', we hear their 'quick suspensive breathings', we are told of their 'long-living faith of youth'. Hardy had carefully designed the contrast between their anxiety on land and their self-confidence once at sea, even after they discover they have no oars. Love and the faith of youth in its own good fortune overturn the clichés about 'all at sea' and 'safe on dry land'. Finally, there is the Wessex detail of St Paul's stone-shipments, and though it might be thought to intrude awkwardly into the narrative of rapid and dramatic action, the reader will by now have accepted such information as an integral part of the fabric of the novel.

Beyond the vivifying of environment and character, there is now also a metaphorical charge in the language. Hardy has chosen to add words, like 'stroke', 'suspensive', 'forbidding', 'united', that work not only within the local context of the phrase, but are also active, with richer associations, in the wider context of the narrative as a whole.

Once Pearston is fished out of the water, the serial ends with his brief, harsh awakening in the sick-room, the annulment of his marriage to Avice the third, and the ultimate grotesqueness of his situation, being cared for by the crone that Marcia his lost wife has now become. As several critics of the novel have pointed out, the last laugh is with the narrator, whose 'Ho-ho-ho!' to the reader are the last words in *The Pursuit*.

For Pierston the ending is more long-drawn-out, and hence thoroughly rewritten. To begin with Hardy has it in mind to offer the reader a reflection upon the idea of the well-beloved. Thus, we see Pierston reviewing his past and examining his future by the side of the corpse of the second Avice, no longer bent on suicide but surrounded by phantoms of the various human forms the well-beloved has inhabited.

In an echo of the reader's first encounter with Pierston, when his deep roots in the island were hidden, a sentence that Hardy added at this point concerning his motivation for planning to marry the third Avice reads: 'Nobody would guess the further sentiment—the cordial loving-kind-ness—which had lain behind what had seemed to him the enraptured fulfilment of a pleasing destiny postponed for forty years' (p. 202). This distinction between loving-kindness and love is one that underlies much of Hardy's later writing on relationships between men and women. His conviction that loving-kindness is to be prized above lover's love here finds its final embodiment in his fiction; another example, this time in *Two on a Tower*, is examined on pp. 205–6 below.

At the conclusion of his reverie Pierston wishes that he too could vanish like the phantoms of the incarnations of his ideal/idol, for his life seems 'but a ghost story', and he longs to cease the involuntary search for the well-beloved. In fact, in a motif similar to Jude's deliberate self-exposure to the elements in the ending of *Jude the Obscure*, Pierston contracts a fever. Marcia, nursing him through it, appears to act the role of the fairy-godmother fulfilling her child's desire, for his sense of beauty and of artistic discrimination is spirited away with the illness—and the well-beloved goes with it too. Pierston's first sight of Marcia's face is an awakening to a harsher reality than any he has yet confronted: 'To this the face he once kissed had been brought by the raspings, chisellings, scourgings, bakings, freezings of forty invidious years—by the thinkings of more than half a lifetime' (p. 212). It is only the last few words that mitigate the identification of the face before him with the rock upon which he and she were born.

He marries this eroded shape, Marcia, and the novel ends with sharp irony as the narrator describes how: 'He was . . . engaged in acquiring some old moss-grown, mullioned Elizabethan cottages, for the purpose of pulling them down because they were damp; which he afterwards did, and built new ones with hollow walls, and full of ventilators' (p. 218). We are offered the spectacle of the erstwhile artist-idealist using the money he has gained from the merchandising of representations of his ideal to buy picturesque and ancient dwellings, only to destroy them and to erect the dismissively described buildings in the approved, utilitarian, modern pattern. It is a more instructive, but perhaps a less original, ending than the serial's hollow, mocking narratorial laughter.

Jude the Obscure: *First-Edition Proofs*

All the proofs of Hardy's fiction that survive contain revisions, and it is certain that the process of transforming *The Pursuit of the Well-Beloved* into *The Well-Beloved* was a two-stage one. However, since no proofs survive for this novel it was impossible in the preceding sections to distinguish between changes Hardy made on his copy of the serial version, and those that he made subsequently on the proofs of the first edition sent from the printer Ballantyne in Edinburgh.

As far as *Jude the Obscure* is concerned, though, such proofs do survive, preserved in the Signet Library in Edinburgh, and study of them reveals the areas of the novel that still dissatisfied Hardy after the mangling of the text for the serial and his original reassembly of it for the book-edition.

In fact these proofs of the first edition of *Jude* are not a homogeneous document. They are made up of sheets from three separate stages—first proof marked by Hardy alone, first proof marked by Hardy and subsequently by the printer's reader, and second proof, or revises. A detailed discussion of the varieties of proof and an explanation for their preservation will be found in Appendix 2. The only detail that is important for an understanding of the material presented in the following discussion is that for most of the first half of the novel only the last, revise stage survives and we have no evidence of the volume or nature of the changes that Hardy made on the now lost first proofs of those gatherings. Hence, generalizations about the extent and direction of the proof-revisions can only be made with the proviso that they do not take into account a substantial amount of the first half of the novel; and for the same reason there are few examples of changes from the early part of the novel.

It is a feature of the last three novels in Hardy's career (as of *A Group of Noble Dames*) that the serialization in a moderately revised form could not form copy for the first edition. In the case of *Jude the Obscure* and *Tess of the d'Urbervilles*, just as for the short story volume, he had to bowdlerize the text so thoroughly in order to make it acceptable to magazine editors that a more substantial process of restoration was needed. What these proofs of *Jude the Obscure* show is that, unless the early pages of proof were very heavily revised, Hardy's reconstitution of the text when preparing copy for the printers of the first edition was fundamentally satisfactory; the proofs as we have them show no large-scale reworking or emendation. What they do show is a concentration on a few aspects of the novel.

There are occasional small alterations made within the larger themes—marriage for instance, where the most striking detail is on p. 417 of the proofs. Sue gives, in the unrevised proof, as her reason why she and Jude never married that they were

terrified at the thought of a second irrevocable union, and the sordid, cruelly compulsory, and nearly utilitarian nature of the contract, yet wishing to be together (p. 349)[6]

It will be unsurprising to learn that 'nearly' was a compositorial mis-

---

[6] Page-references are to Patricia Ingham's World's Classics edition of the novel (Oxford: Oxford University Press, 1985).

reading of 'meanly', and it may be that this error drew Hardy's attention to the passage; but instead of simply correcting the word, he changed the abstract, harsh view of marriage to one that is personal to Sue and Jude, one that still roots the cause in the contract which we have heard so often attacked before this, but which also finds room for the force that binds the two together:

terrified at the thought of a second irrevocable union, and lest the conditions of the contract should kill their love, yet wishing to be together.

Religion as a theme also has its adjustments—in particular the hypocrisies of individual Christians. In his description of Shaston, at the beginning of the fourth part of the novel, Hardy writes how at one time the churches in the town were pulled down and the inhabitants had to 'refrain altogether from the public worship of God; a necessity which they bemoaned in the settles of their inns' (p. 210). This is a slightly cynical remark, but one that is given extra and typically Hardyan edge by the proof-alteration of the second clause to read: 'a necessity which they bemoaned over their cups in the settles of their inns on Sunday afternoons.' This augmentation gives more point to the succeeding sentence: 'In those days the Shastonians were apparently not without a sense of humour.'

A third great theme of the novel centres around the city and university of Christminster, and here too there are a number of proof-changes. In this case there is an opportunity to see again how Hardy can alter the whole flavour of a passage through the change of a single word. The last paragraph of the fifth part of the novel is dense with suggestion. Jude has been severely ill, and wants to return to Christminster—recognizing the perverseness of his feeling that it is for him the centre of the universe, but persisting in the feeling nevertheless: 'His hope that he was recovering proved so far well grounded that in three weeks they had arrived in the city of many memories; were actually treading its pavements, receiving the reflection of the sunshine from its abraded walls' (p. 337). The emotional charge is in the last part of the sentence, in the perfectly judged 'actually', which expresses Jude's surprise and wry veneration, perhaps even his relief at their return, and in the mingling of the beauty and warmth of the light off the walls with the sense that the light is only reflected, and the walls are still excluding. This is Hardy writing at his best, and there does not seem to be any way that it could be improved, until the effect is felt of the proof-change of the perhaps insufficiently simple 'abraded' to the clearer, more pointed, and

alliterative 'wasting'. The present participle has the energy of a continuing process of degradation, and one that in the context of the novel
is to be applied to the institutions as well as the walls that surround
them.

There is, later, a second example of Hardy's ability to re-enter his texts
imaginatively and work fresh life into them with a single word. When
Jude returns to Christminster from his last visit to Sue there is no longer
any hope or buoyancy in his view of the city, though there is a touch of
friendly familiarity in the 'old' at the beginning of what he says to
Arabella: 'This is old Rubric. And that Sarcophagus; and up that lane
Crozier and Tudor: and all down there is Cardinal with its long front,
and its windows with lifted eyebrows, representing the great surprise of
the University at the efforts of such as I' (p. 414). Again Hardy managed
to find in proof the word which expresses precisely Jude's present attitude. He altered 'great surprise' to 'polite surprise', and thus caught the
fresh, clear-sighted detachment with which Jude is able to view his
obsession as he comes close to death.

It seems probable that having completed the work of reassembly of his
novel after the serialization it was easier for Hardy to respond to the
smaller details of the text in proof, and to make changes that in earlier
novels might have been made in copy.

So far, the examples have come from major threads of the novel that
must have been in Hardy's mind at every stage of its progress through
script and print; but there are also a couple of areas of more local concern
which specifically attracted his attention in these proofs.

Considering the development of the relationship between Sue and
Jude by the time Sue has swum the river to escape the training-college at
Melchester and sought refuge with Jude, Hardy decided that they could
no longer simply think of themselves as cousins. In Jude's room Sue herself reflects backwards over their relationship: 'I did want and long to
ennoble some man to high aims; and when I saw you, and knew you to
be my cousin, I—shall I confess it?—thought that man might be you.' It
is probably with the memory of Sue's revelation about her life in London
with her undergraduate friend fresh in his mind that Hardy altered part
of this to read: 'when I saw you, and knew you wanted to be my comrade, I . . . (p. 158). And there are subsequently several other examples
through the novel of the suppression of 'cousin' or the introduction of
'comrade' into descriptions of their relationship.

'Comrade' is a carefully chosen word: it has none of the compulsory
blood-relatedness of 'cousin', which Hardy was trying to get away

from; its early meaning—room-mate—is precisely fitted to the context in which it is first introduced, a sense echoed slightly later in the novel when Jude compares himself and Sue in his imagination to 'priests and virgins of the early church, who . . . became even chamber partners with impunity' (p. 201). Its current (and Victorian) sense—close companion—expresses precisely Sue's meaning throughout the book, though it falls short of what Jude, abandoning his religious aims, later expects from their relationship.

The word was and is used (with one specialized exception) almost entirely of relationships between people of the same sex, and it is a measure of Sue's expectations of personal relationships, and perhaps of her sexuality, that the reader accepts at once the validity of the word in her mouth, while also understanding that the kind of sexless arrangement that it proposes is not often achieved, and that Jude's strongly sensual nature makes its achievement in this particular instance even less probable. The exception is the form of address familiar in communist and socialist gatherings. The first instance of this usage in the OED is dated 1884, and it seems almost certain that Hardy would have come across the use in newspaper reports or elsewhere by 1895; there may well be a deliberate socialist overtone in Sue's use of the word.

One of the later proof-revisions of the idea of cousinship shows how the interested world views their relationship; during a conversation between Physician Vilbert and Arabella at the Great Wessex Agricultural Show they catch sight of Jude and Sue, and originally Arabella says of them 'They are cousins.' Though for the reader this is an established fact, Hardy is not keen for it to be stated so baldly, and with his usual economy he alters the whole impact of the sentence, throwing emphasis upon their loving comradeship and at the same time reflecting Arabella's sexual cynicism. Now her comment is 'They *say* they are cousins' (p. 309).

Hardy is also particularly interested in the relationship between Sue and Phillotson. Most of the changes in this area occur at the time of their remarriage at the end of the novel, but the first comes at the time in the middle of the novel when Sue is begging Phillotson for her freedom from him. The passage originally read:

Sue continued: 'She, or he, "who lets the world or his own portion of it, choose his plan of life for him, has no need of any other faculty than the ape-like one of imitation." J.S. Mill's words, those are. Why can't you act upon them? I wish to, always.'

'Do you mind my saying that I have guessed what never once occurred to me

before our marriage—that you were in love, and are in love, with Jude Fawley!'
(p. 234–5)

Instead of seeming to ignore Sue's erudite self-justification, Hardy
decided in proof to give Phillotson a response to it, and added to the
beginning of his speech: ' "What do I care about J.S. Mill!" moaned he.
"I only want to lead a quiet life!" ' This gives, in a way that nothing else
in the whole debate does, the sense of a nondescript, average, unheroic
man driven into a corner by an extraordinary, impossible woman. Hardy
tried in 1912 to make Sue's quotation less intimidating by adding 'I have
been reading it up' after 'those are.'
     Phillotson is prompted by Arabella, and driven by his ordinary sexual
desires, to want Sue back; in this he provides a low-key parallel to Jude.
When reading through the proofs Hardy seemed unsatisfied by the tone
he had established for Sue's meeting with Phillotson after she has decided
to abandon Jude, and he made several changes. The first words they
exchange are:

'I've come, Richard,' said she, looking pale and shaken, and sinking into a
chair. 'I cannot believe—you forgive your—wife!'
'Everything, darling Susanna,' said Phillotson.
She started at the endearment, though it had been spoken mechanically, and
without fervour. (p. 383)

The first example of Hardy's concern was to remove the suggestion of
lack of enthusiasm from Phillotson's voice, doing what he could within
the constraints of type, ending the last sentence '. . . been spoken
advisedly without fervour.' Now Phillotson has considered what effect
would be least calculated to put off Sue, and we are enabled to imagine
suppressed passion in his brief speech.
     He kisses her on the neck, and she shrinks from him slightly:
'Phillotson's heart sank within him. "You still have an aversion to
me!" ' (p. 384). At this point Hardy decided to make explicit the effect
that Sue's presence has on the schoolteacher, and replaced 'within him'
by 'for desire was renascent in him' in proof. As part of the same
readjustment, he wanted to make Sue slightly less repelled by him, and so
her 'smile of dread' at this speech of Phillotson's became a 'smile of
apprehension'.
     This all occurred on p. 458 of the proofs; four pages later there is a
similar small group of revisions, this time in a conversation between the
schoolmaster and his conservative friend Gillingham. At first there is a

narratorial comment: 'He did not care to admit clearly that his taking Sue to him again had at bottom nothing to do with repentance of letting her go, but was like the first a human instinct flying in the face of custom and profession' (p. 386). Hardy saw an opportunity here of marking again the sexual nature of the motive, and at first revised 'was like the first a human instinct' to 'was, primarily, a physical instinct'; but, reading through the next paragraph, he found a better way of expressing what he needed to, and so revised it again to 'was, primarily, a human instinct'. The subsequent paragraph read:

Gillingham looked at him, and thought it possible, so little did he really know Phillotson, that the reactionary spirit induced by the world's sneers might make him more orthodoxly cruel to her than he had erstwhile been informally and perversely kind. (p. 387)

With careful calculation he changed this to:

Gillingham looked at him, and wondered whether it would ever happen that the reactionary spirit induced by the world's sneers and his own physical wishes would make Phillotson more orthodoxly cruel to her than he had erstwhile been informally and perversely kind.

Social and personal pressures on Phillotson are now nicely balanced in this passage; correspondingly Hardy decided to make him more conscious of his cruelty. As they go to be remarried, the passage reads:

'You do—wish me to be yours, Richard?' gasped Sue in a whisper.
'Certainly, dear: above all things in the world.'
Sue said no more; and for the first time he felt he was not quite following out the humane instinct which had induced him to let her go. (p. 390)

The alteration of 'first' to 'second or third' makes Phillotson at once more honestly self-aware and more culpable. In keeping with this change Hardy also revised something that Sue says in response to Widow Edlin's question about Phillotson:

'What is it you don't like in him?' asked Mrs. Edlin curiously.
'I cannot tell you. It is something . . . I cannot say. The mournful thing is, he doesn't know it himself, so that the excuse of his having concealed something is not left me.' (p. 416)

Hardy changed the last sentence to read: 'The mournful thing is that nobody would admit it as a reason for feeling as I do; so that no excuse is left me.' The effect of this is to remove the hint of some tangible intimate physical or physiological deformity in Phillotson, along with his lack of self-awareness and the patronizing tone of Sue's speech. At the same time, the alteration adds the implication that the problem is more in Sue's head than in Phillotson's body—not that that makes it any the less powerful or valid a reason for her shunning him. Indeed, the final change in this sequence is to the consequence of another kiss that she receives from him when she finally makes up her mind to go back and do what she conceives as her duty: 'he led her through the doorway, and lifting her bodily, kissed her. A wild look of loathing passed over her face, but clenching her teeth she uttered no cry' (p. 419). In the proof copy Hardy altered 'loathing' to 'aversion', taking thus something directly personal from her reaction, and slightly diminishing its intensity; but only slightly, for the overwhelming impression of violation is unaffected.

With Sue's sacrifice of her sexual integrity on the altar of her religious conformity and Jude's death in Christminster the reader reaches the end of Hardy's career as a novelist. But Hardy had no desire to see the children of his pen achieve independence before his own death, and there is still some way for this exploration of his relationship with them to go.

9

Paperback Editions and the Move
to Macmillan

1898–1928

The Relationship Between the Paperback Editions of Far from the Madding
Crowd *and* Tess of the d'Urbervilles *(1900–1901) and Macmillan's
Uniform Edition (1902)*

J. R. Osgood, the moving spirit behind the firm of Osgood, McIlvaine,
had died in 1892, and the younger and less experienced
McIlvaine found it difficult to keep going. In 1898, despite the success of
Hardy's collected edition, the firm ceased trading and their list was taken
over by Harper, with whom Osgood, McIlvaine had always had a close
connection. It was thus under the Harper imprint that Hardy's first two
volumes of poetry appeared in 1898 and 1901. Harper themselves
experienced some financial difficulties in the following years, and this
fact, combined with their being essentially a company based in America,
led Hardy, in 1902, to withdraw his books from Harper and offer them
to Macmillan—the publisher to whom, it will be remembered, he had
sent each of his first three novels (though they did not publish them), as
well as *The Woodlanders* and *Wessex Tales*. They had also published a
colonial edition of Hardy's collected works. Although there were some
difficult negotiations, the transfer was completed and Macmillan made
immediate preparations to issue the plates of the collected edition with
their own title-pages.[1]

Hardy wanted to make some changes to a few of the novels for this
uniform edition; in part, this was his wellnigh automatic response to any
reissue of his work, but for the two novels to which he made the most
substantial alterations there was another stimulus to revision. In 1900
Harper had the idea of bringing out *Tess of the d'Urbervilles* in the paperback format that had recently become popular in Britain for the works of
more newly-established important authors (Scott's and Dickens's novels

---

[1] For a more detailed account of this pattern of events see the introduction to Dale Kramer's
edition of *The Woodlanders* (Oxford: Clarendon Press, 1981); also *Letters*, iii. 5–8, 10–16, 27–30,
and 36.

had long been available in such a form, but Meredith's novels, for instance, were issued by Constable in this way at about the same time). A hundred thousand copies were printed, and sold at 6*d.* a copy. Some three weeks after its publication Hardy was able to report that it had had a great success, and later that it had easily sold out—a success which led Harper to try *Far from the Madding Crowd* in the same format a year later.

It should come as no surprise to anyone who has read thus far to discover that Hardy made substantial alterations for these complete resettings. Though the Macmillan reissue of the collected edition was not to be reset (except, in the end, the preface to *Far from the Madding Crowd*), Hardy felt it was necessary to include some of the changes he had made for the paperback versions in Macmillan's new venture; this, in turn, led to his reconsideration of a few details in other novels, particularly those—*Jude the Obscure* and *The Well-Beloved*—for which Macmillan's edition would provide him with his first opportunity for changes since their publication in book form.

Hardy was always considerate towards his publishers in the matter of revising texts already in type, and although he had made substantial revisions for the paperback editions, when he came to consider these two novels for the Uniform edition, he placed himself under considerable restraint.[2] Of the 280 substantive alterations he made to *Far from the Madding Crowd* in 1901, only thirty-eight were included in 1902, seven of these in the preface, which was reset for the Uniform edition. It is also true that in very few of these thirty-eight instances were the 1901 revisions carried over word for word into 1902. *Tess* shows the same pattern: of 175 substantive revisions in 1900, only twenty-two were made in 1902, and, again, most of these appeared in a different form in the later version of the text.

Hardy was not only highly selective in the changes he wanted to make to the plates for Macmillan's edition, but he also approached the fanatical in ensuring that the disturbance to matter surrounding the revisions should be as slight as possible. He did this by recasting many of the paperback alterations in a form that approximated very closely to the length of the words the revision was to replace. For example, in the 1895 Osgood edition of *Far from the Madding Crowd* Bathsheba Everdene says to Boldwood:

If . . . I can give you happiness by a mere promise without feeling, and just in friendliness, to marry at the end of six years, it is a great honour to me. (p. 407)[3]

---

[2] It may be unduly cynical to add as another possible reason for Hardy's restraint the fact that major changes to a text already plated might result in the author being charged for the corrections.

[3] References are to Robert C. Schweik's Norton Critical Edition of the novel (New York: 1986).

In the paperbound edition of the novel, Hardy added after 'six years' in the passage just quoted, the phrase 'if my husband should not come back'. When he came to consider the change for inclusion in Macmillan's 1902 reissue, he realized that such a long addition would considerably disturb the surrounding text. His solution to the problem was to retain the 1901 addition and to omit from the Osgood version 'without feeling, and just in friendliness,' making it possible for the compositors to fit the revision in with disturbance to only two lines. The passage then read:

If . . . I can give you happiness by a mere promise to marry at the end of six years, if my husband should not come back, it is a great honour to me.

There are other examples like this, but most often the paperback revision itself is adapted or compressed. Section IV of chapter LII begins, in 1895: 'Troy was sitting in a small apartment in a small tavern at Casterbridge' (p. 415). In 1901, following the already established line of topographic revisions made in the Osgood edition, and also removing the repetition, Hardy replaced 'a small' with 'the White Hart'. Although this added only seven characters, in order to retain 'the White Hart' in 1902 Hardy felt it necessary to alter 'small apartment' to 'corner': 'Troy was sitting in a corner in The White Hart tavern at Casterbridge', with the effect of making the new version only two characters different from that in 1895. Most of the thirty-eight paperback changes that were, in one form or another, also made in 1902 suffered from the same restrictions; and this is also the case with *Tess*.

There are several other places where Hardy made a topographical change in 1901 and wished to retain it in 1902, and one of these occurs in one of the best-remembered passages in the novel, the beginning of chapter II which introduces us to Norcombe Hill and the stars. In the Osgood edition the second paragraph begins:

Norcombe Hill—forming part of Norcombe Ewelease—was one of the spots . . .' (p. 8)

In 1901 Hardy added a detail that fixes the location of the lonely spot:

Norcombe Hill—forming part of Norcombe Ewelease and lying to the northeast of the little town of Emminster—was one of the spots . . .

For Macmillan's text there was no way that he could compress the addition to a manageable brevity, but, in keeping with his post-Osgood sense of Wessex, he had to find some alternative to signpost Norcombe Hill, since 'forming part of Norcombe Ewelease' was quite unhelpful. So he replaced the 1895 phrase, and the passage became

Norcombe Hill—not far from lonely Toller Down—was one of the spots . . .

This new version is in itself less helpful to the literary pilgrim than the paperback reading, in that it demands knowledge of Wessex heights rather than towns; but it throws light in another direction. There must be a connection between this revision and the semi-refrain of 'The Homecoming', a poem from *Time's Laughingstocks* that Hardy dated 'December 1901':

> Gruffly growled the wind on Toller Down so bleak and bare,
> And lonesome was the house, and dark, and few came there.

It is unclear whether poem or revision came first, but both are enriched if they are read in conjunction.

The story of the changes to the paperback editions of *Tess* and *Far from the Madding Crowd* does not end with Macmillan's 1902 text; they also form an integral part of the history of the 1912 Wessex edition of the novels. Hardy used an impression of the emended Osgood plates as copy for the Wessex edition, and it might thus be expected that the paperback alterations, having failed to get into the line of transmission, were lost for good; but this is not the case. The situation is different for each novel; as far as *Tess* is concerned there are fifty-five paperback revisions that skip the Osgood plates, and turn up in the 1912 edition in exactly the same form. This seems too large a proportion for memory or coincidence to be factors, and it may confidently be assumed that Hardy had beside him when reconsidering the novel in 1911 a list of the paperback changes, or else the copy on which he made them. A further implication is that he consciously rejected the remaining paperback alterations, though the closeness of his attention to the list of changes may have wavered from time to time.

The case is rather different with *Far from the Madding Crowd*; there are only ten places where an alteration skips the Osgood plates and is incorporated precisely into the Wessex edition. The question then arises whether it is probable or possible that Hardy should, after ten years, remember such a proportion of 1901 changes without notes to refresh his memory. In favour of such an hypothesis it may be said that several of the changes exactly reinstated are of one word, as when 'silver tea and coffee pots' in 1895 and 1902 becomes 'plated tea and coffee pots' in both 1901 and 1912 (p. 265). All of the eight places where the 1912 version adapts a paperback revision are also acceptable individually as the inexact proddings of memory, as when Liddy Smallbury bewails her husband-lessness: 'I stand forlorn. Ah, poor soul of me!' This is how it reads in both the Osgood and the 1902 Macmillan texts; for the paperback edition it became: 'I stand forlorn as a pelican in the wilderness. Ah, poor soul of me!' (p. 63). When he was revising for 1912 Hardy may have remembered the 'pelican' detail, but not the way it was included, and in the Wessex edition the passage runs 'I stand as a pelican in the wilderness!' On the other hand there is the coincidence that the 1912 version is only one character longer than the original reading, and it is possible that it was originally a version of the paperback change intended for incorporation into the 1902 reissue, and then rejected as not worth the bother.

Another example of the uncertain relationship between the paperback text and the revisions made for the Wessex edition is a revision to the moment that Troy kisses the dead lips of Fanny Robin. In both 1895 and 1902 it is introduced thus: 'This is what Troy did. He sank upon his knees—' (p. 230). The melodramatic tone is uneasy, and for the paperback edition Hardy simplified it to 'Troy sank upon his knees'. In the Wessex text there is a sort of half-way version between the artificiality of the earlier and the straightforwardness of the 1901 reading: 'What Troy did was to sink upon his knees'. Perhaps Hardy was, in 1911, struck again by the naïvety of his copy, and simply chose a different way to emend it; on the other hand, there is again a similarity in length between the Osgood and the Wessex readings, and an alternative explanation arises: that when he came to revise *Far from the Madding Crowd* for the Wessex edition Hardy had, not a list of revisions made in the paperback edition, but rather a preliminary list that he had prepared for the 1902 Uniform text, a list that was superseded when he became aware of Macmillan's anxiety about the cost of much alteration to the plates. This explanation seems available for most of the paperback changes added precisely or in modified form to the Wessex edition of the novel, whilst for the two or three others memory may have been at work.

Though this evidence presents a nice academic problem, it is also one of practical interest for the editor of the novel. He may wish to use some of the paperback revisions that appear in no other text, because he perceives their inherent excellence, but he will have to decide whether he can justify such a choice. An argument concerning *Tess* in this respect may be found in the Clarendon edition of the novel (pp. 71–3), in which it is concluded that there is no justification for including paperback changes not distorted by their inclusion in the 1902 Uniform edition. The greater confusion over the relationship of the paperback changes in *Far from the Madding Crowd* to the Wessex edition may be held to give the editor licence to do whatever he likes with them. There does at least seem to be a clear case for the reinstatement in any critical edition of the paperback versions of alterations that were distorted for the Uniform edition.[4]

Paperback Texts: d'Urberville's Conversion and Troy's Disappearance

When making the revision for these paperbound editions Hardy had one large-scale alteration in mind for each novel that involved a considerable number of detailed changes in wording. In *Tess* it was the secularization and vulgarization of Alec d'Urberville's impulse towards religion; in *Far from the Madding Crowd* it was an attempt to make it clear that Bathsheba from the first did not believe in her husband Troy's death. By and large it is changes in these areas that Hardy transferred to the Uniform edition.

The first stirrings of the change in *Tess* have already been looked at on pp. 108–9 above; in the paperback edition Hardy set about making Alec's conversion less sincere, and at the same time making Tess's influence over him seem less powerful, since it had a less genuine faith to overcome. This transformation was for the most part made quite explicitly, as when 'Reason had nothing to do with his conversion' became 'Reason had nothing to do with his whimsical conversion, which was perhaps the mere freak of a man in search of a new sensation' (p. 443).[5] In this case Hardy was prepared to enforce a substantial change in the plates for the 1902 Uniform edition, not only accepting the paperback revision into the text, but also adding 'and temporarily impressed by his mother's death' after 'sensation'.

Sometimes the new attitude was conveyed by depriving Alec's speech of its moral sincerity, as when 'will you put it in my power to do my duty—to make the only restoration I can make for the wrong I did you' became in the paperback edition: 'will you put it in my power to make the only amends I can make for the trick I played you' (p. 432). In this instance Hardy reverted to his care for the plates, and made the minimum change that would retain something of the flavour of the paperback revision: 'reparation' replaced 'restoration' and 'trick I played you' replaced 'wrong I did you'.

At the same time, Hardy had other reasons for revising Alec's speech at this stage in the novel's development, one of the more important

---

[4] For a different view of this problem see Schweik's edition pp. 312–13.
[5] References are to the Clarendon edition of the novel (Oxford, 1983).

being demonstrated in the following change. Where the Osgood edition had:

Why I did not despise you was on account of your intrinsic purity in spite of all; you withdrew yourself from me so quickly

Hardy altered the paperback to read:

Why I did not think small of you was on account of your being unsmirched in spite of all; you took yourself off from me so quickly (p. 441)

which not only diminishes the high moral tone of Alec's discourse, but also removes the highly contentious word 'purity' which had led to so many of the attacks on the novel.

The effect of this radical alteration, completed in the Wessex edition, is to remove from the novel the only aspect of Alec which allows the reader to believe that Hardy had some interest in his character beyond that of the moustache-twirling villain of the most conventional melodrama. As the text stood in 1895, Alec's conversion renders the reader uneasy precisely because it hints at qualities in Alec that would otherwise be quite unsuspected. The emphasis in the novel on Tess herself allowed Hardy little space to develop his understanding of Angel Clare, and it is hardly surprising that he could find no room to go back and reconsider Alec d'Urberville in a constructive way. Though criticism played a part in Hardy's gradually evolved decision to undermine the sincerity of Alec's conversion, Hardy himself must have been dissatisfied with the disturbing ambiguity in his presentation of Alec; and the decision to return him to flatness of characterization throughout, rather than to try to fill him with life earlier in the novel, is consistent with his abiding sense that once his fiction was in book form its fundamentals were fixed. Something of what Hardy might have made of Alec is conveyed in the interpretation of his character in Roman Polanski's film *Tess*; perhaps the only success in an otherwise seriously flawed film is to make Alec reasonably convincing.

In 1911 Hardy looked through the proofs of a Hardy dictionary compiled by F. Outwin Saxelby, and against the entry that summarized the plot of *Far from the Madding Crowd* he wrote 'error analysis'. What Saxelby had written was:

Bathsheba, however, believed herself to be a widow, and some time after, when Farmer Boldwood again pressed her to marry him, she consented to an engagement.

In his copy of the book Hardy amended this to read:

Bathsheba, however, though doubting herself to be a widow, some time after, when Farmer Boldwood again pressed her to marry him, consented to an engagement if she turned out to be one.

Later, in 1921, Hardy made a marginal note in his copy of the first edition of a book by Samuel Chew called *Thomas Hardy, Poet and Novelist*; Chew had written, in connection with *Far from the Madding Crowd*, of 'so stale and out-worn a device for temporarily getting rid of a character as the supposed drowning of Troy while bathing'. Hardy's comment was: 'This is a misrepresentation. Nowhere is he really believed drowned, and such a belief is not necessary to the story: it was introduced to illustrate Troy's character—(G. Moore's "Confessions" originated the misstatement).'[6]

In fact what George Moore had written in *Confessions of a Young Man* (1888) was this:

the moment that Troy told his wife that he never cared for her, I knew something was wrong; when he went down to bathe and was carried out by the current I said 'the game was up,' and was prepared for anything, even for the final shooting by the rich farmer, and the marriage with Oak, a conclusion which of course does not come within the range of literary criticism. (chapter XII)

Not direct criticism of the device in Chew's fashion; but Hardy was familiar with Moore's comments. Indeed, it is possible to guess that his first acquaintance with them was made at some time between 1895 and 1901, since it is in the paperback edition of *Far from the Madding Crowd* that Hardy begins his evidently unsuccessful attempt to make it clear that Bathsheba, at least, does not believe in Troy's death. It can be understood that Boldwood has an interest in assuming that he is dead.

The process begins at the end of chapter XLVIII where, after Bathsheba saying 'I am full of a feeling that he is still alive!' Hardy added in the paperback 'There may be some trick in it'. Although this appears at the end of a section and would thus not have disturbed much type, it did not reappear in the Uniform edition the following year, and indeed it appeared in no other published text. On the other hand, he did add in manuscript precisely those words to his study-copy of the Wessex edition, perhaps stimulated by what he regarded as Chew's misconception in 1921.

Most of the other changes in this area do reappear in some form in the Uniform edition, and most are altered specifically to fit the space taken

[6] Hardy's copies of Saxelby's and Chew's books are in the Dorset County Museum.

up by what they are replacing. Thus 'the universal belief that Troy was drowned' became in 1901 'the hasty belief that Troy was drowned', and in 1902 'the hasty conjecture that Troy was drowned'—which both fits the space of the Osgood 1895 version exactly and adds a further element of doubtfulness. Later in chapter LI Bathsheba originally said 'But . . . I am fully persuaded that I shall see him no more'; in a first version in the copy for 1901 this became 'But . . . I am becoming persuaded . . .', and in a second 'But . . . I am sometimes persuaded . . .'. Both of these were too long for 1902, and there it began 'Even though I am half persuaded . . .'. As usual, in 1912 Hardy revised using the Uniform edition as copy, and the beginning became 'Even were I half persuaded . . .'.

There are some twenty such changes altogether in the paperback edition, and, viewed in isolation, the cumulative effect is quite strong; Hardy has responded to his critics, and though most other people in the story do believe Troy to be dead, Bathsheba at every possible turn expresses scepticism. Nevertheless, the device remains powerfully operative in the structure of the last part of the novel.

Wessex and Dialect in the Paperback Texts

Apart from this common emphasis on one aspect of each novel, the two paperback editions also share elements of the general fabric of Hardy's revision at this time. There is space here to look at two of them—the development of Wessex and adjustments to dialect.

I have already drawn some conclusions about Hardy's developing awareness of Wessex as a fictionally homogeneous environment; the differences between *Tess* and *Far from the Madding Crowd*, in the revisions to aspects of the environment in the paperback texts, go some way to supporting the conclusions. *Tess*, written during the crucial period when Hardy was formulating for himself the all-embracing concept of Wessex, has only seven changes that can be considered to relate to the embodiment of Wessex in all its aspects, social as well as topographical, whereas *Far from the Madding Crowd* has around forty. The task of reconceiving the details of the earlier novels to bring them fully into the Wessex scheme of things was a long one, and, taking into account the pressure Hardy was under to read and revise twelve novels and three collections of stories in 1895-6, as well as to work at the first edition of *Jude the Obscure*, it is not surprising that there remained after the Osgood edition much that Hardy felt still needed alteration.

It must also be remembered that *Far from the Madding Crowd* was the second novel to be revised for the Osgood edition, and some of the changes made in the paperback text might well have been made in 1895–6 if the novel had been revised after *Under the Greenwood Tree* and *The Mayor of Casterbridge*. One of these is particularly revealing. In 1895 Troy tells Fanny Robin to meet him 'on Casterbridge bridge', and the reading was unchanged in the 1902 Uniform reissue of the plates. The copy of this setting that Hardy used to prepare the paperback edition, preserved in the Signet Library in Edinburgh, shows that Hardy had several successive thoughts about how to render more precise this vague reference: the first attempt has been erased and is no longer legible; the second was 'by Grey's Bridge—the stone bridge just outside the town', and the version finally accepted was 'by Grey's Bridge—the stone bridge on Durnover Moor—just this side of the town'. The sequence is quite characteristic in its increasingly detailed location, making identification with the still-existing Dorchester bridge unmistakable. The chief interest, though, of this particular context is provided by the version that eventually found its way into the Wessex edition in 1912: 'on Grey's Bridge, just out of the town' (p. 202). This provides further evidence to support the idea that what Hardy had to hand in 1911 was a list of adaptations of paperback readings made with the intention of introducing them into the Uniform edition a year later, but subsequently rejected. In this instance, I am sure that Hardy would have used the detailed paperback version in 1912 if he had been reminded of it, since he had by then become more interested in achieving where possible a kind of photographic resemblance between his fictional topography and that observable in south-western England.

If this *was* the kind of list that Hardy had by his side when making the revision for the Wessex edition, it would explain why only one of the environmental revisions in the paperback found its way into the later collected edition—and some explanation certainly seems required.

Here is one of many possible examples, the description of the tower of Weatherbury Church at the beginning of chapter XLVI:

a square erection of fourteenth-century date, having two stone gurgoyles on each of the four faces of its parapet

It was altered in 1901 to read:

a square erection of various dates, having a stone gurgoyle on each of the corners of its parapet, and one in the middle of each face

At the same time the location of the gurgoyle relevant to Troy's horticultural activity was altered from the south-eastern to the south-western corner. Hardy re-envisaged Puddletown Church and embodied the appropriate revisions in the paperback text; indeed, in describing the portion of the graveyard in which Fanny was buried, 'sometimes this obscure corner received no inhabitant' became: 'at the date of the story, and before the enlargement of the churchyard, this obscure corner sometimes received no inhabitant'. This is just the kind of detail that Hardy added in many other places for the Wessex edition, and he would hardly have ignored this one had it been within reach as he revised for 1912. Instead, realizing that some reference was needed to the geographical location to which his fictional description corresponded, he added a footnote to the end of the chapter: 'The local tower and churchyard do not answer precisely to the foregoing description.'

If we turn to the changes made to the representation of dialect speech in *Tess* and *Far from the Madding Crowd* there is another discrepancy between the two; in the paperback *Tess* there are twenty-one such alterations, and only two are not also made in the 1912 text. In *Far from the Madding Crowd* there are twenty, and only one of them appears in exactly the same words in 1912. This must indicate, again, a difference in what survived from the two paperback revisions when Hardy was making the Wessex edition.

All but one of the changes in *Tess* replace dialectal forms in Tess's own speech with standard English; there is no comparable pattern in the earlier novel, though there are two or three places where Gabriel Oak's speech is changed from dialect to standard English, returning in a small way to Hardy's original manuscript idea of him, altered in proof for *Cornhill* on Stephen's advice. Most of the other changes add dialect to the speech of the workfolk.

These paperback editions are worth close scrutiny because they contain revisions that we can be sure Hardy thought carefully about, but which have remained unexamined since the last copy was read many years ago. In many cases they may, with some conviction, be held superior to the readings that survive in the standardly accepted Wessex edition.

The Wessex Edition (1912–1913)

Between the publication of Macmillan's Uniform edition and the Wessex edition about which so much has already been said, the publishers brought out a pocket edition. For this they again reused the plates of the Osgood edition, as emended in some cases in 1902, and Hardy made no changes to the text, though he did add to the title-page of *Under the Greenwood Tree* the subtitle *or The Mellstock Quire*.[7] The whole of his creative energies at this time were channelled into the writing of *The Dynasts*, and even had Macmillan offered him the chance, he might well, for the first time in his life, have turned it down.

There is nothing in this book about Hardy's massive drama or about his poetry. It would properly take a separate volume to discuss comparable issues raised by his work in verse, and it is also the case that all of the available material (for the poems at least) is presented to the reader in Samuel Hynes's excellent three-volume edition.[8] It is, perhaps, conventional wisdom to consider that after the turn of the century Hardy abandoned prose entirely, and of course it is true that he wrote nothing fresh in fiction after 1900. And yet during 1911 and 1912, at the age of 71, Hardy devoted almost all of this time to twice rereading and reworking his fiction, once in copies of the Uniform edition on which he made many changes, and again in the proofs of the Wessex edition, on which he made further revisions.

This stage in the development of Hardy's texts brings us to familiar territory, for almost all of the versions of his novels that are currently available are based upon derivatives of the Wessex edition.[9]

The continuation of revisions to aspects of Wessex in this edition has already been discussed in chapter 6, but there are other details common to all the volumes. For most, he revised and added to the 1895-6 prefaces; in almost all of them he adjusted for the last time the representation of the Dorset dialect, and there is to some degree a pattern observable in this adjustment; he took a little further the process of making more explicit or intensifying sexual allusions; and as always there are hundreds of places in each novel where Hardy improved clarity of expression and precision of detail.

The most substantial new material in the Wessex edition is the

---

[7] This detail was pointed out to me by Dr Charles Pettit, to whom I am most grateful. It corrects factually the opening paragraph of my introduction to the World's Classics edition of *Under the Greenwood Tree*, though it does not significantly affect the argument contained therein. The title of *The Mayor of Casterbridge* was also altered at this date (see n. 11 to the introduction of this book).

[8] *The Complete Poetical Works of Thomas Hardy*, ed. Samuel Hynes (Oxford: Clarendon Press, 1982-5).

[9] See Michael Millgate, 'The Making and Unmaking of Hardy's Wessex Edition', in *Editing Nineteenth-Century Fiction*, ed. Jane Millgate (New York: Garland, 1978), 61-82, and Suleiman Ahmad, 'The Genesis of the Wessex Edition of Hardy's Works', *PBSA* 77 (1981), 350-1.

'General Preface to the Novels and Poems' that appeared at the beginning of *Tess of the d'Urbervilles*, the first volume in the series to be published. As far as the novels (and stories) are concerned Hardy had only two points to make in the General Preface: the first was to outline the creation and development of Wessex, the other was to present the classification of his novels that he had made for the edition. This division is now familiar to all more than casual readers of Hardy, and has had an effect beyond that which Hardy could have envisaged when he designed it. The seven novels that were included in the first category, 'Novels of Character and Environment', have become almost exclusively those that are read by the public at large and by students at school or university. If it were true that these were the only seven worth serious consideration there would be no problem, but the reverse is so clearly the case that it seems time to abandon a classification that has imposed a blinkered way of looking at Hardy's novels upon generations of critics and readers.

Many of the individual prefaces of 1895–6 and 1912 concentrate on matters related to the establishment of Wessex and have been mentioned in that context already—but they also raise several other issues. In the prefaces of four out of Hardy's first five novels he apologizes to his readers in various ways for not rewriting the narratives in a more mature or serious way. This apologetic note is some indication of how Hardy, looking back over a now long-completed body of work, felt about the development of his art as a novelist, and it should come as no surprise that it was with his sixth novel, *The Return of the Native*, that he began to feel no need to excuse his work in such terms as 'written . . . at a time when he was feeling his way to a method' (*Desperate Remedies*), 'farcically and flippantly' (*Under the Greenwood Tree*), 'an immaturity in its views of life and in its workmanship' (*A Pair of Blue Eyes*), or 'artificial treatment' (*The Hand of Ethelberta*). Had *Far from the Madding Crowd* (the only early novel whose preface does not contain a similar phrase), not proved so popular it is quite likely that Hardy might have made some deprecatory remark about it, particularly regarding the style.

If we set aside the topographical elements there remains, still, in these prefaces a large commitment to the local history connected with the stories, ranging from the evocation of the Stinsford choir in *Under the Greenwood Tree* to the details that gave rise to the story of 'The Distracted Preacher' in *Wessex Tales*. Indeed, this latter opens out a central theoretical issue that, characteristically, is unconsciously raised by Hardy and not resolved. There is as much assurance in this preface as in that to *The Trumpet-Major* of the historical truth that lies behind the stories. Hardy invites the reader to reimagine a central scene from 'The Withered Arm' because in the story he had incorrectly reported the event as it really happened commenting that his 'misrelation' 'affords an instance of how our imperfect memories insensibly formalize the fresh originality of living fact—from whose shape they slowly depart, as machine-made castings depart by degrees from the sharp hand-work of the mould.' The simile is ambiguous, though suggestive. On the one hand, it implies that memory, and thus by extension the fictional use of remembered details, is less valuable than 'living fact'; on the other hand, it acknowledges that moulds and castings have different functions, while at the same time proposing that the closer memory or fiction comes to 'living fact' the more valuable it will be. What Hardy has asked his readers to do is to incorporate a circumstance from 'living fact' into a narrative deriving from 'imperfect memory'. If this may be thought of as putting a report into fiction, what are we to make of Hardy's statement three paragraphs later: 'However, the stories are but dreams, and not records'? When he notes the decline of copsework in the preface to *The Woodlanders*, or records the disappearance of much of the Puddletown of his childhood in the preface to *Far from the Madding Crowd*, is he introducing a dream or a reality? Hardy's answer would be, I suppose, that his fiction since 1895 partakes of both in different measure in different novels.

The addition of such detail in the prefaces brings the best out in Hardy from time to time. The preface to *A Pair of Blue Eyes* has two memorable passages of personal recollection—one is about church-restoration:

> The following chapters were written at a time when the craze for indiscriminate church-restoration had just reached the remotest nooks of Western England, where the wild and tragic features of the coast had long combined in perfect harmony with the crude Gothic Art of the ecclesiastical buildings scattered along it, throwing into extraordinary discord all architectural attempts at newness there. To restore the grey carcases of a medievalism whose spirit had fled seemed a not less incongruous act than to set about renovating the adjoining crags themselves.

In the light of the mould-and-casting simile it is interesting to wonder to what degree this superbly expressed attack on the very activity in which he was involved forty years before reflects an opinion he held at the time he was working at St Juliot in North Cornwall; another version of his feelings about it in old age may be found in *The Early Life* (pp. 104–5).

The second passage, though dating from 1895, is an anticipation in prose of those most famous of Hardy's poems that he wrote after the death of his first wife:

The place is pre-eminently (for one person at least) the region of dream and mystery. The ghostly birds, the pall-like sea, the frothy wind, the eternal soliloquy of the waters, the bloom of dark purple cast that seems to exhale from the shoreward precipices, in themselves lend to the scene an atmosphere like the twilight of a night vision.

It is pleasing to have this confirmation that images used in those poems of 1912-13 had formed in his mind at least seventeen years earlier, and the impression is that they had been intermittently present to him for fifty years in a similar shape.

The preface to *The Trumpet-Major* has another fine passage of memory-recording:

An outhouse door riddled with bullet-holes, which had been extemporized by a solitary man as a target for firelock practice when the landing was hourly expected, a heap of bricks and clods on a beacon-hill, which had formed the chimney and walls of the hut occupied by the beacon-keeper, worm-eaten shafts and iron heads of pikes for the use of those who had no better weapons, ridges on the down thrown up during the encampment, fragments of volunteer uniform, and other such lingering remains, brought to my imagination in early childhood the state of affairs at the date of the war more vividly than volumes of history could have done.

In a way, this is the whole novel compressed into a few isolated images, and represents vividly Hardy's sense of what an historical novel is, and indeed his sense of what history is. There could hardly be a better introduction to the narrative.

The tone of the prefaces is extremely various, ranging from the intimately personal evocation of Cornwall quoted from *A Pair of Blue Eyes* to the generally uninformative introduction to *The Return of the Native*; from the enthusiastic pursuit after the truth in *Wessex Tales* to this heavily ironic passage from the preface to *The Woodlanders*:

In the present novel, as in one or two others of this series which involve the question of matrimonial divergence, the immortal puzzle—given the man and the woman, how to find a basis for their sexual relation—is left where it stood; and it is tacitly assumed for the purposes of the story that no doubt of the depravity of the erratic heart who feels some second person to be better suited to his or her tastes than the one with whom he is contracted to live, enters the head of reader or writer for a moment.

If this sounds like something from *Jude the Obscure*, it is not surprising, since Hardy was reading the proofs of the first edition of *Jude* at about the same time as he was completing the revision of *The Woodlanders* for the Osgood edition, and writing this preface. And it is in the extended 1912 postscript to the *Jude* preface that a more detailed discussion of the marriage-issue takes place.

Hardy's attacks on critics are also interesting to chart. They first appeared in the preface to the fifth and later editions of *Tess of the d'Urbervilles*, added to the novel in 1892; Hardy's feelings had so far subsided by 1895 that he was able to write: 'The foregoing remarks were written during the early career of this story, when a spirited public and private criticism of its points was still fresh to the feelings. The pages are allowed to stand for what they are worth, as something once said, but probably they would not have been written now.' It seems slightly strange then that the 1895 preface to *Two on a Tower* contained this:

people seemed less struck with these high aims of the author than with their own opinions, first that the novel was an 'improper' one in its morals, and secondly, that it was intended to be a satire on the Established Church of this country. I was made to suffer in consequence from several eminent pens, such warm epithets as 'hazardous,' 'repulsive,' 'little short of revolting,' 'a studied and gratuitous insult,' being flung at the precarious volumes.

By 1912 Hardy had sufficiently relieved his spleen and recovered his judgement, and he deleted the string of quotations from the passage, ending it at 'eminent pens'. He might only have felt able to do this because he had already launched a fresh attack in the preface to *Jude*. Perhaps if Hardy had survived to issue a third revised edition the extended and fiery remarks in *Jude* would have been removed or put into perspective. This pattern of commission and retraction seems, in a small way, a justification for the editorial work on *The Life* by Florence Hardy and J.M. Barrie, and perhaps others, which removed some of the more virulent attacks on critics from Hardy's typescript before publication; given a few years of reflection Hardy might have done the same himself.

Taken together, the prefaces represent above all an insight into the variety of Hardy's interests and approaches to writing fiction, and in almost every case the novel would be the poorer—though not always the less clear—without them. They now form an integral part of the work in the same way as the revisions Hardy made to the texts at the same time. An example of how these prefaces can be used as a point of entry to a discussion of the novels they introduce will be found in Chapter 10 of this book, where the chosen novel is *Two on a Tower*.

Hardy's varying attitude to the dialect elements in his novels is one of the clearest ways of distinguishing in general terms between the Osgood edition and Macmillan's Wessex edition. In 1895–6 Hardy on the whole added dialectal words, spellings, and grammatical constructions; in 1912 on the whole he removed them, with the exception of the change from 'ye' to ''ee'. It is thus a dangerous business to base a judgement of Hardy's attitude to a character in revision on dialectal evidence, as has occasionally been done. *Under the Greenwood Tree* is the best novel to use in illustration of this point: in 1896 about a hundred dialectal forms were added and nine removed, while in 1912 Hardy standardized around a hundred and thirty-five dialect expressions and formulated no new ones (always excluding the 'ye/'ee' change). Thus it is that though the upwardly mobile Keeper Day has his regional expression slightly diminished in 1912, so too does the tranter, and even Michael Mail; and no conclusions can be drawn about the relative social standing of the characters from this kind of evidence.

The greatest interest focuses on situations that reverse the general trends, as for instance with Stephen Smith's parents in the 1895 edition of *A Pair of Blue Eyes*. Rather than adding to their dialectal speech, as would be expected, Hardy removed forty or so such expressions. This may be directly related to the substantial gentrification that they underwent from the first edition of the novel onwards, culminating in the Osgood edition.[10] On the other hand, in the Wessex edition of *Tess of the d'Urbervilles*, Hardy, in his never-ending pursuit of the exceptional in Tess, substantially diminished her dialectal usage (including the change from ''ee' and 'ye' to 'you', which is made nowhere else in this edition), whilst her mother and father and the other dairymaids retain theirs intact.[11]

In the study of individual texts and details of the Wessex edition the obvious novel to use as an example is *The Woodlanders*. This is partly because the copy of the Uniform edition Hardy revised for this edition has survived, along with some page-proofs, but also because Hardy seems to have been particularly impressed with the novel as he reread it.

---

[10] The same pattern of gentrification of some characters as an element of revision is observable in most of Hardy's earlier novels up to *The Trumpet-Major*. A sample of how it works in action is offered in the discussion of the manuscript of *The Return of the Native* in ch. 3.

[11] Anyone particularly interested in this aspect of Hardy's writing would do well to consult two essays by Patricia Ingham: 'Dialect in the Novels of Hardy and George Eliot', in *Literary English Since Shakespeare* ed. George Watson (Oxford: Oxford University Press, 1970), 347–63, and 'Thomas Hardy and the Dorset Dialect' in *Five Hundred Years of Words and Sounds* ed. E.G. Stanley and Douglas Grey (Cambridge: Cambridge University Press, 1983), 84–91.

In *The Later Years* (p. 151), there is a quotation from a letter he wrote to Florence Dugdale: 'On taking up the Woodlanders & reading it after many years I think I like it, *as a story*, the best of all. Perhaps that is owing to the locality and scenery of the action, a part I am very fond of. It seems a more quaint and fresh story than the "Native", & the characters are very distinctly drawn.' An analysis of the changes that he made also suggests that he was particularly attentive to this novel. There are, taken statistically, more alterations than in any other novel, around 360 altogether, of which about sixty were made in proof; and it has more of interest to the critic than any other.

One of the areas with which Hardy is especially concerned at this time is Grace's attitude to Giles after she has run away from her father's house and sought refuge with him. The first of the changes that he made was on the proof-sheets: on the first evening of her occupation of Winterborne's hut Grace, in the Uniform edition, said: 'O Giles . . . I am a woman, and you are a man. I cannot speak more plainly. "Whatsoever things are pure" but—you know what is in my mind, because you know me so well' (p. 285).[12] Hardy wanted to get rid of the biblical priggishness from this speech and removed the quotation, adding in its place 'I yearn to let you in', which gives extra fire to the sexual dilemma Grace experiences at this crucial moment in her life.

Eventually she overcomes her scruples and cries out into the rain 'Giles! You may come in!' For 1912, Hardy intensified it to read 'Giles! You must come in!' (p. 287). Later, when Grace is being questioned by her husband about her recent relationship with Winterborne there are three more changes which reveal in her more sexual independence. One of the places where Hardy made a change in revising copy for this edition, and then revised further in proof, is relevant here: as Giles and Grace sit in Sherton Abbey and consider their future, Grace 'regarded a stained window'. Hardy revised this in his copy of the Uniform edition to 'regarded a high marble tomb to the representatives of an extinct Earldom'; attentive readers might have caught the allusion here to the family of Grace's husband, but Hardy made it impossible for the reader to miss the ominous reminder of Fitzpiers by further revising the passage in the Wessex edition proofs to 'regarded a high marble tomb to the last representative of an extinct Earldom, without a thought that it was the family with which Fitzpiers was maternally connected' (p. 260).

There are similar small changes affecting most of the important characters in the novel: Mrs Charmond becomes deep and lofty rather than

---

[12] References are to the Clarendon edition of the novel (Oxford: Oxford University Press, 1981).

bright and soft; Giles and Marty exchange gestures of intimacy that are otherwise infrequent between them; Fitzpiers is not rich, is more susceptive than energetic, and spends time in nervous misery; Suke Damson laughs at finding herself with Fitzpiers on Midsummer Eve, and has a plump rather than a fine face. There is nothing transforming here, but evidence of a still-maintained involvement with characters already established, and a careful attention to the nuances of their development through the plot.

To end this discussion of the last great revising enterprise that Hardy undertook in his lifetime, one can point to a few changes that have a biographical rather than a literary interest. One, in *The Woodlanders*, is the proof-change to the entry on the scene of a hunted fox that saw 'a fox quietly emerged' become 'a panting fox emerged', with an increase in pathos, a change that reflects Hardy's ever-increasing abhorrence of all kinds of cruelty to animals. This hatred was one of his few remaining links with the inner life of his first wife Emma, and a change made in *A Pair of Blue Eyes* at this time offers a scrap of material for reflection upon how Hardy thought about their relationship in 1911–12. It occurs in the most celebrated scene of the novel, in which Knight is suspended over the edge of the 'Cliff with no Name' and Elfride sets about saving him by taking off her underclothing and twisting it into a linen rope by which he can haul himself back. The rescue once completed, Knight realizes that 'Elfride had absolutely nothing between her and the weather but her exterior robe or "costume".'[13] She blushes from a mixture of gladness at the success of her plan and shame at the state Knight now sees her in; the rain has soaked her remaining outer dress, and Hardy was doubtless being no more than accurate when in 1912 he added 'diaphanous' before 'exterior' in the passage just quoted. Nevertheless, it serves to draw attention to Elfride's all but visible nakedness in a very unVictorian way, and since Hardy was soon to admit, in drafts for *The Early Life*, that Elfride was to a degree based upon his wife Emma when he first met her in Cornwall, the addition stimulates a reader to wonder what was going through Hardy's mind when he made it. There must at least have been a bitter contrast present there between the youngish woman he had married forty years earlier, and the elderly lady who, though Hardy did not know it, was to die within the year and by her death touch off a much more powerful reactivation in his memory of his Cornish courtship.

It will be remembered that Hardy had plenty to say in his prefaces

---

[13] World's Classics edition, p. 216.

about the critics of his work, and on a couple of occasions his changing attitudes are reflected in his revision to the novels themselves. One of these is also in *A Pair of Blue Eyes*, where Hardy altered his description of Knight's profession from a 'reviewer' to 'a man of letters'. In 1873 Hardy felt more benevolently disposed towards 'reviewers' than he can have done by 1912, when the word must have seemed to him like a condemnation of Knight of quite inappropriate intensity. The other example comes from the last paragraph of *The Well-Beloved*, at the end of a chapter freshly written for the first edition of 1897 and thus Hardy's last piece of primary novel-creation. It describes the reputation of the central figure of the story, who has given up the practice of his art as a sculptor: 'At present he is sometimes mentioned as "the late Mr. Pierston" by gourd-like young art-critics; and his productions are alluded to as those of a man not without genius, whose powers were insufficiently recognized in his lifetime.' To this, as the final ironic twist, Hardy added 'and journalists' after 'art-critics'. Whether he intended this sentence as a sufficient comment on his own novel-writing career is quite another question.

The Autograph Edition (1915), the Mellstock Edition (1919–1920), and After

At first it had been intended that the Wessex edition should be a limited *edition de luxe*, but difficulties with Macmillan's American partner in the venture led to a change of plan and the abandonment of the limited aspect of the edition.[14] Nevertheless, the volumes have a handsome appearance and, except for the sometimes excessive show-through of the pages, are extremely pleasant to read, worthy of the respect that is generally accorded to them as representing the authoritative state of Hardy's texts.

This authority rests partly on the recognition that it was the last edition for which Hardy read all the proofs, and partly on the significance that he himself placed upon the edition, requiring, for instance, that writers who wanted to print extracts from his work should use the Wessex-edition text.

It seems, however, that for three novels and two collections of short stories Hardy read proof again three years after the publication of the Wessex edition. It was in America that Hardy first achieved the distinction of a limited signed edition; and in 1915 he undertook to check the

---

[14] For details of these negotiations see Dale Kramer's introduction to the Clarendon edition of *The Woodlanders*, and *Letters*, iv. 123–4, 160–3, 171, 182, 184–6, 195–6, and 198.

volumes of the Harper Autograph edition that were copyrighted in the United States, and thus had to be reset: *Tess of the d'Urbervilles*, *Jude the Obscure*, *The Well-Beloved*, *Life's Little Ironies*, and *A Changed Man* (for the other novels Harper used the plates of the Wessex edition). It is also the case that Hardy made at this time some further very small changes to the texts of at least *Tess* and *Jude*.[15]

It was not until after the first world war that the suggestion for an English *edition de luxe* was revived; Hardy accepted Macmillan's proposal, and the result was the Mellstock edition.[16] The issue of this coincided with the exhaustion of the stock of almost all of the novels in the Wessex edition, and Hardy made more or less the same slight changes to his fictional texts for both the new edition and the reissue of the old. Drafts of the lists of changes that Hardy made for the publishers are preserved in the Dorset County Museum. As far as the prose was concerned it was *A Pair of Blue Eyes* that Hardy took most interest in, for the revision for the Wessex edition had taken place while Emma Hardy was still living, and so he had not felt free to make the precise one-for-one relationships between St Juliot and the fictional church and vicarage which his fully-developed sense of the demands of Wessex required. In 1919 there was no longer any restraining factor and he made some quite substantial changes to the topography of the Cornish parts of the novel. One consequence of these changes was that Hardy read at least some of the proofs of *A Pair of Blue Eyes* in the Mellstock edition, something he did not feel compelled to do for the other prose volumes, even though many of them embodied slight alterations. And as far as we know this was the last time in his life that he read prose proofs.[17]

It was not, however, the last time in his life that he thought about his texts, and in copies of the 1912 impression of the Wessex edition that he kept in his study Hardy continued to jot down the occasional improvement that occurred to him. It is hard to know what stimulated Hardy to make these random and often one-word revisions; what, for instance, made him in 1927, four months before his death, add a manuscript note

---

[15] In a letter of 17 December 1912 Hardy wrote to Florence Henniker: 'Florence Dugdale has also come to help me with the proofs of the American edition of my books, which happen to be in full swing' (*Letters*, iv. 244).

[16] See *Letters*, v. 312–14.

[17] I have no evidence to show whether he looked at the proofs of the one-volume edition of his stories in 1927. In a letter to Sir Frederick Macmillan dated 27 September Hardy wrote concerning this collection: 'If any expression in either of the Prefaces or Introductory notes should not apply to the intended edition I will put it right on receiving a proof of the page on which it occurs.' There is no other evidence to suggest that he read proofs of the collection as a whole.

to the end of 'The Distracted Preacher'. It may, perhaps, have been something connected with work on *The Life*, but that is pure speculation; all that we can be sure of is that Hardy's relationship with his fiction was like that of the most retentive of parents, unable to believe that his influence over his child has ended until the day he dies. It is right that those who edit Hardy's texts, and decide to try to fulfil his final intentions, should respect this relationship and include in their editions these last few fragments of Hardy's paternal care.[18]

---

[18] A further question for the editor is raised by a passage in a letter that Hardy wrote to Arthur Moule on 19 October 1903: 'Your amusing discovery that I was wrong in making a character in "Under the Greenwood Tree" see the *rising* new moon in the evening has been anticipated by other correspondents. I should have said setting of course. I have meant to correct it for years, but have always forgotten when a new edition has been required' (*Letters*, iii. 79). Hardy failed in 1912 and again in 1919 to make this change. Would an editor be justified in taking Hardy's wish for the deed (following the theory expounded in *Tess of the d'Urbervilles*) and making the alteration? Here at least is unimpeachable evidence of authorial intention. As most often in such questions the balance of the evidence is approximately equally weighted—this letter hanging against Hardy's subsequent action (or rather inaction)—and the editor will have to use his own scales to measure the inclination on one side or the other.

10

Two on a Tower
1881–1912

In this book I have combined two aims: to give the reader a chronological sense of the way Hardy's attitude to the various aspects of the novelist's trade developed, and to provide simultaneously an understanding of the various ways in which Hardy approached revision and the significance of the revisions that he made. It has further been my intention to cover as wide a spread as possible of Hardy's fiction in analysing the revisions he made. A consequence of this approach is that to this point there has been no extended study of the development of a single novel. In an essay published elsewhere I tried to show how fruitful such a study could be for understanding some of the characters and themes of *Far from the Madding Crowd*,[1] and I should now like to offer a reading of *Two on a Tower* based upon an analysis of all of the revisions that Hardy made to the novel. The effect of such a study is rather like that of time-lapse photography: discussion of the development of different aspects of *Two on a Tower* over a period of thirty years can be concentrated in a few pages in approximately the way that the unfolding of a flower can be shown in a few seconds. It is perhaps in this way that Hardy the creator can most vividly be seen at work.

The prefaces that Hardy wrote for the collected editions of his novels vary in the directness with which they address important ideas and themes, and in how much they reveal of Hardy's response to the experience of rereading his texts ten or forty years after they were first written. The preface to *Two on a Tower* is especially helpful in these respects, and provides an excellent entry-point for a discussion of the way that the novel grew in Hardy's imagination from the manuscript to 1895 and beyond.

In what follows reference will be made, as occasion arises, to versions of the novel to which Hardy made revisions—stages of development by now familiar: the manuscript prepared for the *Atlantic Monthly* (see Chapter 4); Sampson, Low's first edition of 1882; their one-volume

---

[1] 'Hardy the Creator: *Far From the Madding Crowd*', in *Critical Approaches to the Fiction of Thomas Hardy*, ed. by Dale Kramer (London and Basingstoke: Macmillan, 1979), 74–99.

edition of 1883; the novel's appearance in Osgood, McIlvaine's first collected edition of 1895; and Macmillan's Wessex-edition text of 1912.

The Astronomical Theme

The preface to the novel begins with a paragraph that outlines what Hardy claims was his structuring idea: 'This slightly built romance was the outcome of a wish to set the emotional history of two infinitesimal lives against the stupendous background of the stellar universe, and to impart to readers the sentiment that of these contrasting magnitudes the smaller might be the greater to them as men.' The most striking feature of this formulation is the apparent contradiction between the first four words and the rest of the sentence; it seems inherently improbable that any fiction appropriately defined as a 'slightly built romance' would be able to sustain such a grandiose thematic burden. The implication is either that Hardy is being unduly deprecatory in his description of the novel, or that the novel fails and that Hardy recognizes its failure. It was Hardy's habit publicly to undervalue individual novels, but it is also the case that many critics have felt this novel to be more or less a failure precisely because Hardy has not successfully integrated this astronomical theme into its fabric. Perhaps both Hardy's modesty and his critical insight were at work in the formulation of this apparent contradiction.

One of the theories underlying the whole of this study of Hardy's texts is that when revising he paid the closest attention to those elements in a novel which at that particular time interested him the most, or which he felt most needed restorative care. If this theory is valid, then it must be concluded of *Two on a Tower* either that Hardy felt he had, in the unemended fair copy of the manuscript, achieved as full an expression of his astronomical theme as was possible, or else that he was no longer interested in the theme after its articulation in this first full version of the novel, for there are few revisions to what the preface announces as his primary subject, and of those hardly any is significant.

It is, however, just possible to see Hardy at work trying in revision to integrate cosmic imagery into human affairs and terrestrial imagery into description of the universe. For example, when Swithin St Cleeve, the young astronomer-hero of the novel, is for the first time inside Welland House, he is given the chance by the lady of the manor, Viviette Constantine, to explain some modern astronomical theory. At first the manuscript read: 'The modern Eudoxus now forgot all about Lady

Constantine's great house, magnificent furniture'. But Hardy altered this to: 'The modern Eudoxus now rose above the embarrassing horizon of Lady Constantine's great house, magnificent furniture' (p. 58).[2] Though the purpose here is clear, the effect of the change is to obscure rather than illuminate the original simplicity. Swithin, in the guise of a 'modern Eudoxus', rising like Betelgeuse in the night sky, is not an enlightening picture, and, moreover, the question of how a horizon can be held to be embarrassing is hard to answer.

This revision may be compared with an instance from later in the manuscript, where Hardy describes the phenomena observable by Swithin in the southern skies when he goes to Cape Town. Hardy originally began:

Here, in regions revealed only to the instrumental observer, were suns of hybrid kind, fire fogs, worlds that had just swarmed

But after several attempts at revising the passage in the manuscript, it became:

There, in regions revealed only to the instrumental observer, were suns of hybrid kind, fire fogs, floating world pollen, globes that flew in groups like swarms of bees (p. 299)

The result is that the stars are seen much more concretely in terrestrial terms. In the first edition of the novel, though, the process is reversed, presumably in (what seems to me) an ill-judged attempt to introduce a fragment of astronomical vocabulary—Hardy changing the highly effective though doubtless unscientific 'world pollen' to 'nuclei'.

A second aspect of the astronomical theme, the way in which the characters try to bring themselves into relation with the universe, might be described as rhetorical, though again there are few examples of revision. In one of these Swithin is instructing Viviette:

And to add a new weirdness to what the sky possesses in its size and formlessness, there is added to these the quality of decay. For all the wonder of these stars they burn out like candles . . . The mind may become terrified by plunging among them as they are, but imagine them all extinguished

This is the tone of the lecturer, perhaps, but alterations in the manuscript to the second sentence make Swithin sound more like a preacher:

For all the wonder of these everlasting stars, eternal spheres, & what not, they are not everlasting, they are not eternal; they burn out like candles . . . The

---

[2] References are to the Wessex edition text of the novel (1912), unless otherwise specified.

senses may become terrified by plunging among them as they are, but there is a
pitifulness even in their glory! Imagine them all extinguished (p. 34)

And there is also a touch of impatience with poetic renditions of the
universe in the '& what not'.

One of the things that Hardy is trying to show in the novel is the way
in which Swithin is at first dominated entirely by his relationship with
the cosmos, gradually comes to an understanding that relationship with
a human may be just as powerful, and then fluctuates between the pull of
the two strong forces. During their first conversation Swithin confides
to Lady Constantine, in an addition to the manuscript, that he intends to
be Astronomer Royal if he lives, and then says 'Perhaps I shall not live.'
We are to imagine that his intercourse with the stars has stimulated this
premature anticipation of death, though there are other examples in
Hardy's fiction of youthful characters who have such premonitions, or
even desires—young Jude Fawley is the most celebrated—and it seems to
have been true of Hardy himself. Viviette's response at first was 'I
suppose you will live', which Hardy must have thought rather too easy
and uninterested an acceptance of Swithin's excess, and he changed it to
'I don't see why you should suppose that' (p. 9), which, with its traces
of both impatience and curiosity, suggests more clearly her incipient
concern for the young man.

Swithin makes an important astronomical discovery, but is anticipated
in its publication by a matter of weeks; a chill caught through his self-
abandonment in despair at this set-back turns into a dangerous illness,
apparently through his lack of will to live, and his prediction about an
early death seems about to be justified. A kiss from Viviette Constantine
is not enough to raise him from torpor; it takes the news of the arrival of
a comet in the sky to do that. This celestial visitant is announced by
Hannah, the servant of Swithin's aunt, and Hardy made a couple of
revisions to her startling communication. Swithin asks her the news:
' "Oh, nothing, sir," Hannah replied, looking out of the window with
sad apathy, "only that there's a comet" '; to which Hardy added, 'they
say', to avoid the implication that she might have recognized the comet
herself. This gets 'the dying astronomer starting up on his elbow', and
he demands to know whose comet it is; Hannah originally replied:
'Hush! . . . 'Tis God A'mighty's of course; he's getting bigger every
night', and for the same reason the last sentence was altered to: 'I haven't
seed en myself, but they say he's getting bigger every night' (p. 79).
Swithin is now impatient to recover so that he can observe the comet.
The context of these speeches, at the beginning of chapter X, is one of the

many reminders to the critic that *Two on a Tower* is a tragicomedy, and that one of the reasons Hardy deprecated the novel, and placed it in the category of Romances in 1912 when he was dividing his fiction into groups for the Wessex edition, was its mixture of comedy and pathos. The first paragraph of the chapter is a good example of the characteristic comic tone of the novel, and there is another at the moment of the Bishop's proposal of marriage to Viviette Constantine, where a revision to the passage of narratorial commentary helps to make the effect: 'A blusterous wind had blown up from the west, howling in the smokeless chimneys, and suggesting storms at sea, a tossing ocean, and the helpless inaccessibility of all astronomers and men on the other side of the same' (p. 291). To this Hardy added in the manuscript, after 'suggesting', the pointed phrase that makes, in a characteristically Hardyan way, the reference inescapable: 'to the feminine mind'.

Sexuality

After announcing to the reader the ostensible primary object of *Two on a Tower*, Hardy's preface continues with a summary of the contemporary critical response to the novel;

> But on the publication of the book people seemed to be less struck with these high aims of the author than with their own opinion, first, that the novel was an 'improper' one in its morals, and, secondly, that it was intended to be a satire on the established Church of this country. I was made to suffer in consequence from several eminent pens

He then gave his own response to the two heads of attack; this is the first part:

> That, however, was thirteen years ago, and, in respect of the first opinion, I venture to think that those who care to read the story now will be quite astonished at the scrupulous propriety observed therein on the relations of the sexes; for though there may be frivolous, and even grotesque touches on occasion, there is hardly a single caress in the book outside legal matrimony, or what was intended so to be.

As later writers have pointed out, Hardy's defence here sounds fine until the last two or three lines. Having written, in the interim, *Tess of the d'Urbervilles* and *Jude the Obscure*, he had reason to draw attention to this novel's propriety, but he loses his case at the end, for it is clear to any reader of the novel that the one crucial 'caress' in the narrative was well understood by both parties to be outside legal matrimony, and it is part of the point of the scene in which it takes place that there is indecision about making the union lawful.

In fact, this scene and its consequences were rendered slightly more openly in the edition that the preface first introduced, the revised edition of 1895. Viviette Constantine discovers that the marriage ceremony she went through with Swithin was invalid because her husband's death in Africa did not occur on the date at first thought, but, rather, six weeks after her second wedding. Her first instinct is to arrange an immediate remarriage, but at the same time she also discovers that by marrying Swithin before his twenty-fifth birthday, she would deprive him of a legacy of £600. She decides to send him away from her till he reaches that age, and provokes thereby a critical meeting. In the manuscript's first version the climax of this final encounter read thus:

> They . . . kissed each other, as though the emotion of their whole year-&-half's acquaintance had settled down upon that moment.
>
> Time however was merciless, & the hour came when she was compelled to depart.

On reconsidering the passage Hardy decided to add a scrap of dialogue and a tiny indication of something more; after 'that moment' the manuscript's final reading was:

> 'I won't go away from you,' said Swithin huskily. 'Why did you propose it for an instant!'
>
> Thus the nearly ended interview was again prolonged. Time however was merciless, & the hour came when she was compelled to depart.

In 1895 the last paragraph was further enlarged to reveal the length of the prolongation, and to suggest more clearly how the time was passed: 'Thus the nearly ended interview was again prolonged, and Viviette yielded to all the passion of her first union with him. Time, however, was merciless, and the hour approached midnight, and she was compelled to depart.' This kind of change must be thought of more as making the incident moderately credible than as handling sexual matters with a greater frankness. Viviette's subsequent pregnancy (though the word is still never used) is made more explicit in both 1895 and in 1912 for the Wessex edition by a series of additions. Viviette now thinks of 'that last fatal evening with him'; she says that she has 'physical reasons for being any man's wife', and she recognizes that she 'ought not to have consented to that last interview: all was well till then'. The child is born after Viviette's hasty marriage to the bishop of Melchester and in the revised version Mr Torkingham (who was never in the secret) is made to say of him: 'Remarkably fine boy, and yet he was a seven-month's baby'. But these are still sufficiently indirect indications of the state of affairs.[3]

It is also the case, to refer back to the preface, that Hardy chose to interpret 'improper' on his own terms rather than those of his critics, and it seems more probable that it was the impropriety of foisting a child by one man off on another (a clergyman), as his own, rather than any special sexual licence, that was alleged. Thus, Hardy has separated into two what is essentially one issue—the one that he addresses, in a manner of speaking, in the next paragraph of the preface.

The Church

As for the second opinion, it is sufficient to draw attention, as I did at the time, to the fact that the Bishop is every inch a gentleman, and that the parish priest who figures in the narrative is one of its most estimable characters.

If Hardy argued speciously in the previous paragraph, here he is not arguing at all. The first statement is comic in its irrelevance to the issue (and, indeed, the Bishop's gentlemanliness is itself an element in the satire he is apparently trying to refute); and the second, to anyone who has read the novel, is an inaccurate assessment of the significance of an ineffectual and sycophantic man, though it is true that the characterization of Mr Torkingham, the parish priest of Welland, alters in the last pages of the novel. This is Hardy mocking mockers, using the same tactics to ridicule the critics that he used to satirize the Bishop, and extending into the preliminary matter the satire on the church.

Although Mr Torkingham is not seen sympathetically at first, the earliest passages in the novel that might be called satire directed at the church come when Swithin St Cleeve and Viviette Constantine are married at Bath. The vicar is away on holiday, and his deputy is not exactly reliable. The parish clerk comments, in an addition made for the first edition: 'The best men goes into the brewing, or into the shipping now-a-days, you see, sir; doctrines being rather shaddery at present, and your money's worth not sure in that line. So we church officers be left poorly provided with men for odd jobs' (p. 141). To clarify the reference 'that line' was further changed to 'our line' in the one-volume edition.

---

[3] pp. 281, 282, 296, and 305.

Another change that shows Hardy satirizing the Established Church through its representatives in the novel is the addition in 1912 of 'or a thimble-rigger at a fair' to Hezzy Biles's account of confirmation in his youth: 'The Bishop o' that time would stretch out his palms and run his fingers over our row of crowns as off-hand as a bank gentleman telling money' (p. 166); a detail reminiscent of Parson Grinham in *Under the Greenwood Tree*, who spat on his finger to christen the infants when the font would not hold water.

The first hint that Hardy was interested in increasing the already hostile presentation of Bishop Helmsdale himself comes in a change for the first edition. Viviette says to Swithin: 'I knew him when I was quite a girl, and he held the living of Puddle-sub-Hedge near us' (p. 172). The name of the parish is intended to be mildly comic, but when it is altered to 'Puddle-sub-Mixen' the comedy becomes more pointed ('mixen' is dialectal for dung-heap).

It is possible to see from a study of fos. 325–47 of the Harvard manuscript how the present harsh characterization of the bishop grew. These leaves begin with the visit of Louis Glanville, Viviette's brother, to the bishop in his palace—to suggest that though she has refused him once, it was under the influence of the news that her husband had died much more recently than she had supposed, and that she would be probably be more receptive to a second approach. The bishop explains his position in the first manuscript version:

I am now in a position with regard to Lady Constantine which—in view of the important office I hold—I should not have cared to place myself in, unless I had felt quite sure of not being refused. And hence it is a great grief to me that I unwittingly risked making my proposal at the very moment when she was under the influence of those strange tidings

Subsequently, the second sentence was revised to 'And hence it is a great grief and some mortification to me that I was refused—owing—of course to the fact that I unwittingly risked making my proposal at the very moment when she was under the influence of these strange tidings' (pp. 284–5), adding both the injury to the bishop's self-esteem and his confident assumption of the only motive for Viviette's refusal that would help him to save some of it (though we know that it is the wrong one). And to make sure that the reader does not miss the point Hardy added a paragraph of narratorial analysis at the same time: 'The Bishop's words disclosed a mind whose sensitive fear of danger to its own dignity hindered it from criticism elsewhere. Things might have been worse for

Louis's Puck-like idea of mismating his Hermia with this Demetrius' (p. 285). It is not clear, though, that the Shakespearian allusion is altogether helpful. Further on in the meeting between brother and bishop, Louis informs the prelate that Viviette loves him, and he replies: 'Can you indeed assure me of that. Can it be!' (p. 286). The second sentence was altered to 'Indeed—indeed!', suggesting that he is so smug that he is not at all surprised to hear the (inaccurate) news. The passage continued 'said Bishop Helmsdale' until the one-volume edition of the novel, when it was changed to 'said the good bishop' with increase of mockery.

The scene then moves to Welland Hall, and the bishop's arrival to ask in person for the pregnant Viviette's hand in marriage: 'Dr Helmsdale was standing there with his hat in his hand.' This simple observation was given bite in changes to the manuscript and the first edition; in the manuscript it became: 'Dr Helmsdale was standing there with the air of a man too good for his errand, which was, indeed, not far from the truth.' The pompous self-importance of the man is registered, and at once is undercut by the joke that is being perpetrated upon him. For the book-edition Hardy gives with one hand and takes away with the other: 'Dr Helmsdale was standing there with the air of a man too good for his destiny—which, to be just to him, was not far from the truth this time' (p. 290). This has the air of offering justice, but the clarifying sting of 'this time' more than offsets the greater dignity of 'destiny'; though, indeed, the generalizing quality of the word assists in the impression that such an air was habitual with him. The relationship of the bishop with Malvolio is made more apparent through these revisions—a much more appropriate role for him than Demetrius.

The proposal and Viviette's response to it are made off-stage, and we learn about them from the bishop's report to Louis, who has been waiting about with bated breath: 'She accepts me . . . And the wedding is to be soon. Her long solitude and sufferings justify haste. What you said was true. Sheer weariness and distraction have driven her to me. She was quite passive at last, and she agreed to anything I proposed. A good and wise woman, she perceived what a true shelter my position would afford and refused to despise Heaven's gifts.' The only irony here is unavoidably prompted by the situation, in that the bishop does not know the real reason why Viviette has agreed to marry him, nor why the wedding has to be soon; but Hardy was unwilling to let him off with so venial a folly, and altered the second half of the speech: 'She was quite passive at last, and agreed to anything I proposed—such is the persuasive force of a trained mind! A good and wise woman, she perceived what a true shelter from sadness was offered and was not the one to despise Heaven's gift' (p. 291). In this version Bishop Helmsdale compounds the plot-irony with various evidences of his self-centred arrogance—his conviction that it is his intellect that has persuaded Viviette to marriage, his assumption that he will make her happy, and above all, in the simple change from plural to singular of the last word, the identification of himself as 'Heaven's gift' to her.

Mr Torkingham, the parish priest of Welland, is first seen to some disadvantage in a scene of comedy similar to that in which Mr Maybold was confronted by the Mellstock choir in *Under the Greenwood Tree*, and he is almost immediately recognized by Viviette Constantine as someone to whom she feels unable to entrust a matter of delicacy and importance. Torkingham is weakly in awe of the bishop when he arrives for the confirmation, and we do not meet him again until the last pages of the novel, by which time he seems to have become a somewhat more interesting man.

He welcomes Swithin home, quoting Horace and Shakespeare, filling in details of life in Welland during Swithin's absence, carrying sweets in his pocket for the child that is Swithin's and Viviette's, though of course he is not aware of the boy's true paternity. Or, at least, so we would think, it being hardly likely that Viviette would confide this truth to him; but when he and Swithin meet the boy, Mr Torkingham says 'You know who he is, of course?', and on Swithin replying that he does not, goes on 'O, I thought you did. Yet how should you?' There is here a strong suspicion that Torkingham has made the connection between Swithin and 'the lovely little fellow with flaxen hair, which spread out in a frill of curls from beneath a quaint, close-fitting velvet cap that he wore.' It is no coincidence that in the first edition Hardy altered part of the introductory description of Swithin from 'and his hat was pushed aside for convenience, disclosing a curly head of very light shining hair' to 'and on his head he wore a black velvet skull-cap, leaving to view below it a curly margin of very light shining hair' (p. 6). It seems improbable that the vicar we have seen in the earlier parts of the novel would be capable of drawing such a conclusion, and of not being outraged by it. Perhaps the connection in his mind is unconscious, leading him to make the assumption that Swithin must know who the boy is because they look so alike, without recognizing the possible implications. And yet his attitude to the bishop is a revelation too; in the last of the manuscript revisions that develop Hardy's conception of the prelate's character, he altered Mr Torkingham's mild criticism—'He was not blameless, to speak candidly, but who is'—to something altogether sharper: 'He was not a Ken or a Heber. To speak candidly he had his faults—of which arrogance was not the least. But who is perfect' (p. 204).

There is an acuteness and a kindliness about the vicar in this last phase of the novel that goes a little way towards justifying Hardy's description of him in the preface as 'one of its most estimable characters'.

There is also evidence in the manuscript that Hardy was concerned not to satirize Viviette Constantine's genuine religious feeling. After she has given up Swithin she instructs her servants to say that she cannot see him when he calls at Welland House. However, when he arrives we are told that

Lady Constantine was just above his head, listening to his movements with the liveliest emotions, longing for him to insist upon seeing her.

So it was in the first version, but in the copy eventually sent to America he complicated her response in a way that reflects the essential contradiction in her personality:

Lady Constantine was just above his head, listening to his movements with the liveliest emotions, and, while praying for him to go, longing for him to insist upon seeing her and spoil all. (p. 262)

Five leaves later she has been to see Swithin one last time, at his demand, and they have made love; they return to Welland House together, she goes in alone and, in the earlier reading, 'with her customary devotion to form she had knelt for some time inside the room' before looking out of a window to tell Swithin finally to leave her until his twenty-fifth birthday. The small change that Hardy made is very telling, substituting an analysis of her motive for the notation of conventional observance: 'with her customary complication of feeling she had knelt for some time inside the room'.

These changes were made in the manuscript, but revisions made later seem to turn in a different direction. Hardy had analysed Viviette's 'complication of feeling' earlier in the novel, in a paragraph beginning 'Lady Constantine, by virtue of her temperament, was necessarily either lover or *dévote*'. In the manuscript and serial the heart of the paragraph read:

To be led into difficulties by those mastering emotions of hers, to aim at escape by turning round and seizing the apparatus of religion—which however could only rightly be worked by those emotions already bestowed elsewhere—it was, after all, but Nature's well-meaning attempt to preserve the honour of her daughter's conscience in the trying quandary to which the conditions of sex had given birth.

There is a certain amount of criticism, as opposed to satire, implied in the phrase 'apparatus of religion' but the passage's main thrust is to suggest that Viviette's apparently irrational activity in turning towards religion, and specifically in suggesting to Swithin that he should be confirmed, is instinctive in her, a prompting of Nature and thus beyond her control. By 1912 Hardy was not so sympathetic towards this aspect of Viviette's character, and the effect of the sentence was transformed:

To be led into difficulties by those mastering emotions of hers, to aim at escape by turning round and seizing the apparatus of religion—which could only rightly be worked by the very emotions already bestowed elsewhere—it was, after all, but Convention's palpitating attempt to preserve the comfort of her creature's conscience in the trying quandary to which the conditions of sex had given rise. (pp. 157–8)

The substitution of 'creature of Convention' for 'daughter of Nature' represents a reversal of the trend in the revisions in the manuscript looked at just above. This change is partly a consequence of an alteration in Hardy's view of religion by the time he made the revision for the Wessex edition, but it is also the case that by 1912 Hardy decided to stress Viviette's half-conscious commitment to social forms, already strong in the manuscript, as more powerful in her than instinctive religious sentiment. It is an aesthetic question of some interest to decide the extent to which such a change undermines the fabric of the novel established in the manuscript.

A small but significant change earlier on the same manuscript-leaf provides a more powerful critique of Viviette's turn to religion; Swithin resists her idea that he should be confirmed, and she pleads 'Without the Church to cling to, what have we!' Swithin's reply was originally couched in terms suggested by her religious enthusiasm: 'I am dumb as Pilate at that.' In reading through the passage Hardy was dissatisfied with such evasiveness, and replaced Swithin's words with an echo (to my ears at least) of Matthew Arnold's 'Dover Beach': 'Each other.'

Viviette, Swithin, and Tabitha Lark

This loving response brings the next paragraph of the novel's preface into focus:

However, the pages must speak for themselves. Some few readers, I trust—to take a serious view—will be reminded by this imperfect story, in a manner not unprofitable to the growth of the social sympathies, of the pathos, misery, long-suffering, and divine tenderness which in real life frequently accompany the passion of such a woman as Viviette for a lover several years her junior.

The view that all that had gone before in the preface was playful mockery is confirmed, and the change in tone here can leave the reader in no doubt that he has come to an expression of what Hardy felt, in 1895 and 1912, was really of interest in the novel. That the exploration of the relationship between Viviette and Swithin was Hardy's fundamental purpose in the novel is further indicated by the large number of revisions that different aspects of the relationship attract.

At first Hardy was inclined to explain Viviette's passion for Swithin by saying that her lonely situation and loving nature meant that she would fall in love with any moderately well-looking man who came in her way. Later he recognized that emphasis on this argument diminished her as an individual by tending to deny her free will in the affair, and devalued her attachment to Swithin by making it appear almost automatic.

As a first step towards altering the balance in the narratorial assessments of the growth of Viviette's feeling for the young astronomer, Hardy deleted for the one-volume edition of the novel a part of the last paragraph of the sixth chapter: 'The mental room taken up by an idea depends as largely on the available space for it as on its essential magnitude: in Lady Constantine's life of infestivity, in her domestic voids, and in her social discouragements, there was nothing to oust the the lightest fancy.' Hardy's awareness of the counterproductive effect of this stress upon Viviette's peculiarly retired situation as a kind of excuse for her falling in love with Swithin was a gradual one, and it was not until the revision for the Osgood collected edition that the first paragraph of chapter XIV was removed:

Rural solitude, which provides ample themes for the intellect and sweet occupations innumerable for the minor sentiments, often denies a ready object for those stronger passions that enter no less than the others into the human constitution. The suspended pathos finds its remedy in settling on the first intrusive shape that happens to be reasonably well organised for the purpose, disregarding social and other minor accessories. Where the solitude is shadowed by the secret melancholies of the solitary, this natural law is surer still in operation.

The next paragraph, now the first in the chapter, was substantially emended at the same time. Until 1895 it read:

The laboured resistance which Lady Constantine's judgement had offered to her rebellious affection ere she learnt that she was a widow, and which had taken the form of a sharp remorse, became now an inward bashfulness, that rendered her even more unstable of mood than she had been. However, having discovered herself to love this handsome youth of intellectual promise, she was one of that mettle—fervid, cordial, and spontaneous—who would rather see all her affairs going to rack and ruin than abjure a tender faith in anybody to repair them. But they had already gone to rack and ruin by no fault of hers, and had left her such a painfully narrowed existence as even lent something of rationality to her attachment. Thus it was that her restful and unambitious soul found comfort in her reverses.

In part, the changes made for the collected edition were tidying up, but Hardy also removed phrases like 'discovered herself to love' that might have been seen as ironic comments on the genuineness of her passion, made Viviette less rather than more unstable through her widowhood, and changed the nature of her soul from 'restful' to 'tender'. It is unusual to find Hardy doing so much in so small a space in this edition, unless topography is involved. The revised paragraph reads thus:

> The laboured resistance which Lady Constantine's judgement had offered to her rebellious affection ere she learnt that she was a widow, now passed into a bashfulness that rendered her almost as unstable of mood as before. But she was one of that mettle—fervid, cordial, and spontaneous—who had not the heart to spoil a passion; and her affairs having gone to rack and ruin by no fault of her own she was left to a painfully narrowed existence which lent even something of rationality to her attachment. Thus it was that her tender and unambitious soul found comfort in her reverses. (p. 102)

It was at the end of the previous chapter that the awakening of Swithin to his love for Viviette took place, and the next paragraph in this chapter describes the development of his emotion: 'like a spring bud hard in bursting, the delay was compensated by after speed'; he recognized at once that Viviette was, in the early versions, 'a handsome woman attached to him'. This was clearly inadequate to meet the growing sense that Hardy had of her passion for the young astronomer, and he altered it in the Osgood edition to 'a woman who loved him'—at once less literary and more accurate.

Hardy designed from the beginning that Viviette's love for Swithin should be all in all to her, while his for her should be powerful at times, yet easily diluted by his passion for the stars. However, Hardy's sense of this difference between them led in early versions to his making Swithin too reserved during the first impact of the awakening of his love. For three months he is unable to do any astronomical work, and he writes to Viviette to suggest a solution. Until the Wessex edition his letter read in part: 'This affection I have for you absorbs my life, and outweighs my intentions. The power to labour in this grandest of fields has left me . . . But the desperation of my circumstances has suggested a remedy'. Hardy sensed that this was both too weak and too impersonal, and altered 'affection' to 'longing' and 'circumstances' to 'mind' (though not 'being' or some such all-embracing concept). Later, as Swithin tries to persuade Viviette to marry him, originally he said 'I have neither the power to work nor the honour of your company'; in 1912 'honour' was changed to 'delight'. It can again be seen that Hardy's awareness of the need for change developed slowly, as in the Osgood edition he altered another detail in this dialogue from 'it is you, my dear lady, who have displaced the work', to 'it is you, my dear, who have displaced the work', an effective change of considerable economy.[4]

But it is mostly the way in which Viviette is affected by the relationship that retains Hardy's attention during the revisions. One of the aspects of her behaviour after the marriage that has received most criticism is her frequently renewed request to Swithin that the wedding be kept secret. It is, viewed harshly, a plot necessity for which Hardy has to find some more or less plausible justification. However, though even through the most sympathetic eyes there appears some improbability in her almost frantic demands for secrecy, Hardy does go a long way towards convincing the reader by stressing the importance throughout the novel that Viviette gives to the social surface of appearances required of her class. A revision in the manuscript helps to clarify what Hardy has attempted to do: the pregnant Viviette rushes by train to Southampton to try to catch Swithin before he leaves England; in the earlier reading 'The lovely scenes through which she was dragged had no points of interest for her now'. We have had little evidence of her sensitivity to the natural environment, and, in revising, Hardy saw an opportunity to enhance two aspects of the novel that were important to him. The sentence became: 'The changeful procession of country seats past which she was dragged, the names and memories of their owners, had no points of interest for her now.' In the new version her preoccupation with the affairs of local society is combined with the use of their buildings as emblems of the present and past histories of the families that inhabit them, a detail of interest in the thematic structure of the novel discussed below.

[4] p. 112.

There are many examples of the way in which Hardy in revision tries to show how in her relationship with Swithin Viviette's emotion is for ever at war with her acute sense of the social *convenances*. Even as her love for Swithin is growing, Hardy makes an addition directed towards this aspect of her personality. In chapter VIII she visits Swithin alone, and in response to his thought that she 'might come any evening, and possibly bring company' she says with hypersensitivity: 'Don't quarrel with me for coming alone . . . There are reasons for what I do of which you know nothing.' The crucial change was made in the first edition—the addition of 'social' before 'reasons'—but Hardy also altered 'quarrel with' to 'criticize' in the one-volume edition, so that it finally read: 'Don't criticize me for coming alone . . . There are social reasons for what I do of which you know nothing' (p. 65).

There is another example at the beginning of chapter XI. Before Swithin has been made aware of his emotions, Viviette feels 'that to see St Cleeve again would be dangerous'; and she felt thus until the first edition, when the danger, which might have been to her peace of mind as much as to her standing in society, was replaced, and her feeling became 'that to see St Cleeve again would be an impropriety' (p. 83).

A third example shows that Swithin has learned from Vivette the importance of social standing. As he considers, at the end of chapter XXIV, the effect of their marriage upon her, he feels that she has married him 'at an immense sacrifice'. It was not until the first edition that this became 'at an immense sacrifice of position' (p. 178).

It is the cumulative effect of these changes that makes clearer the importance of the social façade to her. By stressing Swithin's youth and inexperience in other revisions, Hardy makes it clearer why he does not insist on openness. A passage that may be held to stand for others that illustrate the latter point occurs at the beginning of chapter XXXV, as the narrator comments on Swithin's action in telling Viviette about the terms of his legacy. Originally it went in part: 'But the influence over him which eight or nine added years lent her was immensely increased by her wider experiences, and he had yielded the point as he yielded all social points'. Several fragments of this were revised at different times. Hardy added 'immense' before 'influence' in the manuscript, but deleted it again for the first edition; in the surviving manuscript 'eight or nine added' was altered to 'nine or ten outnumbering', but this was reduced in the *Atlantic* serialization to 'seven or eight outnumbering'. The first edition saw the difference confirmed at eight years, but for the Osgood edition it became eight or nine, and for the Wessex edition it finally returned approximately to the revised manuscript reading at 'nearly ten outnumbering years'.

The third revision to the passage was the addition in the first edition of 'her higher position and' before 'wider experiences', making it clear that the experiences in question were those in country-house society of which Swithin knows nothing, so that the passage now reads: 'But the influence over him which nearly ten outnumbering years lent her was immensely increased by her higher position and wider experiences, and he had yielded the point as he yielded all social points' (p. 252).

The preface suggests that a reading of the story might foster growth of 'the social sympathies', a somewhat ambiguous phrase, though it presumably does not refer to the kind of social concerns that are Viviette's preoccupation in the passages just examined. It happens that a revision in chapter XLI provides a key to the interpretation of the phrase. It is while Swithin is in South Africa that the tone of the novel turns decisively against science and astronomy, and his work is effectively diminished through metaphor and analysis. One of the passages of analysis contains the following:

In these experiments . . . important as they were to eye and intellect, there was little food for the sympathetic instincts which create the changes in a life, and are therefore more particularly the question here . . . Swithin's . . . discoveries . . . were, no doubt, incidents of the highest importance to him; and yet from our present point of view they served but the humble purpose of killing time

This is how it was at first, but by the time that Hardy wrote the preface for the Osgood edition it had changed considerably:

In these experiments . . . important as they were to human intellect, there was little food for the sympathetic instincts which create the changes in a life . . . Swithin's . . . discoveries . . . were, no doubt, incidents of the highest importance to him; and yet from an intersocial point of view they served but the humble purpose of killing time (p. 300)

Now, in close association there are 'sympathetic' and 'intersocial'; and, in particular, the change from 'our present' to 'an intersocial' makes it clear that we are to interpret 'social' in the preface as meaning 'of relations between human beings'—quite different from the narrower class-ridden sense that has attached to it through the greater part of the novel.

Hardy's sympathy with Viviette, its intense expression in the preface, suggests that he saw her to some degree as a martyr, a woman who, like Tess, suffers intensely through the inadequacy of two very different men who abandon her, and force her into positions of which she is ashamed. Hardy defined in the manuscript his attitude to the former of these men, her first husband Sir Blount Constantine. Viviette, finding herself falling in love with the young and beautiful astronomer, prays 'to eradicate those impulses towards St Cleeve which were inconsistent with her position as the wife of an absent man'. Originally the sentence ended 'let him be of any sort so ever', but this was revised to 'though not unnatural in her as his victim' (p. 84). It is not hard to see her also as Swithin's victim, sacrificed to the sterile gods of science, and there is hidden in the early version of the manuscript evidence that Hardy consciously connected Sir Blount and Swithin St Cleeve. As, in the third chapter, Lady Constantine is explaining to Mr Torkingham something of the nature of her husband, she describes 'a purpose of his—a mania for African lion-hunting, which he dignified by calling it a scheme of geographical discovery; for he was inordinately anxious to make a name for himself in that field' (p. 25). It is possible to draw a connection between Sir Blount's anxiety for fame as a slayer of wild beasts and Swithin's for fame as an astronomer, but the relationship was originally much more apparent, since 'a mania for African lion-hunting, which he dignified by calling it' was a late addition. Sir Blount as one who charts the terrestrial unknown would parallel Swithin as one who charts the celestial unknown, and Hardy may have felt that the exactness of the parallel was too harsh to Swithin. Nevertheless, when Swithin puts on Sir Blount's fur coat and is thought to be his ghost by the villagers, and when he decides on South Africa as his ultimate destination in his five-year exile from Viviette, the connection is revived, and in the latter decision Hardy judges harshly Swithin's preference for scientific, as opposed to human, discoveries.

Swithin returns to Welland not to look for Viviette, though he knows she is now a widow, but because his work at the Cape is finished; and if a further reminder of the relationship between the heroine's two men were needed, it is supplied in the greeting that Haymoss Fry gives to Swithin on his return: 'I knowed in a winking 'twas some great navigator that I see standing there . . . But whe'r 'twere a sort of nabob, or a diment-digger, or a lion-hunter, I couldn't so much as guess till I heerd en speak' (p. 308).

Although Swithin finally says to Viviette that he will marry her, the news is too much for her wasted constitution, and she dies in his arms. The melodramatic is for once the appropriate ending, and one justification of its rightness is offered in an addition to the last paragraph of the story. In the manuscript and the *Atlantic* it read: 'But he had to do so soon. Sudden joy after despair had touched an over-strained heart too smartly. Viviette was dead. The Bishop was avenged.' When the first edition was published this is how the novel concluded:

> He looked up for help. Nobody appeared in sight but Tabitha Lark, who was skirting the field with a bounding tread—the single bright spot of colour and animation within the wide horizon. When he looked down again his fear deepened to certainty. It was no longer a mere surmise that help was vain. Sudden joy after despair had touched an over-strained heart too smartly. Viviette was dead. The Bishop was avenged.

Hardy evidently wished the reader to make the contrast between the colour and animation of the young Tabitha Lark, and the pale, worn, prematurely ageing Viviette; and, to go further, to feel that Tabitha is the more appropriate mate for Swithin. The conversation that Swithin and Tabitha have in the orchard at Welland Bottom, her development into independence and a certain amount of celebrity on her own account, even his solicitude towards her at the time of her accident during the confirmation service—all these seem now to have led to her appearance at the climax of the novel. Viviette alive could not now, we are asked to think, have fought successfully for Swithin's love against the youth and vitality and new cosmopolitanism of Tabitha Lark.

A revision in 1912 draws attention to a passage that points the contrast between the two women even more sharply. Viviette feels momentarily a pang of jealousy of Tabitha as her brother affirms without justification that the young organist must be in love with Swithin; and, as soon as she can, she hurries to the hut at the foot of the tower where Swithin is working. The narrator describes her as she goes: 'She appeared a mere spot, hardly distinguishable from the grass as she crossed the open ground, and soon became absorbed in the black mass of the fir plantation' (p. 185). The passage describing Tabitha that was added to the last paragraph of the novel in the first edition seems deliberately designed as a parallel to this description; and the dullness of Viviette's appearance is further emphasized by the revision for the Wessex edition of 'grass' to 'sod'.

Though Hardy does further emphasize the cruelty of Swithin at the end of the novel, he also recognizes that it is inevitable that one so inexperienced as he should be unable to value rightly the mature Viviette. It must also be remembered that the 'loving-kindness' that motivates Swithin's final return to Viviette is described by the narrator as 'a sentiment perhaps in the long run more to be prized than lover's love' (p. 312).

Places

Viviette dies at the top of the tower, her tower, the predominant feature of the landscape of her estate. The last paragraph of the preface that has provided so full an introduction to the novel is concerned with this landscape:

> The scene of the action was suggested by two real spots in the part of the country specified, each of which has a column standing upon it. Certain surrounding peculiarities have been imported into the narrative from both sites, and from elsewhere.

The last three words were added as a kind of postscript in 1912, one more small example, to set alongside those discussed above in Chapter 7, of the increasing influence that public attention to Wessex had over Hardy's thought—he felt he had to cover himself from the discoveries of the scene-searchers who had been unable to pin down Welland to any particular spot in Dorset.

The novel begins with a reference to Wessex: 'On an early winter afternoon, clear but not cold, when the vegetable world was a weird multitude of skeletons through whose ribs the sun shone freely, a gleaming landau came to a pause on the crest of a hill in Wessex.' The detail from the vegetable world and the mention of Wessex suggest that this might be the first sentence of a novel like *The Woodlanders*; but the presence of a 'gleaming landau' represents the true note of the novel more accurately. The reference to Wessex is especially misleading, for the novel might have been located anywhere, and, as Hardy's note in the preface implies, the precise topography of its action in relation to any map of Wessex is undiscoverable, being both vague and inconsistent. On the other hand, the imagined topography is centrally important as a structuring element in the novel, thematically as well as formally. The salient features of this landscape are two groupings: the tower on Rings Hill, the temporary hut at its foot, and the farmhouse in Welland Bottom which lie to the north of the turnpike road; and Welland House and church to the south. The crest of the road on which Viviette causes her landau to be halted at the beginning of the novel divides her great

house from the column in which much that is most intense in her future
will be enacted.

Briefly stated, tower, hut, and farmhouse are Swithin's territory,
while House and church are Viviette's; the tower is Swithin's aspirational home, the farmhouse the home for his body, until Viviette has the
hut built for him; the church is Viviette's aspirational home, and the
House the home of her body. The structure of the novel is based on these
associations; and the action, both literal and metaphorical, can be charted
with reference to the intrusions of one character into the other's
buildings, or their escape to their own. This is a highly simplified
description of Hardy's organization, and I have discussed it at some
length in 'Middling Hardy', an essay in the fourth volume of *The
Thomas Hardy Annual*. On the whole, Hardy had this fundamental
structure well developed in his imagination from the beginning of the
manuscript, and it required little amendment, though there are one or
two significant changes. The interested reader will find these detailed in
my essay.

The last word in the preface to this novel, as in many of the others, is a
note of when the novel first appeared in three volumes. By 1912 Hardy
was interested in thus ensuring that the attentive reader should know
how much time had passed between the novel's primary creation and this
second collected edition of his work. For *Two on a Tower* the gap was
thirty years, a period filled for Hardy with fresh writing, latterly in
different directions, and it is as if he were trying with this note to prompt
the reader into recalling that he was now a dramatist (of a sort) and a
poet, rather than a novelist.

On the other hand, this preface, like all the others (and unlike those
that Henry James appended to the New York edition of his works),
offers no hints of the revisions that the novel had undergone during those
thirty years—some of which this section has chronicled—and the note in
question might be thought more significant to anyone who has studied
the texts of *Two on a Tower* as a reminder that in some ways the 1912
version offers a different novel from that which was first written in 1882.
Hardy's sense of most of the more important characters has undergone
subtle changes since he first committed the story to paper, his attitude to
the thread of religious sentiment running through the novel has similarly
altered, but the most substantial refocusing of Hardy's vision of his novel
was away from the astronomical theme and towards the purely human
dilemma faced by his heroine. Whether, as a matter of aesthetics or of

principle, we prefer to read the novel of 1882 or that of 1912 is a question of individual taste. Aesthetically, I think that most, though certainly not all, of the changes Hardy made are improvements, and that on the whole the 1912 version is superior to that of thirty years earlier. As far as principle is concerned, particularly the principles of authorial intention and authority, some of the implications are brought together in the next chapter.

11

Editing Hardy

Scattered in various places throughout this book have been brief discussions of the implications for anyone interesting in editing Hardy of the evidence presented. It seems worthwhile to draw this dispersed material together through a more generalized analysis of some of the problems that an editor will face.

What I am concerned with in this chapter is the critical editing of Hardy, the process by which all versions of a work are collated, and some conclusion is reached on the basis of these collations about (a) the relationship between the versions, (b) the version or versions that should form part or all of an edited text, and (c) errors in these versions that may need to be eradicated.

The basis upon which my understanding of the priorities involved in the process of critical editing rests is that in the last resort the particular text that is established by the editor is unimportant, in that in many situations several different texts might be justifiable. The crucial point is that whatever the text it should be scrupulously accurate according to clearly enunciated principles, and the record of the development of the work presented in the apparatus should be complete. If I can reform all the significant versions of the work from the edited text and the apparatus, then I am free to make my own edited text.

However, in qualification of this basic position there are several things to be said. The first is that, however strong-minded the user of the edition, and however convinced of the misjudgements of the editor, it is always the case that the printed text has an inbuilt authority that it requires an effort to resist. Then, it is further true that critical editions do not exist in a vacuum, and it is highly probable that after all the labour expended upon the establishment of the text the editor and his publisher will want to issue a cheap impression of the text, without the apparatus. Once that happens the text indeed carries authority to the reader. Thus, the critical editor in the establishment of the text is in practice obligated to make decisions based upon as full and acute an analysis of all the evidence offered by the different versions of the work as possible, and further, to take into account, as far as possible, all other conditions external to the particular work that may have affected its development—from other work by the same writer to the socio-economic conditions of the day.

In many instances such analysis will support more than one acceptable procedure, and it is then that the theory of editing held by the editor will prove a determining factor. The dominant editorial theory of the last decades has been that developed and elaborated by Walter Greg, Fredson Bowers, and G. T. Tanselle, which pays particular attention to the significance of authorial intention, and in particular authorial final intention, in the establishment of a critical text. This emphasis leads most often, for those whose work utilizes the theory, to the creation of an eclectic text which draws (for sufficient and announced reasons) material from different versions of the work. My editorial practice has been guided by this theory, and so, much of what follows has to be understood as proceeding from within such a theoretical framework.

The Greg-Bowers-Tanselle theory has, however, recently been under attack from two sides; one (which might be represented by Jerome McGann) that (put very crudely) denies the author authority over his work once it has been published since it is then a social rather than an individual product, and the other (which might be represented by Herschel Parker) that (put equally crudely) denies the validity of the author's apparent authority over his text as he revises it, since once the text has been uttered it is a whole thing, and unless the text is wholly rethought any revision, however intentional, is a deforming intrusion.

I am not here intending a theoretical debate, but I do want to show how both of these divergent theories about the value of final authorial intention may reasonably be held to have a place in the editing of Hardy's fiction.[1] In effect this chapter will be an abbreviated guidebook for editors of Hardy.

Punctuation

I shall begin with a matter that has hardly arisen so far in the book, Hardy's punctuation, and with the associated question of copy-text or

---

[1] I have here summarized all too briefly arguments developed at length in Jerome McGann's *A Critique of Textual Criticism* (Chicago: University of Chicago Press, 1982) and Herschel Parker's *Flawed Texts and Verbal Icons* (Evanston, Ill.: Northwestern University Press, 1983). The distinctive approaches to editing have recently been summarized with wit and clarity by Peter Shillingsburg in his *Editing in the Computer Age* (Athens: University of Georgia Press, 1986).

base-text. (In what follows I accept as given the value of an eclectic text in which punctuation and substantives are treated separately and may derive in a critical edition from different versions of a text, thought I shall subsequently have one or two things to say about alternative procedures.)

As far as the work of Hardy is concerned this area of editorial discussion has already produced some debate. In an essay entitled 'Hardy, House-Style, and the Aesthetics of Punctuation' I made two suggestions in relation to the transmission of Hardy's prose texts from manuscript to print. One was that though most printing houses in the last third of the nineteenth century instructed their compositors to apply standard rules of punctuation to manuscripts they set, in fact, the application of such house styles by individual compositors employed by the same printing shop was subject to wide personal variation. The other was that the imposition of the compositorial style, both standard and individual, upon Hardy's manuscript punctuation resulted in the loss of much rhetorical significance, especially in speech.

One conclusion I drew from these arguments was that Hardy's manuscripts should form the copy-texts for critical editions of his fiction. The bulk of the material in the essay came from only two novels, *Under the Greenwood Tree* and *Tess of the d'Urbervilles*, and recently Robert Schweik and Michael Piret, in an essay entitled 'Editing Hardy', the relevant part of which has been reprinted in Schweik's Norton edition of *Far from the Madding Crowd*, have suggested that, as far as *Far from the Madding Crowd* is concerned, the manuscript punctuation is so haphazard and incomplete that it cannot adequately form the basis for a critical text.[2]

In response to their argument I should like first of all to reaffirm the value of Hardy's manuscript punctuation. Consider this short speech taken from the manuscript of *A Pair of Blue Eyes*:

'Yes—indeed you are!'

There is nothing particularly remarkable about it taken thus out of context, but I want to consider it in comparison with the version of the same speech found in the novel's serialization in *Tinsley's Magazine*:

---

[2] Gatrell, 'Hardy, House-Style, and the Aesthetics of Punctuation' in *The Novels of Thomas Hardy*, ed. Anne Smith (London: Vision, 1979), 169–92; Schweik and Piret, 'Editing Hardy' *Browning Institute Studies*, 9 (1981), 15–41. See also the Clarendon edition of *Tess of the d'Urbervilles* (Oxford: 1983), 88–99.

'Yes, indeed, you are!'[3]

Though exactly the same words are used, the speeches are quite different: from the manuscript version the reader learns precisely how the words were spoken—emphasis on 'Yes', a longish pause after it, and another slightly lesser stress on the second syllable of 'indeed'. From the serial version the reader learns nothing helpful about how the words were spoken; the two commas divide the sentence so impartially that almost any pattern of stresses would be possible.

Here is another example from the manuscript of *Two on a Tower*:

'Well Hezekiah, & Samuel! And Nat, how are you?'

When the speech was printed in *The Atlantic Monthly* it ran:

'Well, Hezekiah, and Samuel, and Nat, how are you?'[4]

The vivid sense that the reader of the manuscript has of the way in which Swithin greets the first two men, and then notices the third and addresses a different remark to him, all the liveliness of the moment, is quite lost in the monotone conflation of the serial.

In the first edition of *Under the Greenwood Tree* Fancy Day says in response to a more or less innocent remark of Dick Dewy:

'Now, Mr. Dewy, no flirtation, because it's wrong, and I don't wish it.'

All those commas again give the reader no help at all in recreating the cadences of Fancy's speech. What she said in the manuscript was:

'Now Mr Dewy—no flirtation, because it's wrong and I don't wish it.'[5]

The rhythm of her voice in speaking is at once apparent.

The most satisfactory way of explaining these differences between Hardy's manuscripts and what the compositors thought he should have written is to say that Hardy put on the page as close a representation as he could of the voice he heard in his imagination, while the compositors set what convention suggested the reading eye would most readily accept.

It is also the case that in narrative Hardy's manuscript punctuation often has a meaning that is obscured by compositorial changes. In *Tess of the d'Urbervilles*, for example, as Tess is returning from her unprofitable journey to Emminster, in the manuscript

---

[3] World's Classics edition, p. 58.
[4] Wessex edition, p. 98..
[5] World's Classics edition, p. 118.

she began to grow tired; and she leant upon gates, and paused by milestones.

Her weariness is much more effectively caught by what Hardy wrote than by the version that appeared in the *Graphic*:

she began to grow tired, and she leant upon gates and paused by milestones.[6]

In fact, in thousands of instances in every novel for which most of the printer's manuscript survives, Hardy's punctuation and paragraphing was ignored by the compositors who first set his work in type; and though I have, naturally, chosen examples in which the destructive effect of compositorial interference is clear, there are hundreds of others in the novels that could have replaced them just as effectively. Here I should like briefly to consider the situation in *Far from the Madding Crowd*.

Schweik and Piret, in commenting adversely on the adequacy of Hardy's manuscript punctuation in the novel, have presented examples that are completely convincing in themselves. They have, however, also chosen the illustrations that most thoroughly support their argument, and another view is possible using other evidence.

There are a couple of places in the first four leaves that show quite vividly the effect of the compositorial addition of commas required by convention, but not by rhythm or sense. One is in a simple sentence:

In short he was twenty-eight and a bachelor. (p.8)

In the *Cornhill* serialization it becomes:

In short, he was twenty-eight, and a bachelor. (p.8)[7]

It is not that Hardy's is particularly preferable to the compositor Dutton's punctuation—indeed, a good argument could be made for a sole comma after 'twenty-eight'—but that the particular pace of the sentence in the manuscript is characteristic of Hardy as a writer.

The second is a little more complex:

Mr Oak carried about with him by way of a watch what may be called a small silver clock: in other words it was a watch as to shape and intention, and a small clock as to size.

This is how it was in the manuscript, and the compositor Granger altered it to:

---

6 Clarendon edition, p. 413.

7 Page references to *Far from the Madding Crowd* are to the Norton Critical edition, ed. Robert Schweik (New York, 1986).

Mr. Oak carried about with him, by way of watch, what may be called a small silver clock; in other words, it was a watch as to shape and intention, and a small clock as to size. (p. 7)

It is a fundamental characteristic of Hardy's punctuation that it is lighter than any later Victorian compositor would be prepared to accept (though, as will be seen later, some were more prepared to accept it than others), and this is a representative example of how one of them copes. The added commas are all unnecessary, and they alter the tone and rhythm of the sentence. It is also common to find places where Hardy is not permitted to use a colon in such a context, though it is a mark he employs quite often in his manuscripts.

Hardy's lightly punctuated sentences can lead to a stretching of the reader's attention beyond his expectations, but I would argue that to encounter even such an extreme example as the following is not unacceptable, especially when the eye is attuned to Hardy's idiosyncracies: 'Bathsheba having previously been living in a state of suspended feeling which was not suspense now lived in a mood of quietude which was not precisely peacefulness.' And in the same paragraph there is the sentence: 'She looked back upon that past over a great gulf, as if she were now a dead person having the faculty of meditation still left her by means of which, like the mouldering gentlefolk of the poet's story, she could sit and ponder what a gift life used to be' (p. 253). This is what has to be accepted if Hardy's punctuation is accepted. For comparison it should be noted that Longman added commas to the first sentence after 'Bathsheba' and 'suspense' and to the second after 'person' and 'her'.

There were something in the region of two thousand commas added in the *Cornhill* to Hardy's manuscript text, and there are many repetitive situations in which for the most part Hardy has no comma and the compositors add one—situations such as 'said Gabriel, indignantly' or 'Now, listen', or 'Thank you, Joseph'. It is, however, quite easy to find places where Hardy does have a comma in such positions; and occasionally there are places where the compositor removes one of Hardy's commas—it is evident that neither Hardy nor the compositors were consistent in such situations. The point made here is not that Hardy's usage is superior to that of the compositors (though in many cases it may be thought to be so), but that it is different, it is acceptable, and it is Hardy's.

There are, in fact, plenty of occasions on which it does seem possible to claim that the compositor in adding his own particular variety of conventional punctuation has obscured something valuable in what Hardy wrote. Most often (as with all his manuscripts) this happens in speech. When Bathsheba is led to confide in Gabriel her troubles about Boldwood's renewed courtship after Troy's disappearance, he says of Boldwood: 'He'll never forget you, ma'am; never' (p. 271). The pause represented by the semicolon gives an emphasis to the last word that seems required by the context, but Longman replaced it with a comma.

Earlier in the novel, during Oak and Jan Coggan's pursuit of Bathsheba towards Bath, Gabriel in the manuscript said:

"Very well, we are better mounted and must overtake 'em".

Longman ignored the excitement of the situation, and slowed down the pace of Gabriel's exhortation with formally balanced punctuation.

"Very well; we are better mounted, and must overtake 'em". (p. 164)

After they had discovered that it was Bathsheba they were following, Hardy wrote:

"A strange vagary this of hers, isn't it Oak?" said Coggan.

which Scotter altered to:

"A strange vagary, this of hers, isn't it, Oak?" said Coggan. (p. 167)

Doubtless, the *Cornhill* version is pointed according to convention, but in the fragmentation into four breath-groups Hardy's sense of how the words were actually spoken to Gabriel has been lost. In both of these cases Hardy has represented the speeches as he heard them in his imagination, and the effects have disappeared in the *Cornhill* conventionalizations.

A final example shows the compositor—Simpson in this case—speeding up something Hardy had indicated was to be spoken deliberately or hesitatingly. Bathsheba meets Gabriel during a night-time tour to check her farm, and replies to his concern for her safety:

"Thank you indeed. But I am not very fearful."

The manuscript reads thus, but it was changed in the serial to:

"Thank you, indeed, but I am not very fearful." (p. 148)

In part, this alteration must have been made because Simpson's conscience or his house rules would not allow him to begin a sentence with 'but'; however, the running together of the two sentences makes it appear as if Bathsheba had the reply ready on her tongue, something Hardy certainly did not intend.

It would be possible to offer further examples taking in every mark of punctuation, but I believe that this brief sample makes good the initial case, that Hardy's often sensitive punctuation was distorted by the work of the compositors who first set the manuscript. The second stage is to suggest that these compositors were guided not only by an authoritative uniform system of pointing, but also consulted their own preferences in altering Hardy's punctuation.

In 'Hardy, House-Style and the Aesthetics of Punctuation' I demonstrated, through a statistical analysis of the work of individual compositors of *Under the Greenwood Tree* and *Tess of the d'Urbervilles*, that though the printing house may have instructed them in the use of a house style of punctuation, they acted far from uniformly in its application. Some compositors were considerably more receptive of Hardy's punctuation than others, and most had some individual quirk, in altering Hardy's punctuation, followed by none of the others. It is possible to show the same is true of some of the compositors who set *Far from the Madding Crowd* for its serialization in the *Cornhill*.

In all, twenty-seven compositors worked on the manuscript, and I have chosen to look at the five who set the most text—about 40 per cent of the whole. As with the other two novels the addition of commas accounts for over half of all the differences noted between the manuscript and *Cornhill*. In this sample there were 795 added commas, which amounts to between twelve and thirteen extra commas in every hundred lines of Wessex text (in order to make it possible to compare results from novel to novel it seemed best to use the Wessex edition as a basis of comparison). If house style were a rigorously applied strait-jacket on the compositor one would expect to find that each man conformed reasonably closely to this proportion—allowing for variation in the nature of the text he set. The contrary, however, is the case. While Scotter added sixteen commas per hundred lines, Simpson added only eight, Ellis ten, Longman twelve, and Dutton fourteen.

It is also worth noting a few individual idiosyncracies. Scotter was the only compositor to replace Hardy's colon with a dash, while Dutton was the only one never to replace a colon with a semicolon (something the others did quite frequently). Simpson added significantly more semicolons to the text (significantly, that is, in statistical terms), and Dutton removed significantly more of Hardy's commas and dashes than any other compositor. These results are the most striking, but the body of the statistical analysis all tends to the same conclusion: that it is not one of the advantages of the punctuation of the printed versions of Hardy's novels that it is uniform and consistent, but rather that it is subject to the whim of compositors who have no creative responsibility for the state of the text.

The decision of an editor of *Far from the Madding Crowd* who chooses to ignore the available manuscript punctuation in favour of the overlay of heavier pointing from the printing house has strong arguments to support it. It is certainly the case that Hardy showed less care with this manuscript than with almost any other: it is reasonably common to find throughout Hardy's prose manuscripts stretches of speech without quotation marks, with no full stops at the end of sentences, and the occasional passage that is so lightly punctuated that the sense is not immediately clear, but the situation is at its worst in parts of *Far from the Madding Crowd*. Schweik has suggested that there are fifty or so places where ambiguity is caused by the omission of necessary punctuation and, though no two readers would agree about every instance, such an estimate is not excessive. He has drawn attention to places where Hardy omitted essential question marks, and again there is no doubt that this happens more frequently than is consistent with care for the whole structure of the pointing. The proportion of speech without quotation marks is extremely high. All this is evidence of carelessness, of reliance upon the printer for setting him right, and of awareness that there would be proofs that might be corrected. It is also true, as Schweik has pointed out, that Hardy is inconsistent in his punctuation of apparently identical constructions, but this lack of uniformity is less significant as evidence of carelessness, in that where alternative methods of pointing are acceptable no writer has an obligation to stick to one. The compositors do not bring consistency to such situations either. Nevertheless, there is no doubt that Hardy was in this novel copying under greater time-pressure than usual, and left more necessary punctuation to be supplied by compositors than elsewhere in his fiction.

To add weight to the argument against the manuscript punctuation, there is the evidence that Hardy revised the pointing of his novels for the Wessex edition. It is possible with justification to argue that the alteration of over four hundred marks in *The Woodlanders* for the edition of 1912, repeated on a similar though somewhat diminished scale in other texts, indicates a level of attention which, combined with the relative inattention demonstrated in the manuscript, makes the Wessex edition a preferable choice as copy-text for a critical edition of *Far from the Madding Crowd*.

On the other hand, it is also possible to argue that, as far as the revisions for the Wessex edition are concerned, Hardy was altering texts full of corrupt non-authorial punctuation; that since the overwhelming majority of the revisions at this time were the removal of commas, Hardy was concerned in 1912 with only one feature of the pointing and not with the whole fabric, and further that such changes in any case returned the text towards the manuscript.

And as for the manuscript, the examples furnished on the previous pages lend support to the view that, despite the noted lapses, Hardy's punctuation is on the whole coherent, distinctive, and substantially different from what it became in *Cornhill*. And above all, of course, it is his own.

An editor might, then, want to argue that the best choice of copy-text would be the manuscript emended where essential from the serialization; this would put a pressure on him to scrutinize every mark, and to make a decision several thousand times, and to justify those decisions where necessary. What Hardy intended is unknowable, though he cannot have intended his manuscript to be printed exactly as it stood. Perhaps he thought of it rather as he did the manuscript of *Two on a Tower* that he sent to the editor of the *Atlantic Monthly* in America with his licence to correct obvious errors. Such a procedure by a latter-day editor with regard to the punctuation and paragraphing of *Far from the Madding Crowd* would be defensible, and would have the virtue of preserving as much as possible of what Hardy initially wrote.

The evidence here presented can be applied with greater force to the other of Hardy's novels for which a more or less complete manuscript survives. A separate question, though, arises with those manuscripts which have had random pages removed by Hardy. Here it may be suggested that a similar procedure should be adopted, and that the first setting from the manuscript should be followed as being the nearest to what Hardy wrote. There is, though, an additional possibility that might be pursued by an editor thoroughly familiar with Hardy's manuscript practice; he might use his knowledge and judgement to emend such of the printed punctuation as offends against demonstrable preferences elsewhere in Hardy. This procedure would undoubtedly remove some compositorial punctuation, but the very inconsistency of Hardy's practice in some commonly occurring situations should limit the editor's options.

Where no manuscript survives, or only a fragmentary one, the problem of copy-text becomes more difficult, and the revisions that Hardy made for the Wessex edition assume a larger significance—indeed they may well be held to push the balance in favour of choosing that edition as copy-text. It would, however, be perfectly respectable to choose the earliest printed version, since in some resettings of some novels there is evidence of considerable compositorial inattention, especially by Ballantyne's men in setting for the Osgood, McIlvaine edition, and the choice of the serial will at least eliminate such disturbance.

The whole of the preceding argument has been directed towards establishing the value and adequacy of Hardy's manuscript punctuation, and arguing for its retention in a critical text of those of his novels and stories for which it is available. It is possible, however, to argue against the retention of Hardy's manuscript punctuation on quite different grounds than inadequacy. The argument would run something like this. Hardy's novel only existed as a work when the first printed copies were in the hands of the first readers; before that act of publication it was a private and tentative thing, only given, as it were, posthumous authority by the publication of a version of it. It is the interaction of writer, printer, publisher, and reader that makes a work, not the author alone. Hence an edition of the work should not go back to a time before the work existed, back to the manuscript or to the pre-publication proof-sheets, for any aspect of its identity. Though I respect the argument shadowed by this brief summary, its acceptance seems to me a matter of ideology that I cannot share.

Substantives

A corollary of this argument would be further to stress the historical importance of the first and subsequent versions of the published text—to say that, taking *Under the Greenwood Tree* as an example, it is important to know what was read and responded to in 1872, what was read and responded to in 1896, and what was read and responded to in 1912, and to recognize that each version of the novel offers a different face to a changed world. As a consequence it can then be argued that the concept of author's final intention should be modified by the addition of 'at any particular time', and a case made on such grounds for producing a critical text that represents the first edition of a novel purged of error in so far as it can be identified.

On the other hand, it has generally been accepted that an eclectic critical edition of Hardy should include his latest revisions, in particular those made in the revised collected editions of 1895–6 and 1912–13 (though the case has also been made—by myself amongst others—for the inclusion of those last handwritten alterations Hardy made in his study-copies of the 1912–13 edition). This position is readily defensible, but it seems more and more clear that it is not the only defensible position available to the editor of Hardy.

The discussion in Chapter 7 of the effect of several kinds of revision on the texts of Hardy's novels and stories offers the most substantial argument against the incorporation of those revisions in a critical text. The Greg–Bowers–Tanselle editing theory allows that when revision is such that it makes the work a different work then the editor may chose to edit either work. This is fine, but the theory can offer no help in defining what makes a revised work a different work.

It would seem, on the one hand, possible to argue that one revision makes a different work, and, on the other hand, to say that not until there is evidence that the whole fabric of the work has been rethought and revised does it become a different work. The former position would seem in practical terms ridiculous when applied to a work the length of a Hardy novel, until the effect is measured of changing, for instance, the last word of D.H. Lawrence's *Sons and Lovers* from 'quickly' to, say, 'hesitantly'. It may be that in reading the hypothetical new version, our apprehension of the present and future state of the central character, Paul Morel, as the novel ends, would amount to no more than uncertainty, through the reception of conflicting signals from the text. Yet we would be left with 'hesitantly' and the final impression of the novel—so positive as it stands—would be quite different.

There is material in the history of Hardy's works to provide an illustration of an author at work on the whole of his text. It can be argued that the revisions made after 1895 to the texts of some and perhaps most of his novels and stories show sufficient signs of overall rethinking to constitute, by the most rigorous tests, different works. It was only in 1895–6, after gradually developing within himself the concept of Wessex, that Hardy was able fully to see his separate novels and stories as part of a whole single work, a single enterprise, and to revise them accordingly. Thus, an editor might well be held free to edit the earlier work rather than the later. However, the argument is not equally applicable to all novels and stories. In particular, if the account I have given of the development of Wessex as a concept in Hardy's work is satisfactory, then the different-work argument is weak for *Tess of the d'Urbervilles*, and is invalid for the two novels published after it, *Jude the Obscure* and *The Well-Beloved*. It is also hard to make a case for novels such as *A*

Laodicean which are only tenuously caught into the web of Wessex.

One reason why an editor might wish to edit the earlier rather than the later work, supposing the distinction to have been established, would be that, for instance, to call *Under the Greenwood Tree* a novel of 1872, as most critics do, ought to mean amongst other things that the text embodies Hardy's intentions for his novel at that date—something that the 1912 version of the novel in some ways emphatically does not, since it has shed a number of the characteristics of 1872 and been wrapped in others of forty years later. The landscape in which it was set in 1872 was vaguely representative of the observable reality: now it is as sharply focused as a photographic print of the area. The rather self-conscious language in which some of it was couched has been modified. Hardy has allowed himself expressions that it would not have occurred to him to use in 1872, and he has added phrases to the novel that express his mature sensibility. He has prefaced the text with a discussion of matters that he could not have conceived of discussing in 1872.

In some ways, though, *Under the Greenwood Tree* is a special case, in that Hardy did not revise the novel between the first edition and the Osgood collected edition in 1896. Most of his other novels were so revised, and the question of what an editor rejecting the revisions for the collected editions should do with these changes is a separate issue. Certainly, for none of the novels is it possible to make a convincing case that these intermediate changes have made the novel a different work on the same scale as those he made for the collected editions. For the most part, as I have suggested in Chapter 6, they are excisions of material Hardy must have thought of as redundant, and the motivation may well have been his sense that the requirements of serialization had led him into overwriting—as they undoubtedly did with *The Mayor of Casterbridge*.

The editor wondering whether to exclude Hardy's later revisions has also to take into account the powerful fact of Wessex, and in particular the relationship between generations of readers and that idealized concept known as 'Hardy' who is the embodiment of Wessex. The idea of Wessex that Hardy had evolved by 1895 and refined in 1912 has tremendous strength: it colours every critical response, published or not, to his writing, it is a context the absence of which is likely to leave the reader accustomed to it quite disorientated. Hardy decided, for better or for worse, that he wanted to see his early novels by the light of his later creation. He must have been aware of the degree to which he was altering aspects of his work that had seemed important to him at the time it was written; but the new, the almost overwhelming, sense of himself as recorder of Wessex was more powerful. The question then becomes whether an editor should allow a middle-aged author to have his own way with his early texts. The editor must be powerfully convinced of the rightness of his course who will overturn custom and thwart the readers' expectations by presenting them with a critical text incorporating the substantives only from the first edition or the first one-volume edition.

An editor deciding for an eclectic text would also have to consider the question of stranded variants, variants that for one reason or another did not find their way into the sequence of transmission of the text, but which may be thought to have value as representing Hardy's intention at a particular stage. I have discussed such variants in the manuscript of *Two on a Tower*, the American serialization of *A Group of Noble Dames*, and the paperback editions of *Far from the Madding Crowd* and *Tess of the d'Urbervilles*, and it is clear that each situation is different, and no valid generalization can be made about a procedure to follow. What can be said, though, is that unless there is strong evidence to the contrary, it is statistically probable that any given instance of the stranded readings would not have been revised further by Hardy. As always, the editor will come to a decision after considering all the evidence for each particular novel; but I would hope that the intrinsic value of the variants under examination would be taken substantially into account.

The ideal situation would be to have available two scholarly texts of *Under the Greenwood Tree*, or *Far from the Madding Crowd*, or *The Return of the Native*, one based on the first-edition substantives, the other on the Wessex edition. But the economics of publication make this an improbability, and if I were driven from the comfortable fence, I would have to say that I would bow to the pressure of Wessex; but that I would do so reluctantly and casting rueful glances over my shoulder at the youthful thing I left behind on the other side. I would do so because what is implied in Wessex is the whole relationship between man and his environment that is at the heart of Hardy's writing, and it is ultimately impossible not to acknowledge its authority.

12

Conclusion

After all this analysis, all these examples what synthesis can ultimately be made? Perhaps a brief summary is first in order. For Hardy the manuscript that went to the printer was always still a working document, never a final copy. Though some are cleaner than others, there is often the sense on examining one of the manuscripts that it was unwillingly released—not exactly ripped untimely from the womb, but sent into the world without those endless final reviews that would for ever refine and eliminate; that it is work still in a state of becoming. It feels as if only economic necessity and the publisher's deadline halted Hardy's revising ear, eye, and hand.

Proof for the serial fixed the text to a degree, but Hardy came early in his career to recognize that he could never think of a serialized novel as a finished thing, and it is for most novels the first book-edition that is the earliest version to give the impression of a work completed. Though a combination of factors lead to the conclusion that for *Tess of the d'Urbervilles* it was not until the cheap one-volume edition that Hardy drew some kind of a mental line under the development of the novel, in the cheap editions of his other novels Hardy rarely gave consistent thought to their larger issues.

This might have been the pattern for Hardy's relationship with his novels throughout the remainder of his lifetime, were it not that the influence of Wessex became powerful over him. Then he became restless again for change, not change to the plot or characterization, but to the fabric of life out of which these elements in his novels grew. The first collected edition of his work gave him the opportunity to revise the fourteen novels and three volumes of stories as if they were each fragments of a whole, and he took it eagerly. He maintained and even increased his interest in the unification of his work through a common background-texture into the second collected edition, and though some novels proved resistant to the process, Wessex as we read of it now is a vital force structuring our response to all of Hardy's fiction.

It is perhaps simplistic to imagine that there is one convincing reason for Hardy's perennial concern for what he had created forty or fifty years earlier, but a reading of the first two volumes of his collected letters does offer some suggestive material for the imagination to work upon.

It is probably true of most novelists that what they ultimately publish bears only a moderate resemblance to the image, trailing clouds of glory, that they had of each work in its infancy. There can, though, have been few writers who were so haunted by these successive images as Hardy. He wrote to Coventry Patmore, who had praised his novels: 'It is what I might have deserved if my novels had been exact transcripts of their original irradiated conception, before any attempt at working out that glorious dream had been made—& the impossibility of getting on paper had been brought home to me' (*Letters* i. 157). And there are similar passages in letters referring to all his novels from *Two on a Tower* onwards, of which this, concerning *Jude the Obscure*, may be taken as representative: 'You have hardly an idea how poor & feeble the book seems to me, as executed, beside the idea of it that I had formed in prospect' (*Letters* ii. 93).

This platonic idea might have had the power to drive Hardy to the effort of revision that accompanied each fresh setting of each of his novels—revision made not in the hope of achieving the ideal form, for he knew that to be unattainable, but in the hope of reaching the best possible human approximation to the ideal. Not something perfect, but something finally satisfying. I imagine Hardy remained always unsatisfied; but for him in many fields the journey was the thing, not the arriving.[1]

In what seems to me an important essay on *The Well-Beloved*, 'Hardy and the Hag', John Fowles has an insight about the nature of fictional creation that might indicate a slightly different account of Hardy's drive

---

[1] This may well be thought a characteristic romantic and post-romantic view of the nature of inspiration and the creative process. Shelley in his 'A Defence of Poetry' wrote: 'When composition begins, inspiration is already on the decline, and the most glorious poetry that has ever been communicated to the world is probably a feeble shadow of the original conception of the Poet.' Henry James, in his New York edition preface to *The Spoils of Poynton*, expresses a similar, though characteristically much less personal and direct, account of this problem for the author. He too generalizes, suggesting that for all artists the completed work is 'ever the sum, for the most part, of so many lapses and compromises, simplifications and surrenders. Which is the work in which he hasn't surrendered, under dire difficulty, the best thing he meant to have kept? In which, indeed, before the dreadful *done*, doesn't he ask himself what has become of the thing all for the sweet sake of which it was to proceed to that extremity?' (World's Classics edition, ed. Bernard Richards (Oxford: Oxford University Press, 1982), p. xlv). The truth still remains, however, that the sequel to such laments at the loss of the primary vision has only rarely been so remarkable a sequence of revisions as Hardy's. James's own New York edition is a celebrated Edwardian example of an author reworking his texts, in some cases many years after their original publication—and a comparison with Hardy's Wessex edition would prove instructive, though beyond the scope of this book.

to revision.[2] Fowles suggests that 'beyond the specific myth of each novel, the novelist longs to be possessed by the continuous underlying myth he entertains of himself' and that this possession is: 'a state that withdraws as the text nears consummation; and its disappearance, however pleased one is with the final cast, is always deeply distressing . . . one other sense of loss, or reluctant return to normality, that every novelist-child has to contend with.' In applying this thought to Hardy's perpetual revision it could be argued that until the first book-edition of a novel was published, Hardy kept the text's initial consummation at bay—with *Tess of the d'Urbervilles* even longer—and that the growth of the matter of Wessex was an attempt to reopen the stories, to provide them with another, recreative myth, the consummation of which could be hindered until he was near his death.

It seems in any case certain that for Hardy the impulse to assure himself that his tales were never finally complete was a deep-seated psychological need, only partially diminished by his growing commitment to poetry.

There remains one final question that is worth trying to answer in the context of this kind of study: Why did Hardy give up writing novels? First of all I do not think it was a conscious decision taken at any moment; he published a couple of stories in 1900, and seemed not to reject out of hand the possibility of a novel in the future. It must have been rather like his loss of faith in the doctrine of Christianity in the 1860s, a gradual process of growing awareness of the impossibility of believing any longer, or of writing another novel. There are several perceptions that would have contributed to that growing awareness. His letters and notebook-entries show that he found the criticism of his last three novels more and more damaging to his sensibilities, more and more couched in the form of personal attacks. The poems that he wrote in the early nineties would have suggested to him that he could say what he now wanted to say more clearly and less controversially in poetry, where his ideas and observations did not have to become entangled with the demands of plot-invention, or with the need for verisimilitude of character and action. The financial success of *Tess of the d'Urbervilles* and the collected edition provided security for at least a limited experiment in commitment to verse.

Hardy must also have been aware that the gap between concept and achievement which had concerned him increasingly in his fiction from 1881 onwards could be made much narrower in poetry; he understood

---

[2] The essay is in *Thomas Hardy After Fifty Years*, ed. Lance St John Butler (London: Macmillan, 1978), 28–42.

that poetry's conventions, its compression and variety, would allow the precise embodiment of his vision, distorted only by the limits of his talent and the inevitable imprecision of language. He was not anxious or able to experiment with the form of the novel any further than he did in *The Well-Beloved* in order to shape a suitable vehicle for his imaginative insights.

Gradually, as his early volumes of poetry were admired by those whose opinion he respected, as he began work on *The Dynasts*, fresh creation in prose must have seemed a more and more remote possibility. Eventually he began to resent those who still thought of him as primarily a novelist.

And yet, as we have seen, the pressure to improve the detail and fabric of his novels and stories never slackened. He was truly, to adapt a line from one of his most famous poems, a man who used to care for such things.

Appendix I

A Chronology of the Writing of Hardy's Fictional Prose

1865	March	'How I Built Myself a House' published in *Chamber's Journal*.
1867	August	Hardy began writing *The Poor Man and the Lady* (*PML*) at Bockhampton.
1868	July	The MS of *PML* sent to Macmillan. Read by John Morley and Alexander Macmillan.
	December	*PML* sent to Chapman and Hall.
1869	March	George Meredith, as reader for Chapman and Hall, advised Hardy to withdraw the novel and write a different one.
	April	*PML* offered to Smith, Elder, and rejected.
	June	*PML* offered to Tinsley, who also rejected it.
	September?	*Desperate Remedies* (*DR*) begun at Weymouth.
1870	March	The MS of *DR* sent to Macmillan.
		[Hardy went to St Juliot for the first time, meeting there Emma Lavinia Gifford, who would become his first wife.]
	April	Tinsley received *DR*.
	May	Tinsley agreed to publish *DR* on advance of £75.
	Autumn	Hardy made revisions to *DR*—fair copy made by E.L. Gifford.
	December	Resubmission of *DR* to Tinsley; acceptance confirmed 19 December.
1871	March	*DR* published anonymously in three volumes.
	Spring and Summer	Hardy was writing or completing *Under the Greenwood Tree* (*UGT*); the novel was conceived in 1868, but how much was written then is unclear.
	August	The MS of *UGT* offered to Macmillan.
	September	Macmillan responded, temporizing.
	October	*A Pair of Blue Eyes* (*POBE*) probably conceived or even begun. Hardy enquired of Tinsley about the accounts of *DR* (and again 3 January and 20 February 1872). He also mentioned working on a novel 'the essence of which is plot, *without crime*'.

1872	April	Tinsley accepted *UGT*, offering £30 for the copyright.
	June	*UGT* published.
	July	Hardy agreed to provide serial for *Tinsley's Magazine*; he was to be paid £200 for serial- and first-edition rights. This was *POBE*.
	August	Copy sent for first instalment of *POBE*, due to be published 15 August.
	November	Stephen asked for a *Cornhill* serial.
1873	March	Final chapters of *POBE* sent off.
	May	First edition of *POBE* published by Tinsley in three volumes.
		Holt produced *UGT* and *POBE* in USA.
	July	Hardy perhaps began *Far from the Madding Crowd* (*FMC*) though he had been thinking about it since before November 1872.
	September	Probably the first ten chapters of *FMC* sent to Stephen. The serialization was to begin in *Cornhill* January 1874, and Hardy was to get £400 for serial- and first-edition rights.
1874	January to April	Hardy struggling to keep ahead of the printer of *FMC*.
	February	*Spectator* review of first episode of *FMC*. *New York Times* contract for 'Destiny and a Blue Cloak'.
	July	Hardy finished writing *FMC*.
	August	Hardy corrected proofs for first edition of *FMC*.
	September	Hardy 'finishing off' 'Destiny and a Blue Cloak'. [Hardy's wedding to E.L. Gifford.]
	November	*FMC* published by Smith, Elder in 2 volumes.
	December	Hardy agreed to write a new serial to begin July 1875 in *Cornhill*.
1875	January	A rough draft of the first part of *The Hand of Ethelberta* (*HE*) sent to Stephen.
	March	Smith offered £700 for serial- and first-edition rights to *HE*.
	March	*New York Times* agreed to pay £50 per installment of *HE*, in the end paying £550 overall. [Hardy's first published poem, 'The Fire at Tranter Sweatley's', in the *Gentleman's Magazine*.]
1876	March	Hardy enquired about the possibility of Smith, Elder issuing cheap editions of *POBE* and *FMC* during the summer.

	Winter	Hardy may have begun writing *The Return of the Native* (RN). Tinsley issued illustrated one volume *UGT* (but Hardy, having sold the copyright, had no interest in it).
1877	February to July	Hardy was writing and trying to find a magazine to accept *RN*. It was turned down by *Blackwood's*, *Temple Bar*, and probably by Stephen for *Cornhill*.
	July	*Belgravia* accepted *RN* at £240 for the English serial rights; Hardy was paid £3 per page of *Harper's New Monthly Magazine* for American serial- and book-rights, a total of £472; and Smith, Elder paid £200 for the English book-rights—in all, considerably less than he was paid for *HE*.
	December	'The Thieves Who Couldn't Help Sneezing' published in *Father Christmas*.
	During the year	Hardy arranged for the publication of one-volume editions of *POBE* (Henry King), and *FMC* and *HE* (Smith, Elder). None of these editions was particularly profitable for author or publisher. He also sold the continental rights in *FMC* to Tauchnitz.
1878	March	Hardy probably finished *RN*. [The Hardys moved to London, thus ending the 'Sturminster Newton idyll', bound up with the excitement of writing *RN*.]
	April	'The Impulsive Lady of Croome Castle' published in *Light*, and in *Harper's Weekly* in America. [Hardy was intermittently working in the British Museum library, researching details for *The Trumpet-Major* (TM) for at least a year.]
	First half of year	Corrected proofs for *RN* in *Belgravia*; he corresponded with Hopkins about the illustrations for the serial.
	July	*An Indiscretion in the Life of an Heiress* published in the *New Quarterly Magazine*, and in *Harper's Weekly* in America. Hardy received £20 for the latter issue.
	September	Agreement with Smith, Elder for book-edition of *RN*: he was to receive £200, they were to print 1000 copies.
	December	*RN* published in America by Henry Holt.
1879	February	Hardy wrote to Stephen about the possibility of serializing *TM* in *Cornhill*.

	April	'The Distracted Young Preacher' published in the *New Quarterly Magazine*, and in *Harper's Weekly* in America.
	May	Hardy may have sent a portion of the manuscript [of *TM*] to Macmillan, presumably in the hope of serialization in *Macmillan's Magazine*.
	June	Hardy wrote to Blackwood about *TM*, and to Macleod, the editor of *Good Words*, where the novel was eventually serialized.
	September	Hardy was about half-way through the final draft of *TM*.
	December	Kegan Paul agreed to publish one-volume edition of *RN*.
1880	January	*TM* began its serialization in *Good Words*.
	April	'Fellow Townsmen' published in the *New Quarterly Magazine*, and in *Harper's Weekly* in America. For the latter issue Hardy received £40.
	April	Hardy agreed to provide a serial for the new European edition of *Harper's Monthly Magazine*, if they would pay him £100 an episode (which they did, totalling £1300).
	July	Smith, Elder agreed to publish first edition of *TM*, Hardy to receive £200 for an edition of 1000 copies.
	August	Hardy sent the manuscript of the first episode of *A Laodicean* (*L*) to R.R. Bowker, Harper's agent in London, though, since the illustrations of the first two serial episodes were finished in July, the writing must have been fairly well advanced by then.
	September	Revised copy for first edition of *TM* sent to Smith, Elder. Manuscript of second and third parts of *L* sent to Bowker.
	October	[Hardy fell seriously ill.]
	November	Part four of *L* sent to Bowker.
	December	*Harper's* began serializing *L*.
1881	January	Parts five to eight of *L* sent to Bowker.
	September	A serial novel requested of Hardy by the editor of the *Atlantic Monthly*, to which he agreed.
	December	'Benighted Travellers' published through the syndicated fiction bureau of Tillotson and Son in the *Bolton Weekly Journal* (at the rate of £7 per 2000 words), and also in (as usual) *Harper's Weekly* in America.
		First edition of *L* published by Sampson, Low.

1882	January	Tauchnitz enquired about publication of *L*; eventually paid Hardy £60 for the European rights.
	February	The first part of *Two on a Tower* (*TT*) sent to America for the *Atlantic*.
	May	First episode of *TT* published in the *Atlantic*.
	July	Hardy finished 'A Legend of the Year Eighteen Hundred and Four'.
	September	Hardy sent last part of *TT* to America.
	October	First edition of *TT* published by Sampson, Low, who were also gradually acquiring the one-volume rights to most of Hardy's novels.
	November	'A Legend of the Year Eighteen Hundred and Four' published in *Harper's Christmas*. Hardy got £20 for it.
	December	*TT* ended its run in the *Atlantic*.
1883	January	Probably the second impression (slightly revised) of the first edition of *TT* issued (see Purdy pp. 45–6). It is also probable that the Tauchnitz European edition of *TT* was published early in the year with the text of the second impression of the first edition, though since I have not seen a copy I cannot be sure.
	March	'The Three Strangers' published in *Longman's Magazine* and in *Harper's Weekly*. Harper paid Hardy just over £20.
	April	One-volume edition (revised) of *TT* published.
	June	'The Romantic Adventures of a Milkmaid' published in the *Graphic* and (June–August) in *Harper's Weekly*. Harper paid Hardy £100. Published in volume form in America in June, but never published separately in Britain.
		[The Hardys moved to Dorchester, to live there for the rest of their lives.]
	July	'The Dorsetshire Labourer' published in *Longman's Magazine*.
	November	Hardy sent the manuscript of *Our Exploits at West Poley* to the editor of *Youth's Companion* in Boston, though its appearance in print (in a different magazine) was delayed until 1892–3 (q.v.).
1884	February	The second incarnation of 'The Impulsive Lady of Croome Castle' appeared in the New York *Independent* as 'Emmeline, or Passion versus Principle'.
	May	'Interlopers at the Knap' published in the *English Illustrated Magazine*.
	Spring	Purdy (p. 53) suggests that Hardy may have begun

work on *The Mayor of Casterbridge* (*MC*) at this time, though there is no evidence for this other than the apparent lack of any other writing on hand (unless his reading of back numbers of the *Dorset County Chronicle* begun in March can be taken as evidence).

October   Ward and Downey asked if they might publish an edition of *Desperate Remedies*. Hardy turned them down.

1885   March   'Ancient Earthworks and What Two Enthusiastic Scientists found Therein' published in the *Detroit Post* (see below, 1893).

April   *MC* manuscript completed.

June   [The Hardys moved to Max Gate, the house just outside Dorchester, designed by Hardy and built by his brother Henry, that became his permanent home. It soon became Hardy's standard practice to spend the winters there writing, and to visit London for parts of the spring and summer.]

October   'A Mere Interlude' published in the *Bolton Weekly Journal*.

November   First evidence of work on the manuscript of *The Woodlanders* (*W*).

1886   January to May   *MC* serialized in the *Graphic* and *Harper's Weekly*. I do not know how much the *Graphic* paid Hardy; Harper's, at the rate of £2 per 1000 words, paid him £239. 8*s*. 10*d*.

May to April
   1887   *W* serialized in *Macmillan's Magazine* and *Harper's Bazar*. Hardy was paid £600 by Macmillan and £272 by Harper.

May   First edition of *MC* published by Smith, Elder in two volumes, and by Henry Holt in America.

June   Macmillan gained permission to publish a Colonial edition of *MC*, the first of Hardy's novels to be issued in this form.

1887   February   The manuscript of *W* finished, only two months before the final episode appeared in the magazine.

March   First edition of *W* published by Macmillan in three volumes, in an edition of 1000, the first for which Hardy received a royalty (7*s*. a copy) rather than a cash payment. It was also published by Harper in America. Tillotson offered Hardy 1000 gns. for a serial novel.

June   Hardy accepted Tillotson's offer, the first part of the manuscript to be delivered in June 1889.

September	First one-volume edition (revised) of *W* published by Macmillan (at a royalty of one-sixth of the published price).
October	'Alicia's Diary' published in the *Manchester Weekly Times*. At some time during this year Sampson, Low issued the first one-volume edition (revised) of *MC*.
November	Locker solicited a serial for the *Graphic*; Hardy refused, pleading work on hand.
December to January 1888	'The Waiting Supper' published in America in *Harper's Weekly*, and in January and February 1888 in *Murray's Magazine* in Britain. Harper's paid Hardy £50.

1888	January	'The Withered Arm' published in *Blackwood's Edinburgh Magazine*. Hardy received £24.
	February	Locker renewed his request for a serial for the *Graphic*; Hardy still had too much work.
	March	'The Profitable Reading of Fiction' published in *Forum*. Hardy was paid 40 gns.
	May	*Wessex Tales* (*WT*), Hardy's first collection of stories, published by Macmillan in two volumes, and by Harper in America. It included 'The Three Strangers', 'The Withered Arm', 'Fellow-Townsmen', 'Interlopers at the Knap', and 'The Distracted Preacher'. Hardy received as British royalty one-sixth of the published price, and £50 for a Colonial edition. The edition was of 750 copies, of which more than 100 were remaindered.
	July	Hardy began working on 'A Melancholy Hussar', but soon switched to 'A Tragedy of Two Ambitions'.
	September	Hardy at work on 'The First Countess of Wessex'. The first signs of work on the Tillotson novel that was to become (eventually) *Tess of the d'Urbervilles* (*TD*).
	December	'A Tragedy of Two Ambitions' published in the *Universal Review*. J.R. Osgood began negotiations with Hardy about the publication of a collected edition of his works.
1889	January	Hardy agreed to allow Ward and Downey to publish *DR* on a five-year lease for £100. He revised the novel slightly.
	February	First one-volume edition of *WT* published by Macmillan. Locker of the *Graphic* asked for a long story.
	March	Hardy offered Locker a Christmas story of the same

	length as 'The Romantic Adventures of a Milkmaid', to be written some time in 1890.
April	Hardy asked £125 for the Christmas story.
July	A title for the Tillotson serial sent to Bolton.
August	A different title sent to J.R. Osgood as Harper's representative, together with a brief sketch of the story. Scenes from the early part of the story outlined for Tillotson's illustrator.
September	Hardy informed Locker that he could send the Christmas story to the *Graphic* by 1 July 1890.
	About half of the new serial ('Too Late Beloved', as it was then called) sent to Tillotson.
	After reading the first sixteen chapters in proof Tillotson requested changes. Hardy declined and the contract was cancelled, though Tillotson asked for a short story instead.
October	'The Melancholy Hussar' sent to Tillotson.
	The manuscript of the rejected novel sent to the editor of *Murray's Magazine*.
November (perhaps October)	Hardy offered to substitute a serial story for the long short story that he had agreed to write for the *Graphic* (though the manuscript of 'Too Late Beloved' or *TD* was still with Arnold of *Murray's Magazine*). Arnold turned it down on 15 November.
	Hardy offered terms on 18 November to Locker of the *Graphic* for an untitled, undescribed serial to begin publication in July 1891. Terms were agreed on 21 November: £550 for British serial rights, £50 for Australian, and £20 for Indian serial rights.
	On 25 November, Morris, the editor of *Macmillan's Magazine*, sent a detailed rejection of the manuscript of *TD*, Hardy having already reached agreement with the *Graphic*.
December	Tillotson asked for a serial!
	'The First Countess of Wessex' published in *Harper's New Monthly Magazine*.
1890 January	'Candour in English Fiction' published in the *New Review*. 'The Melancholy Hussar' published in a number of English newspapers.
	'The Lady Penelope' published in *Longman's Magazine*.

		Hardy negotiated with Harper about the American magazine-rights for the two *Graphic* pieces.
February		Signed agreement with Tillotson for a 60000-word serial at some future date.
March		Hardy accepted Harper's offer of £2 per column of *Harper's Bazar* (to include book rights also) for *TD*. Eventually they paid £298.8s. for the serial alone, and a 15% royalty on the book-issue, since International Copyright legislation was passed in the United States prior to the book's appearance.
April		Agreement with Harper for the publication of 'Wessex Folk'; Hardy to receive £120 for serial use on both sides of the Atlantic.
May		The manuscript of *A Group of Noble Dames* (*GND*)—a linked story-sequence—sent to the editor of the *Graphic* for their Christmas number, nearly two months earlier than agreed.
June		The *Graphic* requested bowdlerizations of *GND*; Hardy agreed.
July		Bowdlerized stories accepted.
September		'To Please His Wife' sold to McClure's Syndicate for £50.
October		First half of the manuscript of *TD* sent to the *Graphic* on the eighth, eight days late, the remainder by the end of the month.
November		Agreed to provide story for the *Independent* at the rate of £10 per 1000 words. The story was 'The Doctor's Legend'.
December		*GND* appeared in the Christmas number of the *Graphic*; and (beginning on 29 November) in *Harper's Weekly*—in a more or less unbowdlerized form, for which Hardy was paid £74. Hardy began to receive proofs for *TD*.

1891	March	'For Conscience Sake' published in the *Fortnightly Review*. Hardy was paid £17.
		'Wessex Folk' begun in *Harper's New Monthly Magazine*, to conclude in June.
	April	'The Science of Fiction' published in the *New Review*.
	May	'The Midnight Baptism' (a fragment of the original *TD*) published in the *Fortnightly Review*.
		First edition of *GND* published by Osgood, McIlvaine in one volume. The collection included the original six *Graphic* stories restored almost entirely to their original

form: 'Barbara of the House of Grebe', 'The
Marchioness of Stonehenge', 'Lady Mottisfont', 'The
Lady Icenway', 'Squire Petrick's Lady', and 'Anna,
Lady Baxby'. To these were added 'The First Countess
of Wessex', 'The Lady Penelope', 'The Duchess of
Hamptonshire' (originally 'Emmeline, or Passion
versus Principle'), and 'The Honourable Laura'
(originally 'Benighted Travellers').

June   'To Please His Wife' published in *Black and White*.

July   *TD* began in the *Graphic*, and in *Harper's Bazar* in
America, to finish in December.

August   Hardy prepared for publication 'Saturday Night in
Arcady', a second fragment of the original *TD*
manuscript left out for the serialization.

September   Hardy expected to finish preparing the text of the first
edition by the first week of the month.

October   Shorter, the editor of the *Illustrated London News*, asked
for a serial story, and Hardy promised him the next one
he should write.

November   As he was reading the proofs for the first edition of
TD, Hardy decided to write a new title page for the
novel, including for the first time the contentious
subtitle 'A Pure Woman'. The three-volume first
edition was published by Osgood, McIlvaine at the end
of the month. Tauchnitz paid £100 for the European
rights.

'Saturday Night in Arcady' published in the *National
Observer*.

'On the Western Circuit' published in *Harper's
Weekly* in America, and in December in the *English
Illustrated Magazine* in Britain. The simultaneous
publication was arranged by A.P. Watt, the literary
agent.

December   Hardy at work on *The Pursuit of the Well-Beloved*
(*WB*), which was apparently promised both to Shorter
and to Tillotson—presumably to the *Illustrated London
News* in the metropolis, and to Tillotson for provincial
publication. 'The Son's Veto' published in the
Christmas number of the *Illustrated London News*.

1892   January   A revised and partially reset second impression of *TD*
called for. The writing of *WB* delayed by this
unexpected success.

TD published in America by Harper; the text taken
from a variety of sources. (It was the first of Hardy's

		novels to benefit from copyright in America.)
February	In negotiating with Harper about *WB* Hardy was already aware that the novel would have to be rewritten if it were to be published in volume form at all.
March	Hardy was supposed to send copy of *WB* to Tillotson by the end of the month, though he had asked in January for a delay of three weeks.
May	*TD* reissued in America with some, but not all, of the text of the English first edition.
June	Copy for the much-revised one-volume edition of *TD* with the printer.
September	The revised one-volume edition of *TD* published (17000 printed by the end of the year).
	Arranged with McIlvaine for the bringing together of the rights to publish his fiction into his hands as a preliminary to the issue of a collected edition.
	Hardy imaginatively at work on the story that was to become *Jude the Obscure* (*JO*).
October	*WB* began its run in the *Illustrated London News*, ending in December; it appeared in *Harper's Bazar* during the same period.
	Heinemann prepared to issue a cheap edition of *DR*.

1893	January	'The Fiddler of the Reels' completed.
	March	'Master John Horsleigh, Knight' sent to Shorter for the *Illustrated London News*.
	April	Agreement to supply through W.M. Colles, the literary agent, a 6000-word story for the *Pall Mall Gazette*, Hardy to receive £100. This would be 'An Imaginative Woman'.
	May	'The Fiddler of the Reels' published in *Scribner's Magazine*. [Hardy met Florence Henniker for the first time.]
	June	During difficult negotiations with Macmillan over his withdrawal of their right to publish *W* and *WT* Hardy discovered that there was still a debt of nearly £200 against the titles in the publisher's accounts.
		'Master John Horsleigh, Knight' published in the summer number of the *Illustrated London News*.
	July	The first suggestion of a collaboration in a story between Hardy and Florence Henniker.
	September	'An Imaginative Woman' sent to Colles.
		Hardy at work on the collaborative enterprise with Florence Henniker.

In a letter to Florence Henniker Hardy records that he has 'already jotted down a few notes for the next long story' (*JO*).

Agreement to rewrite 'Ancient Earthworks at Caster-bridge' (see under March 1885) for Shorter's *Illustrated London News*.

October — Collected stories together for *Life's Little Ironies* (*LLI*). Collaborative story 'The Spectre of the Real' all but finished.

November — Shorter (editor of the *Illustrated London News*) told that Hardy's new serial story (to be *JO*) was in chaos, but would probably run the same length as usual.

December — 'Ancient Earthworks at Casterbridge' published.

Hardy told Shorter that he had agreed to let Harper have the complete serial-rights to his next serial (*JO*).

1894 January — In a letter to Florence Henniker Hardy wrote that he was working slowly at *JO*.

Hardy agreed to a bowdlerization in 'An Imaginative Woman' as published in the *Pall Mall Magazine*, writing that he always allowed editors a free hand with serials, as he always restored the original readings in book-editions.

February — *LLI* published in one volume by Osgood, McIlvaine, and by Harper in America (where Hardy's royalties were to be 15 percent). It contained the following stories: 'The Son's Veto', 'For Conscience' Sake', 'A Tragedy of Two Ambitions', 'On the Western Cricuit', 'To Please His Wife', 'The Melancholy Hussar of the German Legion', 'The Fiddler of the Reels', 'A Tradition of Eighteen Hundred and Four', and the story-sequence 'A Few Crusted Characters' (serialized as 'Wessex Folk').

March — Hardy renegotiated his contract with Harper and Osgood, McIlvaine for the first edition of *JO*, so that he obtained 20 per cent royalty on copies after the first 5000 had been sold.

April — Hardy wrote to Harper to say that the serial he was writing for them was not after all conforming to the certification of inoffensiveness that he had given them, and offered either to cancel the contract, or to allow them to emend for the serialization as they saw fit. Harper chose to ask for changes, and Hardy made them, as he had made them for *TD* and *GND*.

May — Hardy in the midst of arranging for his novels to be

		published in a Colonial edition by Macmillan.

July — Sampson, Low's rights in Hardy's novels ended.

Part III (up to chapter 16) of copy for *JO* sent to Osgood, McIlvaine for *Harper's New Monthly Magazine* (due to begin publication in December, so Hardy was back to his old position of having to complete a novel while the opening was already set in type—something his connection with the *Graphic* had saved him from).

September — Hardy at work on the revisions for Osgood, McIlvaine's collected edition—in this month *FMC*—as well as on *JO*.

November — 'The Spectre of the Real', the story on which Hardy had collaborated with Florence Henniker, published in *To-day*.

December — Macbeth Raeburn, the illustrator of the Osgood, McIlvaine collected edition, visited Hardy for the first time, in order to make sketches 'drawn on the spot' for the frontispieces.

JO began its run in *Harper's New Monthly Magazine*, to end in November 1895. For the first instalment the novel was entitled *The Simpletons*; it was then altered to *Hearts Insurgent* for the remainder of the serialization.

1895 February — The first volumes of the collected edition at press. The new preface for *TD*, the first volume, dated January 1895.

March — Macbeth Raeburn stayed with the Hardys at Max Gate and made more drawings under Hardy's direction.

Hardy finished last chapters of *JO*.

April — *TD* published in the Osgood, McIlvaine collected edition. Volumes appeared thereafter at monthly intervals, including substantial revisions, new prefaces, and frontispieces by Macbeth Raeburn.

To *WT* in this edition Hardy added the story 'An Imaginative Woman'.

August — Hardy wrote to Florence Henniker that he could not write the stories editors requested from him.

He was restoring the text of *JO* for the first edition, and wrote that he was more interested in the story than in any he had written.

October — Hardy wrote of correcting a proof-sheet every day for the collected edition.

November — The first edition of *JO* published as volume 8 in the collected edition (dated 1896). It was published by Harper in America, also dated 1896.

		To Colles Hardy described himself as 'vague' about another serial story.
1896	February	Hardy completed a dramatization of *TD*.
	May	To Arthur Symons as editor of *The Savoy* Hardy wrote that he hoped to write some short stories soon, but he could not say when.
	July	In process of writing 'A Committee-Man of "The Terror" '.
	August	Manuscript of 'A Committee-Man of "The Terror" ' sent to Shorter.
	September	The last regular volume of the collected edition, *UGT*, published.
	December	'A Committee-Man of "The Terror" ' published in the Christmas number of the *London Illustrated Magazine*.
		'The Duke's Reappearance' published in the Christmas supplement of the *Saturday Review*.
		Hardy sent much-revised copy for the first edition of *WB* to the printer.
1897	January	Finished correction of proofs of *WB*.
	March	*WB* published, as volume 17 of the collected edition.
	July	Rough draft of 'The Grave by the Handpost' completed.
	December	'The Grave by the Handpost' published in the Christmas number of *St. James's Budget*.
1898	April	Hardy considering collecting his remaining short stories. (This came to nothing until 1913.)
	November	To William Archer Hardy wrote that he did not incline to the writing of a novel, saying 'There is no enlightened literary opinion sufficiently audible to tempt an author, who knows that in the nature of things he must always come short of real excellence.'
	December	[*Wessex Poems* published. The collection, which Hardy had been working on for at least a year and a half, effectively marked the end of his interest in writing new long fiction.]
1899	October	To Edward Clodd Hardy wrote that since fiction had got on to wrong lines of late he was not stirred to novel-writing.
	November	Hardy trying to write 'Enter a Dragoon'.
	December	Hardy agreed to write a short story for Shorter.
		Macmillan informed Hardy that Harper were in financial difficulty and were transferring books to other publishers. As Harper had recently assumed

control of Osgood, McIlvaine, and were now issuing Hardy's works in England under their own imprint, Macmillan wondered whether—if Harper contemplated relinquishing Hardy's books—they might take them on. Hardy, without committing himself, answered favourably, but also needed more information.

1900   January   Hardy reported that he had finished 'Enter a Dragoon' and 'A Changed Man'—his last works in prose fiction. Hardy received £100 for 'A Changed Man'.

April   'A Changed Man' published in the *Sphere*.

July   *TD* published in paperback by Harper; 100000 copies at 6*d*. were sold. Hardy's royalty was 1*d*. per copy.

December   'Enter a Dragoon' published in *Harper's Monthly Magazine*.

1901   [Summer]   Harper published a sixpenny paperback-edition of *Far from the Madding Crowd*, for which Hardy had revised the text.

July   Wrote to Shorter that he was thinking of doing some stories 'some day'.

August   Hardy negotiated an agreement with the American branch of Harper for the issue of a cheap Uniform edition of the Wessex novels. His royalty ranged between 6c. and 1c. a volume—the former for copyright volumes sold to booksellers and the latter for non-copyright volumes sold by subscription.

November   [*Poems of the Past and the Present* published in England (in December in America), though dated 1902.]
              Hardy told Shorter that he hoped to write two stories next year, since both already existed in outline.

1902   February   The story for the persistent Shorter still not written, but not yet abandoned.
              Negotiations begun between Hardy and Clarence McIlvaine (who had become, once Harper had taken over the firm of Osgood, McIlvaine, Harper's representative in Britain) over the continuance with Harper of the rights to publish Hardy's work in England. The initial seven-year agreement was about to expire.

March   Hardy wanted a British-based publisher to be responsible for the issue of his books in England, and, after taking legal advice, reached agreement with Macmillan to take up publication of his work from October 1902.

	April	Again to Shorter Hardy wrote that his story materials were 'in statu quo as yet'.
	June	To Shorter Hardy reported that the story he had thought of 'getting into shape' would not after all work.
	July	Hardy told Macmillan of his desire to revised scattered details in *FMC*, *TD*, and *JO* for the publishers' reissue of the collected edition of his work. In the end his revisions were rather more substantial.
	December	To Maarten Maartens Hardy wrote that he did not 'know at all' about writing another novel.
1904	September	Hardy wrote to Gerald Maxwell that for years past he had not written a line of fiction or thought of the subject.
1906	August	Hardy's lecture 'Memories of Church Restoration' published in *Cornhill*.
	September	The first volumes of the pocket edition of Hardy's work published by Macmillan, one appearing every fortnight thereafter. New impressions were frequently called for during Hardy's lifetime and afterwards.
1907	July	To H.W. Massingham Hardy wrote his opinion that 'a dozen or so years ago the English novel . . . was developing on sound lines in the direction of a real grasp of life, which would I think have resulted in the formation of a school unequalled in any other literature . . . However, the English & American press set itself with a will to stamp out the torch on the grounds of morality'.
	September	In a letter to Macmillan Hardy wrote that he did not feel up to a novel at present. It is perhaps surprising that he was not more emphatic or decided, though it may be that he did not like baldly to tell his publisher that he would never write another novel. On the other hand, the comment might be a scrap of evidence to suggest that he himself had not entirely given up the prospect of one day returning to fiction.
1908	March	Hardy sent his novel manuscripts to Shorter, who had offered to have them bound in return for the gift of one of them—*RN*.
1909	January	In a letter to Macmillan about the publication of *The Dynasts* in one volume, Hardy added a plaintive note: 'I suppose I shall never reach the dignity of an edition-de-luxe!'
1910	July	[Hardy appointed to the Order of Merit]

	October	Macmillan forwarded a proposal from an American publisher, Hinkley, to issue an *edition de luxe* of his books. Hardy asked for a set of Macmillan's edition so that he could make corrections for the edition.
1911	June	Hardy received books to revise and opened the question of dividing his novels into two groups. He decided to correct the proofs himself. By now the arrangement was for co-publication between Hinckley and Macmillan.
	September	Hardy at work on the revision, and making additions to the prefaces.
	October	With the assistance of Sydney Cockerell Hardy distributed many of his manuscripts to public collections in Britain and the United States. Macmillan increased their share of the new edition from 250 to 500 copies. Hardy sent revised copy for *TD* and *FMC* to Macmillan.
	December	Macmillan suggested a purely English edition, to which Hardy agreed.
1912	January	The joint arrangement between Hinckley and Macmillan finally abandoned. The now purely English edition to be called the Wessex edition. Hardy's royalty was to be 1s. 6d. on each volume. The initial print run for each title was 1000 copies; hence Hardy would eventually have received £1575 from this first impression. All titles were subsequently reprinted.
	February	Hardy corrected proofs of *TD*.
	March	Proofs of *RN*.
	April	Revised *W*. *TD* and *FMC* published. (On each succeeding month two further vols. were published, until the edition was complete.)
	August	Hardy sent copy to Macmillan for the volume of stories, to be called *A Changed Man* (*CM*). Proofs arrived at the end of the month.
	October	*CM* published by Macmillan and Harper. Hardy's royalty from Harper was 20 per cent. The volume contained 'A Changed Man', 'The Waiting Supper', 'Alicia's Diary', 'The Grave by the Handpost', 'Enter a Dragoon', 'A Tryst at an Ancient Earthwork', 'What the Shepherd Saw', 'A Committee-Man of "The Terror"', 'Master John Horsleigh, Knight', 'The Duke's Reappearance', 'A Mere Interlude', and 'The Romantic Adventures of a Milkmaid'.

	November	Agreement for Tauchnitz to divide *CM* into two for publication in Europe. One volume was called *CM*, the other *The Romantic Adventures of a Milkmaid*. Hardy was to be paid £30 for the first 3000 copies and £10 for each further 1000 copies sold of each volume.
	December	It was decided that *CM* should initiate a new grouping of Hardy's novels—mixed novels—since (as Hardy wrote to Macmillan) the volume was made up of specimens from every class.
1914	February	[Hardy married Florence Dugdale.]
	March	To the literary agent Colles Hardy wrote that there was no likelihood of his writing any more prose stories.
	July	Macmillan proposed a limited edition of Hardy's work. Hardy was keen. He suggested the names Casterbridge edition or Mellstock edition. The First World War prevented this proposition from bearing fruit until 1919.
	August	[The First World War began.]
1915	November	Hardy wrote to Macmillan that he would like the texts of the cheaper editions of his work to be brought into line with those of the Wessex edition—or a cheaper impression of the Wessex edition itself to be issued—after the war was over.
1919	June	Agreement reached with Macmillan for the publication of an *edition de luxe*, to be known as the Mellstock edition. Hardy was to receive £2,775 for the edition as a whole.
		He sent up five pages of corrections for the edition, primarily in *POBE*. He read proof only for *POBE* and the volumes of verse.
	December	The first volumes of the Mellstock edition published, the remainder at intervals during 1920.
1920	January	Hardy read proofs of *POBE*.
	April	Hardy sent to Macmillan details of revision for reprints of the Wessex edition.
1921	August	A representative example of Hardy's public (and partly private) attitude to his prose fiction at this date comes in a letter to Ruth Head, who was preparing an anthology of Hardy's writing: 'I don't care an atom what prose you select'. To set against this there are the revisions mentioned in the previous entry, which seem to suggest a continuing care for his prose texts. Hardy's denigration of his fiction in many letters in the

post-war years must have derived at least in part from the continuing attention his novels and stories received from critics and lecturers at the expense of his poetry.

1922	January	Macmillan proposed an Indian edition of some of Hardy's novels: *FMC*, *RN*, *TM*, and *MC*. The Macmillan edition-books suggest that *UGT* was also later included in the series. Hardy was to receive 10 per cent royalty on the published price (which I do not know).
	July	Hardy's royalties for July 1921–June 1922 were about £2300.
1923	July	For this year Hardy's royalties had increased by approximately £200. The Globe Publishing Company, a Macmillan subsidiary, selling the pocket edition of Hardy's works on the instalment plan.
1924	July	In this year Hardy's receipts increased by almost 50 per cent, marking 1923 as the year when his reputation really took off (see the schedule of printings at the end of this chronology).
	December	The first suggestion for an illustrated edition of *TD*. The illustrations (woodcuts) were to be done by Vivien Gribble; Hardy suggested that she might like to see Gertrude Bugler perform Tess in his stage adaptation of the novel currently being performed by the Dorchester Hardy Players. This she did.
1925	October	*TD* serialized from the Wessex edition by *John o'London's Weekly*, ending in July 1926. Hardy received £1,000 for the serialization.
1926	April	The illustrated edition of *TD* published in large-page format, each of 325 copies signed by Hardy.
	July	1500 normal-sized copies of the illustrated *TD* published.
1927		Macmillan gradually abandoned the plates used for most of the novels in the Uniform and pocket editions, and reset the texts, probably using the 1920 or later impression of the Wessex edition as copy. There is no evidence that Hardy played any part in this work.
1928	January	[Hardy died]
	March	The one-volume edition of Hardy's short stories published.
	November	*The Early Life of Thomas Hardy* published. It was ostensibly written by Hardy's wife Florence, but in truth dictated to her and subsequently revised by

Hardy himself. There were also alterations made by Florence and others after Hardy's death.

1930   April   *The Later Years of Thomas Hardy* published. Hardy's work on the full draft ended with the year 1918. Though often working from Hardy's notes, the last four chapters are Florence's work. As with *Early Life* other hands were also responsible for additions and excisions.

1935   January   On the seventh anniversary of Hardy's death, the copyright of *UGT*, the only one of his works of which he did not retain the rights, reverted from Chatto and Windus to his estate.

Hardy's Works as Published by Macmillan 1895–1939

(based on information gathered from the Macmillan edition-books in the British Library. NB These figures do not include details of impressions published in the Cottage Library from 1932 onwards).

Note: The numerals following the equals sign represent the number of thousand copies printed in that year. Titles are listed here in chronological order of first publication.

Title	Copies Per Year	Total Copies
Desperate Remedies		
Colonial edition	1896 = 2	2000
Uniform edition	1903 = 2, 1911 = 1, 1926 = 1, 1934 = 1	5000
Uniform edition (large paper)	1919 = 1	1000
Pocket edition	1906 = 2, 1910 = 2, 1915 = 2, 1918 = 1.15, 1922 = 3, 1923 = 3, 1925 = 3, 1926 = 3, 1928 = 5	24150
Wessex edition	1912 = 1, 1923 = 1	2000
Mellstock edition	1920	525
TOTAL		34675
Under the Greenwood Tree		
Uniform edition	1903 = 2, 1906 = 1, 1910 = 1, 1914 = 1, 1919 = 1, 1924 = 1, 1928 = 1.5, 1938 = 2	10500

Title	Copies Per Year	Total Copies
Pocket edition	1906 = 2, 1909 = 2, 1911 = 2, 1913 = 2, 1915 = 2, 1918 = 1, 1919 = 2, 1919 = 3, 1921 = 3.2, 1922 = 5, 1924 = 9, 1925 = 10, 1927 = 9.6, 1929 = 20	72800
Wessex edition	1912 = 1, 1920 = 1, 1931 = 1	3000
Mellstock edition	1920	525
Indian edition	1925	3000
TOTAL	(NB No Colonial edition)	89825

A Pair of Blue Eyes

Title	Copies Per Year	Total Copies
Colonial edition	1895	3000
Uniform edition	1902 = 2, 1905 = 1, 1907 = 1, 1911 = 1, 1914 = 1, 1919 = 1, 1927 = 2(reset), 1938 = 2	11000
Pocket edition	1906 = 2, 1908 = 2, 1911 = 2, 1913 = 2, 1916 = 2, 1917 = 2, 1919 = 2, 1920 = 3, 1921 = 5, 1923 = 5, 1924 = 10, 1928 = 10	47000
Wessex edition	1912 = 1, 1920 = 1	2000
Mellstock edition	1920	525
TOTAL		63525

Far from the Madding Crowd

Title	Copies Per Year	Total Copies
Colonial edition	1894	3500
Uniform edition	1902 = 2, 1903 = 2, 1906 = 2, 1908 = 3, 1913 = 2, 1921 = 1, 1924 = 1.5, 1927 = 2, 1934 = 1.5	17000
Uniform edition (large paper)	1918	1000
Pocket edition	1906 = 5, 1909 = 3, 1911 = 3, 1912 = 3, 1914 = 3, 1916 = 2, 1917 = 2, 1918 = 2, 1919 = 5, 1920 = 5, 1921 = 5, 1922 = 5, 1923 = 5, 1924 = 10, 1925 = 20, 1927 = 20.3, 1929 = 30	128300
Two shilling library	1930 = 10, 1931 = 10	20000
Wessex edition	1912 = 1, 1919 = 0.5, 1922 = 1, 1931 = 1	3500
Mellstock edition	1920	525

Title	Copies Per Year	Total Copies
Indian edition	1930	1000
TOTAL		174825

The Hand of Ethelberta

Title	Copies Per Year	Total Copies
Colonial edition	1896	2000
Uniform edition	1903 = 2, 1910 = 1, 1922 = 1, 1927 = 1	5000
Uniform edition (large paper)	1918 = 0.5	500
Pocket edition	1906 = 2, 1910 = 2, 1912 = 2, 1918 = 1, 1919 = 2, 1920 = 3, 1923 = 5, 1925 = 5, 1928 = 5	27000
Wessex edition	1912 = 1, 1922 = 1	2000
Mellstock edition	1920	525
TOTAL		37,025

The Return of the Native

Title	Copies Per Year	Total Copies
Colonial edition	1895	3000
Uniform edition	1902 = 2, 1906 = 1, 1909 = 1, 1912 = 1, 1916 = 1, 1921 = 1, 1924 = 1, 1927 = 2(reset), 1935 = 2	12000
Pocket edition	1906 = 2, 1907 = 2, 1910 = 2, 1912 = 2, 1912 = 2, 1917 = 2, 1918 = 2, 1919 = 3, 1920 = 5, 1922 = 5, 1923 = 10, 1924 = 10, 1926 = 20, 1929 = 12.5, 1933 = 5	84500
Wessex edition	1912 = 1, 1920 = 1, 1928 = 1	3000
Mellstock edition	1920	525
Indian edition	1929	1500
Two shilling library	1930	15000
TOTAL		119525

The Trumpet-Major

Title	Copies Per Year	Total Copies
Colonial edition	1895	3000
Uniform edition	1903 = 2, 1906 = 1, 1910 = 1, 1914 = 1, 1920 = 1, 1925 = 1, 1929 = 2	9000
Pocket edition	1906 = 2, 1909 = 2, 1911 = 2, 1914 = 2, 1917 = 2, 1919 = 2, 1920 = 3, 1922 = 5, 1923 = 5,	

Title	Copies Per Year	Total Copies
	1924 = 5, 1925 = 10, 1928 = 10,	
	1933 = 5, 1934 = 5	60000
Wessex edition	1912 = 1, 1920 = 1	2000
Mellstock edition	1920	525
Indian edition	1924 = 1, 1925 = 2.5	3,500
TOTAL		78025
A Laodicean		
Colonial edition	1896	2000
Uniform edition	1903 = 2, 1911 = 1, 1919 = 1,	
	1926 = 1, 1935 = 1.5	6500
Pocket edition	1906 = 2, 1910 = 2, 1914 = 2,	
	1918 = 1.5, 1919 = 2, 1921 = 3,	
	1923 = 3, 1924 = 5, 1926 = 10	30500
Wessex edition	1912 = 1, 1922 = 1	2000
Mellstock edition	1920	525
TOTAL		41525
Two on a Tower		
Colonial edition	1895	3000
Uniform edition	1902 = 2, 1906 = 1, 1910 = 1,	
	1916 = 1, 1927 = 1(reset), 1934 = 1	7000
Pocket edition	1906 = 2, 1909 = 2, 1912 = 2,	
	1915 = 2, 1918 = 1, 1919 = 2,	
	1920 = 3, 1922 = 3, 1923 = 5,	
	1925 = 5, 1926 = 5, 1928 = 5	37000
Wessex edition	1912 = 1, 1920 = 1	2000
Mellstock edition	1920	525
TOTAL		49525
The Mayor of Casterbridge		
Colonial edition	1895	500
Uniform edition	1902 = 2, 1905 = 1, 1908 = 1,	
	1911 = 1, 1914 = 1, 1919 = 1,	
	1923 = 1, 1926 = 1.5, 1930 = 2	11500
Pocket edition	1906 = 2, 1907 = 2, 1910 = 2,	
	1913 = 3, 1916 = 2, 1918 = 1,	
	1918 = 1, 1919 = 3, 1920 = 5,	
	1922 = 5, 1923 = 5, 1924 = 10,	
	1925 = 10, 1926 = 20, 1929 = 20,	
	1939 = 2	93000

Title	Copies Per Year	Total Copies
Wessex edition	1912 = 1, 1920 = 1, 1929 = 1	3000
Mellstock edition	1920	525
TOTAL		108525

The Woodlanders

Uniform edition	1903 = 2, 1906 = 2, 1913 = 1, 1918 = 0.5, 1920 = 1, 1924 = 1, 1928 = 1.5, 1936 = 1.5	10500
Pocket edition	1906 = 2, 1908 = 2, 1911 = 2, 1913 = 2, 1916 = 1, 1917 = 1, 1918 = 1, 1918 = 2, 1919 = 3, 1920 = 5, 1923 = 5, 1924 = 10, 1926 = 10, 1929 = 10, 1934 = 3	59000
Wessex edition	1912 = 1, 1920 = 1, 1931 = 1	3000
Mellstock edition	1920	525
TOTAL		73025

Wessex Tales

One-volume edition	1893	500
Uniform edition	1903 = 2, 1910 = 1, 1923 = 1, 1928 = 1, 1938 = 1	6000
Pocket edition	1906 = 2, 1910 = 2, 1913 = 2, 1917 = 2, 1919 = 2, 1920 = 2, 1921 = 3, 1923 = 5, 1924 = 5, 1926 = 10, 1930 = 10	45000
Wessex edition	1912 = 1, 1920 = 1	2000
Mellstock edition	1920	525
TOTAL		54025

A Group of Noble Dames

Colonial edition	1894	3000
Uniform edition	1903 = 2, 1914 = 1, 1924 = 1, 1934 = 1	5000
Pocket edition	1906 = 2, 1911 = 2, 1917 = 1, 1918 = 1, 1919 = 2, 1925 = 5, 1928 = 5	18000
Wessex edition	1912 = 1, 1922 = 1	2000
Mellstock edition	1920	525
TOTAL		28525

Title	Copies Per Year	Total Copies
Tess of the d'Urbervilles		
Colonial edition	1895	3000
Uniform edition	1902 = 2, 1903 = 2, 1904 = 2, 1906 = 2, 1907 = 2, 1910 = 3, 1914 = 2, 1916 = 2, 1919 = 2, 1923 = 2, 1925 = 3, 1929 = 3	27000
Pocket edition	1906 = 5, 1908 = 3, 1910 = 3, 1912 = 3, 1913 = 3, 1914 = 3, 1916 = 3, 1917 = 3, 1918 = 3, 1919 = 5, 1920 = 5, 1920 = 10, 1922 = 10, 1923 = 20, 1925 = 25, 1925 = 30, 1928 = 23.9, 1929 = 30	190900
Wessex edition	1912 = 1, 1917 = 0.5, 1920 = 1, 1926 = 1	3500
Mellstock edition	1919	525
Illustrated edition (large paper)	1926	325
Illustrated edition	1926	1500
TOTAL		226750
Life's Little Ironies		
Colonial edition	1894 = 3, 1894 = 2	5000
Uniform edition	1903 = 2, 1909 = 1, 1915 = 1, 1923 = 1, 1928 = 1	6000
Pocket edition	1906 = 2, 1910 = 2, 1913 = 2, 1916 = 2, 1918 = 1, 1919 = 2, 1920 = 3, 1922 = 3, 1923 = 5, 1925 = 10, 1928 = 5, 1937 = 3	40000
Wessex edition	1912 = 1, 1920 = 1	2000
Mellstock edition	1920	525
TOTAL		53525
Jude the Obscure		
Colonial edition	1896	5000
Uniform edition	1903 = 2, 1905 = 1, 1908 = 1, 1910 = 1, 1913 = 1, 1918 = 0.5, 1920 = 1, 1923 = 2, 1929 = 2	11500
Pocket edition	1906 = 2, 1907 = 2, 1910 = 2, 1911 = 2, 1913 = 2, 1914 = 3, 1917 = 2, 1918 = 1, 1918 = 2, 1919 = 3, 1920 = 3, 1921 = 5,	

Title	Copies Per Year	Total Copies
	1922 = 5, 1923 = 5, 1924 = 20,	
	1927 = 10(reset), 1928 = 20	89000
Wessex edition	1912 = 1, 1919 = 1, 1929 = 1	3000
Mellstock edition	1920	525
TOTAL		109025

The Well-Beloved

Colonial edition	1898 = 3, 1898 = 1	4000
Uniform edition	1903 = 2, 1911 = 1, 1919 = 0.5,	
	1923 = 1, 1927 = 1, 1935 = 1.5	7000
Pocket edition	1906 = 2, 1910 = 2, 1913 = 2,	
	1917 = 2, 1919 = 2, 1920 = 3,	
	1922 = 3, 1924 = 3, 1925 = 5,	
	1927 = 10	34000
Wessex edition	1912 = 1, 1922 = 1	2000
Mellstock edition	1920	525
TOTAL		47525

A Changed Man

First edition	1913	10000
Wessex edition	1914 = 1, 1925 = 1	2000
Uniform edition	1915	5100
Pocket edition	1919 = 3, 1920 = 3, 1923 = 5,	
	1926 = 5	16000
Mellstock edition	1920	525
TOTAL		33625

The Collected Short Stories of Thomas Hardy

Collected edition	1928 = 10, 1928 = 10	20000

SUMMARY
TOTALS
(in descending
order of no. of
copies published).

Tess of the d'Urbervilles	226750
Far from the Madding Crowd	174825
The Return of the Native	119525
Jude the Obscure	109025
The Mayor of Casterbridge	108525

Title	Copies Per Year	Total Copies
Under the Greenwood Tree		89825
The Trumpet-Major		78025
The Woodlanders		73025
A Pair of Blue Eyes		63525
Wessex Tales		54025
Life's Little Ironies		53525
Two on a Tower		49525
The Well-Beloved		47525
A Laodicean		41525
The Hand of Ethelberta		37025
Desperate Remedies		34675
A Changed Man		33625
A Group of Noble Dames		28525
Collected Stories		20000

The pocket edition is the most satisfying to use as an index of Hardy's sales as a writer of fiction. The total printing of fiction in this edition between 1906 and 1939 was 1096150 copies. The pattern of printing reflects very clearly a curve of demand for Hardy's writing:

Totals of volumes printed by five-year periods:
1906–1910 = 83000
1911–1915 = 69000
1916–1920 = 162650
1921–1925 = 407200
1926–1930 = 351300
1931–1935 = 18000
1936–1939 = 5000

The dramatic drop after 1930 was apparently caused by a combination of rapidly declining demand and the reasonably large number of copies printed in the two years after Hardy's death in 1928—for instance, the last printing recorded for *Tess of the d'Urbervilles* was of 30000 copies in 1929, and the same was true of *Far from the Madding Crowd*. It was presumably for this reason that, while it took only four years between 1925 and 1928 to sell 54000 copies of the pocket *Tess*, it took at least ten years to sell the 30000 printed in 1929. Such, perhaps, is often the consequence of an author's death: momentary high celebrity, and then rapid decline in popularity.

Appendix II

The Proofs for the First Edition of Jude the Obscure

Though in the surviving document there is a single sequence of the volume's pages, there are in fact three different stages of proof represented—first proof marked by Hardy alone, first proof marked by Hardy and subsequently by the printer's reader, and second proof, or revises.

The first proofs without any annotation by the printer's reader occur at the end of the novel (gathering 2D–2K), and are substantially revised by Hardy; machine collation of a 50 per cent sample of these leaves with their counterparts in the published volume showed that there was a fair amount of alteration of punctuation and lineation between the two, alteration of a kind consistent with that made by the reader on other proof-sheets. On the other hand, there are no substantive changes, other than those indicated by Hardy on the proofs. It was most probably the case, then, that a revise of these pages was subsequently pulled for the reader, and that Hardy did not see them. The first leaf of each gathering is marked 'press'.

The proofs seen by both Hardy and the reader (gatherings F, H, I, M, P–S, and X–2C) are also quite heavily revised by Hardy, but in addition have notes from the reader to the compositors about how Hardy's additions or deletions should be accommodated within the paragraph or the page, and some punctuation changes in a style and ink different from Hardy's. A similar sample-collation with the published book revealed no differences between the two, attributable to either author or reader, other than those indicated in the proofs; so the probability is that either no revises were made of these gatherings, or else neither Hardy nor the reader made alterations to them. On the first leaf of each of the gatherings there is the notation 'press' and 'Last', implying that no revises were to be made for the author, though presumably a reader checked the fresh copy made after Hardy's changes had been incorporated.

The revises, or second proofs (preliminaries and gatherings A–E, G, K, L, N, O, T, and U), have only occasional revisions by Hardy on them, and it seems certain that antedating these were first proofs on which Hardy made many more changes. The first leaf of each gathering also has 'press' and 'Last', which makes it even more likely that Hardy saw no revises for the leaves in the previous group. Why this should have been so is not clear, though it should be remembered that this important first-edition proof-reading came in the midst of proof-reading for Osgood's collected edition, and it is possible that there was urgency in the printing house. On the other hand, the non-consecutive nature of the gatherings for which it appears that there were no revises makes it less easy to find a satisfying account of their state—unless, indeed, Hardy was not sent proof in the narrative sequence, or did not revise it or send it back in sequence (a possibility which would underline the disjointed nature of the proof-reading experience). It is also possible that the gatherings for which Hardy saw revises were those that he had most heavily revised in first proof. The proofs and revises are dated, and the dates provide a certain amount of further information about the way Hardy read proof during this hectic year.

In a note in *The Later Years* (p. 37) Hardy says that the 'restored copy' for the first edition of *Jude* was sent off about the end of August 1895. This may have been the case; the earliest dates stamped on the gatherings show that from 2–6 September proofs of F–I and revises of A–D were printed, so it seems likely that Ballantyne had some copy well before the end of August. There is, however, a gap from 7–17 September when no surviving proofs were pulled (though K at least must have been proofed during this period), and revises were made only of E–K; and although it may have been that there was urgent pressure on the compositors for other jobs at this time, it is also possible that Hardy did not send the second part of the copy until the middle of the month. From 18 September it is possible to infer a regular schedule of two gatherings of proof every day until the work was complete on the 30th. Revises were made, presumably as the proofs returned from Hardy, sometimes singly, three or four days apart, sometimes in a batch of three or four at a time.

For most of this time, as far as it is possible to tell, Hardy was at Max Gate, and we can thus picture him receiving on most days during the second half of the month a packet with two gatherings of proof for him to correct; from the dates on some of the revises it took on average something in the region of a week to get from proof to revise, and if two or three days are taken off for time in the post, then it seems Hardy was pretty prompt in working through and sending them back. It is a reasonable further assumption that the whole of the Osgood, McIlvaine collected edition was proof-read in this piecemeal manner.

Index